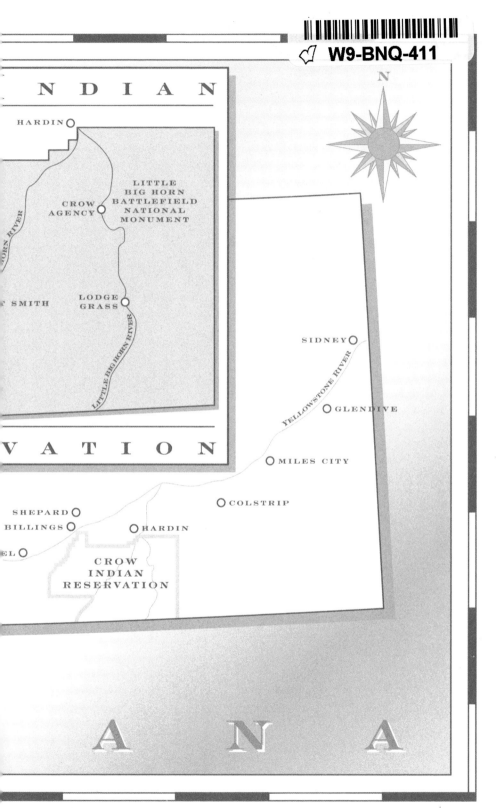

N

N D I A N

HARDIN

CROW
AGENCY

SMITH

LITTLE
BIG HORN
BATTLEFIELD
NATIONAL
MONUMENT

LODGE
GRASS

HORN RIVER

LITTLE BIG HORN RIVER

V A T I O N

SIDNEY

YELLOWSTONE RIVER

GLENDIVE

MILES CITY

COLSTRIP

SHEPARD
BILLINGS
EL

HARDIN

CROW
INDIAN
RESERVATION

A N A

Map illustration by Ellen Shively Neureuther

COUNTING COUP

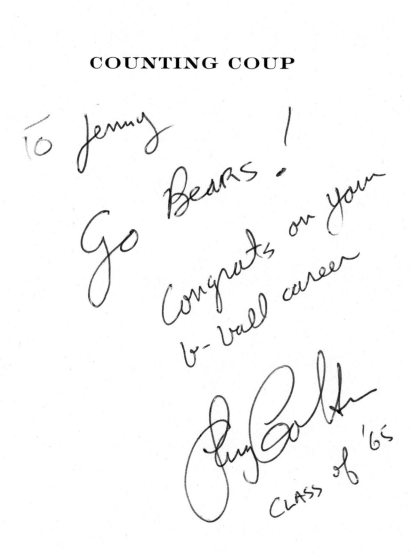

To Jenny

Go Bears !

Congrats on your
b-ball career

[signature]
CLASS of '65

COUNTING COUP

A True Story of
Basketball and Honor
on the Little Big Horn

LARRY COLTON

WARNER BOOKS

A Time Warner Company

Warner Books, Inc., 1271 Avenue of the Americas, New York, NY 10020

Visit our Web site at www.twbookmark.com

(w) A Time Warner Company

Printed in the United States of America

First Printing: September 2000

10   9   8   7   6   5   4   3   2   1

Library of Congress Cataloging-in-Publication Data

Colton, Larry.
     Counting coup : a true story of basketball and honor on the Little Big
Horn / Larry Colton.
          p. cm.
     Includes index.
     ISBN 0-446-52683-5
     1. Basketball for women—Montana—Hardin. 2. Hardin High School
(Hardin, Mont.)—Basketball. 3. Indian athletes—Montana—Hardin. 4. Crow
Indians—Montana—Hardin. I. Title.

GV886 . C65 2000
796.323'62'0820978638—dc21

                                                                    00-024987

To Marcie

ACKNOWLEDGMENTS

The early believers: Richard Pine and Herman Golub

Friends in Billings: Pam and Keven Richau and Bob Lee

Friends in Hardin: Mary Koyama, Katy Lytle, Ron and Eunice Koebbe, Ron and Hjordis Johnson, and the Dawn Patrol Ratballers

Tribal friends: Tim Bernardus, Bill and Maggie Yellowtail, Carson Walks Over Ice, and especially Janine Pease Windy Boy (Pretty On Top)

Hardin High: Principal Jerry Slyker, staff, and students

The boys' team: Coach John Whiteman and his players

The Fallsdown family: Karna, Marlene, Blaine, and especially Danetta

The coaches: Don Gordineer, Dave Oswald (my buddy), and especially Linda McClanahan

The families: all the mothers and fathers of the players

Young friends: Kate Lundberg, Cammie Weaver, Brian Oswald, and Amylynn Adams

Special motivation: Gerry Pratt and Arlene Schnitzer

Editorial help along the way: Mark Christensen, John Strawn, Tom Lang, Marcie Olson, Paula Dougherty, Don and Wendy Cobleigh

New York editor supreme: Rick Wolff

Portland word doctor supreme: David Kelly

Portland Assistance League: Larry Frager and Julie Strasser Dixon

And of course: the Hardin Lady Bulldogs and Sharon LaForge

Author's Note

During my fifteen months on the Crow Reservation, I rarely heard a tribal member refer to him/herself as a Native American. They called themselves Indians. "Because our ancestors most likely came across the Bering Sea, we're not really natives," explained John Pretty On Top, a Crow Sun Dance leader. "It's more accurate to call us First Americans." For the most part, the word *Indian* is used in this book.

The characters and events depicted here are real. The names of a small number of minor characters, however, have been changed because of issues of privacy. Otherwise this is a true story.

Counting Coup

Long ago it was possible for young warriors of the Plains Indian tribes to gain honor and respect by *counting coup*. There were four primary ways to accomplish a coup: touch an enemy in battle, steal an enemy's horse, lead a successful war party, or capture an enemy's weapon. Of these, the bravest was to touch an enemy—not kill him—but touch him on his chest. The more coups a warrior scored, the more glory and dignity he achieved. Often it was the one with the most coups who was chosen as chief.

"Somehow, in the mindless ways that rivers sculpt valleys and shame shapes history, the Montana Indians' purest howl against a hundred years of repression and pain had become . . . high school basketball."

Gary Smith
Sports Illustrated

PART I

PRESEASON

CHAPTER ONE

Tar paper shacks, abandoned junk heaps in front yards, rutted and littered streets—all the outward signs of people living on the margin. Down the block from where I park, a pack of mangy dogs mosey across the street, pacing themselves in the heat of this August day in Crow Agency, Montana.

The only sign of energy in the town is the ubiquity of basketball hoops . . . on telephone poles, sides of houses, scrawny trees. These hoops aren't fancy Air Jordan NBA specials purchased at the Rim Rock Mall in Billings—they have rotting plywood backboards and flimsy rims drooping toward the hardened dirt. Rare remnants of net, shredded by heavy use and the fierce winds that blow off the prairie, hang loosely.

At the park in the center of town—a luckless patch of dried grass with a well-used outdoor basketball surface in the middle—Norbert Hill, Paul Little Light, and Clay Dawes, three seniors on the Hardin High varsity, are playing a lazy game of half-court crunch. I know their names because I studied their photos in the showcase in the lobby of the high school gym. These are the guys I've traveled to this remote corner of southeastern Montana to write about, the athletic young men who carry the hopes of the Crow Tribe on their shoulders. In the heat, they move at half speed. I sit down to watch.

A burgundy Mercury Cougar riding out of the dusty Montana summer eases to the curb, and a young woman—I guess her to be seventeen—grabs a basketball from the back seat and walks onto the vacant end of the court, dribbling the ball between her legs with a casual ease, her eyes fixed on the guys at the other end. She shyly waves to them, then throws up a halfhearted shot from the free throw line, the ball sailing perfectly through the netless rim, hitting the support pole and bouncing onto the dead grass. Slowly, she retrieves it, picking it up with a tricky little flick of the foot, then returns to the court.

Tall and slender, she has a quiet beauty—high cheekbones, dark hair, mahogany eyes—yet she is not a celluloid Pocahontas or a black velvet rendition of an Indian princess. Her appeal is subtler. It is the way she moves, a grace, languid, fluid, sexy. All without effort. She seems mysterious, detached.

From the other end of the court, one of the boys beckons her to come play some two-on-two. He is Paul Little Light, a charming, handsome, crew-cut seventeen-year-old who dreams of Hollywood. He'll be a movie star with a Beamer, a Benz, and a mansion.

She rolls the ball off the court and walks to the other end, silent, serious. Her teammate will be Norbert, a young man slated to be captain, star player, and class clown. Twenty years earlier his uncle Darrell Hill had also been a star player at Hardin High, good enough to win All-State honors. After the season Uncle Darrell and his brother got into a fight outside a bar in Hardin with two men from another clan with a long-standing feud against the Hill family. When it was all over, the Hill brothers were dead on the sidewalk of stab wounds and the other two men were arrested, although one eventually walked free and the other spent only ten years in jail. Whites took the double murder as further proof that the Crows were their own worst enemy.

On the first play, the girl dribbles to her left, then zips a no-look pass to a wide-open Norbert, who scores. Little Light, her defender, grins, embarrassed. She shows no expression. Instead, she fakes left, then cuts backdoor, leaving Little Light flatfooted with his Hollywood smile. Norbert's pass is perfect and she scores an easy layup. She still doesn't smile, but she looks at home, as comfortable as the old T-shirt and shorts she wears.

At this moment, a red Chevy 4x4 with a young Indian man behind the wheel cruises by the park. The girl turns and watches it disappear around the corner, then flips the ball to Little Light and takes off running toward her Cougar, picking up her own ball on the way.

"Wait," pleads Little Light. "Let's finish the game."

She doesn't look back or bid them farewell. She just gets in her car and vanishes around the corner.

My journalistic journey to the Crow Indian Reservation, and my own fascination with sport, date back several decades. Back in the late 1960s, when America was going nuts in the streets, I was a professional baseball player, skilled enough to make it to the major leagues with the Philadelphia Phillies, but stupid enough to blow it one game after I got there, injured in a mindless bar brawl, my dream cut short. I played for the Phillies on a Tuesday.

But not a day has gone by since then that I haven't thought about the pursuit of fickle athletic glory and our national obsession with sports. It's hard not to: we've got fans in cheese hats, Dennis Rodman on the best-seller list, endorsement fees bigger than school district budgets. I always read the sports news first.

After I left baseball and took a turn at high school teaching, I wrote a book about pro basketball, as well as basketball stories for a number of magazines. Somehow along the way I became fascinated, then mystified and alarmed, at the plight of young Native American athletes. For reasons that were beyond me, these intelligent, very capable young men seemed to have their lives explode at the time when most young men's lives are just taking off. On the Crow Reservation, where the passion for basketball is legendary and star high school players are the heroes of the tribe and often the best players in Montana, these young athletes invariably finish their high school careers with no hope for a scholarship and no skills for the future.

Before coming to the rez to explore this phenomenon, I knew enough to understand that this is not just some funky little social trend. This is a whole culture that is backsliding, and has been for a very long time. Why, I wondered, is Native American society failing, leaving its people so hopeless at such an early age?

The story I've come looking for, however, is not at all the story I will write. The story I find is the girl who just dropped the ball and took off in pursuit of the 4x4.

At the end of my first week in Montana, I head off for another journey to Crow Agency, this time to check out Crow Fair, a huge tribal powwow. I decide to take the long way from my newly rented duplex in Hardin, a border town on the edge of the rez. The route will take me south on Montana State Highway 313, across the Big Horn River, then east through the heart of the rez. On my bicycle. Out of shape.

I've never been on a rez before, not even to gamble. I'm not a Native American scholar or New Age wannabe in search of becoming one with the tribe. I've come to Big

Horn County only because Indians and sport seem like a good story and an interesting way to spend a year.

Riding through Hardin, I pass two Indians in front of the Mint Bar, angry, pointing fingers at each other. They interrupt their discourse to glare at me. I speed up.

Indians, I've been led to believe, are very emotional people who tend to score big from fat government handouts, then blow their windfall money. They are people with rocky family lives and major booze problems. Doesn't everyone know that?

Odd. That sounds familiar. Though I am, by DNA and upbringing, a WASP, I can identify. As an athlete and a writer, I've scored nice bonuses on occasion, and hey, why not buy a couple of rounds for everybody in the place— only to find myself months later scrounging cash for rent and a cup of coffee. And perhaps the best thing to be said about my family life is that it's been eventful. I've been married a couple of times, and although I put in a decade doing the single-dad thing seeing two daughters through high school and on to college, I'm still baffled by parenting. As for alcohol, I no longer drink, but back when I did . . . let's just put it this way: I've seen the inside of a drunk tank.

So, in some ways, I expect to feel right at home here.

As I head south out of town, the land is flat, the air thick with the smell of fresh-mown alfalfa. I take a deep breath. Riding a bike across the landscape is quickly changing the first impressions I'd gotten a week earlier when I arrived on I-90 from my home in Portland, Oregon. From the Interstate that first day, eastern Montana appeared intimidating, mile after relentless mile of empty space—no trees, no houses, no Burger Kings. Why had I left my girlfriend and our cozy tree-lined neighborhood for these cutbacks and ravines, this dead dirt and buffalo grass, these low-pinched hills and dry creek beds? But now, from my bicycle seat, I can smell the alfalfa, see the horses, hear the river. A sign reads: "Good Luck Fishermen." What at first seemed hostile land now breathes of life and adventure. It feels good . . . except that after only an hour on the road my butt hurts and it feels like I'm riding in a kiln.

An empty sugar beet truck barrels past, nearly blowing me into the irrigation ditch next to the road. I keep pumping, past an abandoned homestead, the landscape crawling by, land rich with beets, wheat, barley, and corn, the crops providing the area with its economic lifeline, at least to its white farmers. I wave to a farmer on a tractor. He doesn't wave back.

After crossing the Big Horn River, I turn onto a county road toward Crow Agency ten miles to the east. The rich farmland that hugs the river now gives way to mile after mile of open range, herds of cattle grazing their way to the slaughterhouse. At first glance, the terrain seems smooth and flat, but soon I encounter slow winding hills that loom like invisible Himalayas. The fact that the temperature on this cloudless prairie day just passed the plutonium meltdown point doesn't help. I pass an Indian mending a fence. He doesn't wave either.

The closer I ride to Crow Agency, the more garbage and litter I notice next to the road: discarded pop cans, junk food wrappers, disposable diapers, Styrofoam cups. It seems contradictory. I've just read a poignant account of the Indians' kinship and harmony with the earth and nature and how that relationship had been disrupted by the white man and his pollution of the land and the rivers . . . and yet the deeper I ride into the reservation, the uglier the trail of trash. I doubt farmers have thrown it there.

A car filled with Crow teenagers zooms by and an empty pack of Marlboro Lights sails out the window. "Get a car," the driver yells. In the distance, I see Last Stand Hill.

Finally, I stop at the top of a rise, and down below is

dusty little Crow Agency, the political and cultural center of the reservation, a town with a population of one thousand, give or take a couple dozen on any day. Off to the left is the Big Horn Carpet Mill, a government-subsidized tribal business that has been abandoned and boarded shut since going belly-up in 1974. Prior to its failure it was the largest entrepreneurial venture ever tried on the reservation, but now it is just an ugly hunk of concrete alongside the freeway, an eyesore, a grim testimonial to yet another Crow failure in business.

Entering town, I stop at the Crow Mercantile to get something to drink. Of the ten customers, I'm the only white. "Do you have any bottled water?" I inquire.

The clerk doesn't respond.

I ask again.

Still no response. She stares at me as if I'm speaking French. I wonder if they only speak Crow in Crow Agency during Crow Fair week. Finally, she turns and points to the rear of the store. "Gatorade's down there," she advises.

I quench my thirst, then ride south, past the rodeo arena and tribal headquarters, and past the proposed site of Little Big Horn Casino, a project that, depending on whom you ask, is either going to be the salvation of the tribe— "it'll bring jobs and revenue"—or its ruin—"just what they need, another addiction."

At the Custer Trading Post, I turn onto the road leading up to Custer Battlefield, and fall in line behind the caravan of campers and urban assault vehicles bringing needed tourist revenue into the area. Struggling to catch my breath, I slowly make my way up the incline leading to the entrance, swerving onto the shoulder to avoid a Winnebago from Minnesota.

Inside the park, I lock my bike and walk up the hallowed hillside to the monument marking the spot where the Indians had massacred General Custer and his troops back in 1876. A warm wind ripples through my T-shirt. Looking at the clusters of white headstones scattered in the undulating meadows of parched mustard and buffalo grass, I wipe away the sweat. I want to know more about the Battle of Little Big Horn and Custer's demise, but on this day and in this heat, I'm not in the mood to take the tour. Maybe on another day when the tourists are thinned out, and the sun is low, and the park rangers aren't looking like Marine DIs in their olive green uniforms and reflector shades. So I head back down the hill, stopping at the Custer Trading Post to buy another drink.

Sitting on a bench out back, I stare down the hill and across a dirt road at a small brown house, probably built by HUD. It stands alone and weary, and has all the architectural flair of an inflated shoe box. There is something melancholy about it, like the sacred ground that surrounds me. Next to the drab house a teenage girl nonchalantly shoots hoops at a netless rim nailed to a telephone pole beside a rusty abandoned trailer. She is too far away to see her face, but it is impossible to miss the grace and elegance of her movement. When the ball rolls away, she moves to retrieve it, picking it up with a tricky little flick of the foot. It is that same girl.

From where I sit, I can't even tell if the ball goes through the hoop or not, yet as I sit and watch, transfixed, I forget that I am in the middle of one of the most famous places in American history. There is something enchantingly beautiful in what I'm seeing—the girl's movements, the setting, the arc of the ball, the cavalry gravestones in the background. It all seems to momentarily fit together in some sort of American mosaic, old and new, sport and culture, form and purpose, sorrow and hope.

* * *

Crow Fair is the tribe's five-day powwow held the third week in August, an event the recently fired boys' basketball coach at Hardin High describes as "a place where a bunch of Indians run around drunk and nothing starts on time." Known in Crow as *umbasax-bilus,* or "where they make noise," the fair is the most anticipated happening of the year on the reservation. For five days, Crow Agency becomes the "Teepee Capital of the World," with spirited competition for prize money in horseracing, rodeo, and tribal dancing. I've never seen so many pickups.

At the fairgrounds located above the banks of the Little Big Horn River, a river the Indians call the Greasy Grass, I lock up my bike again and start meandering on foot, soaking up the culture: men in full-length headdresses; fancy dancers in beaded dresses; the Nighthawk drummers pounding out tribal rhythms; kids in braided hair riding bareback on pintos; hundreds of teepees with lodge poles extending so high above the covering they resemble giant hourglasses. I feel like a tourist in New York City trying not to let the natives see me gawking up at the skyscrapers. Judging from the dearth of white faces in the crowd, Crow Fair is not big on the social calendar of local farmers and ranchers.

I check the Crow Fair program and according to the schedule of events it is almost time for the Grand Entry, a colorful parade into the arbor, the circular outdoor arena that serves as the centerpiece of the fair. The Grand Entry, I've been told, is something not to miss, a spectacular display of pageantry and culture that serpentines its way down an adjoining roadway before entering the arbor. I walk to the roadway to get a good view, surprised to find nobody there, no spectators, no participants. I wait ten minutes, and still nobody appears.

Finally, an elderly woman carrying a folding chair arrives, her face creased with many lines. I imagine her to be full of wisdom and stories. Slowly, she sets her chair down next to the roadway and takes a seat. Dressed in the clothes of the traditional Crow woman—long-sleeved T-shaped cotton dress, wide leather belt, high-top moccasins, head scarf, shawl—she is one of a handful of elderly women on the reservation still clinging to the old tribal customs and trying to maintain the vanishing culture. Whites call these women "blanket squaws."

"What time does the parade start?" I ask.

She stares straight ahead toward the east and the direction from which the earliest Crows migrated two centuries earlier. No words come, no acknowledgment of my presence or my question. Just like earlier at Crow Mercantile. I wonder if she even speaks English. For many on the reservation, Crow is still the first language, and to a few, it is still the only language.

Just as I'm about to turn and walk away, she raises her head and points down the roadway, away from the arbor. "The parade will start," she says, "when you see it coming."

My patience is no match for hers, so I make my way back to the arbor to wait there for the Grand Entry and the start of the tribal dancing competition. I join the waves of fairgoers circling the perimeter. It is like a carnival midway—craft booths, food vendors, teenagers. If there is a litter patrol, I don't see it.

I purchase a slice of fry bread, a puffy pancake-shaped pastry fried in lakes of grease, then sit down to rest and people-watch. Pretty soon I see a familiar face—the mystery girl from the outdoor court in Crow Agency. At her side is a white girl, wearing tight jeans and a dark blue Montana State sweatshirt. She is pretty, if maybe a little trailer park naughty, her reddish brown hair teased skyward. They are sitting on a bench, deep in conversation, oblivious to everyone around them.

The conversation seems intense. Not angry, just earnest.

Intuition, sharpened by raising two daughters and spending tons of hours around high school kids, advises me that they are up to no good, especially when they high-five each other, then hurry off, arm in arm, laughing, two girls on a mission, escorted out of sight by the rhythmic pounding of tribal drums.

In time—Crow Time—the Grand Entry parades into the arbor. Accompanied by a cacophony of bells, drums, and chanting, and led by a color guard of Crow Vietnam vets, hundreds of dancers dressed in native costumes stream into view. Men, women, children. I have never seen such color, such beadwork, such magnificence. Some of the children are no more than four years old. How do they know the steps?

I watch the dancers majestically circle the arbor, and I am moved by the beauty and spirit. The parade has indeed started.

It is twelve miles back to Hardin along the frontage road next to I-90, twelve long miles, not uphill, just long. I pedal hard.

The land around me is at the center of the enmity between the Indians and whites. From a territory once the size of Pennsylvania, the Crows' land has been reduced by the U.S. government to a mere 2.2 million acres, smaller than Connecticut. And if that isn't bad enough, whites now lease or own 95 percent of the Crows' allotted reservation land, acquiring it for pennies on the dollar from tribal members desperate for a buck. Small wonder the Indians are pissed and suing to get it back, a case that seems destined to idle in the courts forever.

But it isn't the struggle for the land I'm thinking about as I pedal along. It is that Indian girl. She is in my karass, a term Kurt Vonnegut used in *Cat's Cradle* to explain recur-

13

ring chance encounters with a stranger. I've been in town for a couple of days and already I've spotted her three times. She stands out. Maybe it's her athleticism, or maybe it's her good looks. Whatever it is, she's in my karass.

I will soon learn she is Sharon LaForge, a fifth-generation relative of one of the six Crow scouts that rode with General Custer on his fateful day. And as I sense, she will turn out to be special, a person who will be the focus of my attention during my time on the rez, as well as after I leave. I will see her in school and talk to her daily when she finally allows it. I will yell myself hoarse watching her try to win a scholarship and carry Hardin High to the State Championship. I will become inexorably involved in her life as she struggles against the seemingly endless forces working against her. I will marvel at her bravery, recoil at her bad choices.

I can't foresee any of that, of course, as I continue to pedal, continue to hurt. I'm not exactly sure how far I've ridden this day, maybe forty miles, maybe 750. For a guy fast approaching his AARP card, it feels like the Tour de France over the Pyrenees. I still have five miles to go. Even worse, a nasty wind has come whipping in off the prairie. It feels as if I'm losing ground. I have to pedal on the downslopes.

I try to think of anything rather than how badly I hurt or how slowly I'm moving. An eighteen-wheeler rumbles by on the Interstate and I'm reminded of a sad story I heard about two Crow teenagers who decided to play a modern-day version of counting coup. On a rainy night these two boys stood on the edge of I-90, leaning out into the right lane to count coup by slapping the sides of eighteen-wheelers rolling by. These trucks, evidently, were the enemy. But the boys had been drinking and leaned out too far and got hit. They both died instantly.

With three miles to go and the wind still blowing hot and

hard, I spot a beat-to-shit pickup turning onto the frontage road. It is headed in my direction. As it gets closer I see that it is limping along on a flat tire, the torn tread flopping against the pavement. An older Indian couple are inside, and as we pass, they check me out, not just a quick glance but a real eagle-eye stare-down.

They go a few yards farther down the road, then turn around, nearly driving off the shoulder. I can hear them behind me, closing ground, the sound of their flopping tire getting louder and louder, closer and closer.

Being new to these parts, I'm a bit nervous. I know it's irrational, but my heart doesn't. I can't outrun them, not even with their wounded tire. I strain into the wind.

In a few seconds they are right alongside me, almost close enough to touch. I glance over, just as the woman in the passenger seat rolls down her window. We travel side by side for several more yards, then she speaks. "In case you're interested," she says with a toothless smile, "you're going four miles an hour."

CHAPTER TWO

I awake feeling stiff—my shoulders, back, butt. Especially my butt. I abandon my plan to go for another bike ride, and decide instead to take a walk through Hardin to the Chat and Chew Cafe for breakfast. Maybe after that I'll head over to the high school to catch the first day of the girls' varsity practice. (In Montana, the girls' and boys' basketball seasons are separated, the girls playing in the fall, the boys in the winter.) The girl from the court in Crow Agency will be there, I hope.

I've been in Hardin a few days now, settling into my prosaic little unfurnished two-bedroom duplex behind the empty lot adjacent to Hardin Bowl. I found the place only through a chance conversation at the Big Horn County Historical Museum with a sweet grandmotherly woman who said that property owners never list their rentals in the *Big Horn County News* because they don't want to rent to Indians. "They make bad tenants," she explained.

That isn't the only thing explained to me during my first couple days in town. At Sevons, a junky secondhand shop and Tupperware graveyard where I'd gone to pick up some home furnishings, I stopped to buy a snow cone from a cherubic ten-year-old in front of the store. He took the opportunity to inform me that the Indians in Hardin "wouldn't be so bad except they all think they own the place."

At the Hardin Community Center, a nice clean facility where $50 bought me a year's membership to use the exercise equipment, Jacuzzi, and Olympic-size indoor pool, the assistant manager looked me square in the eyes and set the record straight. "All you need to know about these Indians around here is that they were all born with basketballs in their hands."

Despite the mistrust and misunderstanding between the two cultures, I like the prospect of spending a year in a place that is an underdog, a gritty town fighting the odds. I've always wanted to live in a small town, I guess in the same way I've always wanted to live in New York—not forever, just to do my thing for a while and move on. Hardin is indeed a small town. It has an abundance of churches and bars, but only one traffic signal and no MTV in its cable package. "Why no MTV?" I ask the cable guy.

" 'Cause folks around here said they'd rather have the two Nashville stations," he answers.

So far, I've seen no car phones, gang graffiti, or business suits. At Hardin Ford, the only vehicles on the lot are pickups, and during the day, the only radio station I can get on my secondhand radio is KTCR "Cat Country." This is Montana, real wrangler country. The Chamber of Commerce's promotional video boldly declares the town "The Heart of the American West," and those are real cowboys and real gun racks, and that's a real Indian pissing over there in the shadows next to the Mint Bar.

To the storekeepers, these drunken Indians are ruining business, driving away customers. Merchants regularly complain to tribal leaders about the problem, but the leaders say it isn't their jurisdiction, and besides, the drunks aren't really bothering anyone, they are just "a benign presence." So nothing ever changes, including perceptions. It is these Indians, the visible ones, the ones peeing in the shadows and sleeping on the sidewalks, whites think of first. They are the ones perpetuating the stereotype of the drunken Indian staggering down America's Main Street.

In the town's early days, saloonkeepers learned in a hurry that money could be made selling booze to the Indians. But there was an obstacle—it was a federal crime to sell liquor on the reservation, and Hardin was within the reservation boundaries. So town leaders asked the government to move the boundary. The government obliged, moving the line to the edge of town, taking Hardin off the reservation. The saloonkeepers were then free to sell liquor to Indians, and in time, everybody else was free to complain about the "Indian drinking problem."

But is it really the drunken Indians who are hurting the local economy? Or is it the "disloyal whites" in town, the ones who take their money and drive fifty miles to shop at the supermarkets and malls in Billings? In the past month, the corner drugstore closed its doors, and the owner of the jewelry store, who is also the mayor and brother of my landlord, has announced he is looking for a buyer. So far, he's had zero offers.

Or is Shell Oil the real culprit? Back in the 1970s, predictions of huge oil and coal discoveries swept across eastern Montana. Practically overnight Big Horn County was supposed to change from a cattle and crop place into a huge energy empire. Hardin's population would swell to twenty thousand. Even Safeway bought into the prediction, building an oversize store to handle all the wildcatters who'd rush to town with money to burn. Then a funny thing happened on the way to the oil rush. The boom fizzled and Shell Oil pulled up stakes. Safeway shut its doors and Hardin merchants went back to trying to make a go of it selling to the farmers, ranchers, and Indians.

Or is it the rest of America screwing up the town's fight

for survival? Except for Custer Reenactment Week in June, tourists blast by on the freeway, pausing only to grab some gas or a quick bite at Pizza Hut or Taco John, the franchise chains that are the town's only viable new businesses. To the outside world, Hardin is nothing more than a dot on the map.

Yet somehow the town is growing, and its growth is . . . Indians.

Over the last two decades, a steady stream of Crows has moved off the reservation into town. Indians now constitute 49 percent of Hardin's population of 2,990. This migration wasn't because Hardin was so beautiful; it had more to do with a housing shortage on the rez. Indians attend its schools, shop at the IGA, gas up at Conoco. They now even have a voting majority in the county, gaining footholds on the school board and the county commission, as well as the voting booth. What's next?

Entering the Chat and Chew, I sit next to a table with four farmers. I assume they're farmers because of their John Deere hats. On the other side of me sit two Indians, weathered and worn, chins down, stoic, silent, staring into their coffee cups. It wasn't that long ago, only twenty-five years, that shops in town still hung "No Dogs or Indians Allowed" signs in their windows. Now merchants welcome the Indians' money, if not their presence.

I wait for the large woman behind the counter to bring me some coffee, but she seems preoccupied. I believe she's Margaret, the owner. Rumor has it that she recently caught her husband, the cook, in the kitchen after hours with one of the waitresses. In Hardin, rumors travel fast.

A couple minutes pass and she still hasn't waited on me, or even looked in my direction. I try to act patient, staring at the blood red carpeting, then at the black velvet paintings of a Spanish galleon and a flamenco dancer. Finally, one of the farmers leans in my direction.

"You gotta pour your own around here, stranger," he says.

So I get up and pour a cup of coffee that looks like it's left over from the covered wagon days. I check the menu. The Chat and Chew is a biscuit and gravy joint, not exactly the best place to be on the first day of my new diet. I order a couple soft-boiled eggs. I want donuts.

Sufficiently caffeinated and still hungry, I head for the door, stopping on my way out to read the notices on the bulletin board. One has a picture of a broken-down old sorrel for sale. "Best offer," the ad says.

In the lobby of the Hardin High gym, I stop at the showcase to check out the pictures of the Hardin Lady Bulldogs, and there she is, smack dab in the middle, number 24, senior Sharon LaForge. Beneath her name it reads, "Co-Captain." In her photo she is standing with a basketball under her arm, looking as serious as a snakebite.

There are also pictures of several former Hardin High basketball stars, like the legendary Larry Pretty Weasel and Jonathon Takes Enemy, players who were as good as anyone in the state, but didn't last in college. Conspicuously absent in the showcase, however, is any state championship trophy since 1941. There are none, which is a sore spot on the rez. The boys' teams from the two smaller high schools in Big Horn County, Class B Lodge Grass High and Class C Plenty Coup High, both of which are 95 percent Crow, have shelves full of state championship trophies—ten in the last decade to be exact. These championships have brought great honor and glory to the tribe. But against the tougher competition of Class A, Hardin High, a school with a 49 percent Crow population out of its enrollment of 395, has won no state titles, not the boys, not the girls.

Inside the gym, a sparkling clean facility built in the

1960s with a seating capacity slightly larger than the town's population, Linda McClanahan, the girls' varsity coach, impatiently waits for her players to exit the locker room. This is the day she's waited for since the end of last season. The first day of school is still a week away; Crow Fair is still in full swing; and the sugar beets and wheat aren't yet harvested. But the balls are inflated, the hardwood waxed.

McClanahan, or Coach Mac as her players call her, looks the part of the coach—black gym shorts, gray T-shirt, black high-top Reeboks, whistle, clipboard. She is forty-one, unmarried, slightly out of shape. Her looks are plain and unadorned—shoulder-length dishwater blond hair, blue eyes, dark-rimmed glasses. She is starting her eighth year at Hardin High, her fifth as the girls' varsity coach. She also teaches physical education and health, but that is work. Everybody in town knows that basketball is her life.

Slowly, her players straggle out onto the court. "Has anyone seen Sharon?" she asks. No response.

She checks her watch. Still two minutes to nine, the official starting time . . . still two minutes for Sharon to show up. She takes a deep breath. For her, this day is filled with all the hope of a new beginning, a new season. She's been awake since 4:30, wired, staring at the ceiling. In her fifteen years of coaching, she's never arrived on a season with such high expectations. Normally she is conservative in predicting her teams' chances, but with four returning starters, including two potential All-Staters, she is convinced this year's Lady Bulldogs will be her best team ever, with a real chance of making it to State, something no girls' team at Hardin has ever done. She even has visions of an undefeated season.

But where is Sharon?

She takes another deep breath. In years past, she has waged a losing battle with her Scotch-Irish temper, throwing chairs, clipboards, water bottles, anything that wasn't

21

nailed down. A Bobby Knight with estrogen. Nobody escaped her wrath—players, refs, opposing coaches, Sharon. She has never kicked or hit a player, but she has yelled and screamed at many—in practices, in games, on the bus. Players have quit because of her. Not surprisingly, the stress affected her health. In her first year as head coach, a season of only three wins, she developed an ulcer. Sometimes that first season it hurt so much that she doubled over in pain on the bench. She chugged Mylanta. Her doctor finally issued an ultimatum: either learn to relax or quit coaching. Since then, she's worked hard at controlling her emotions, even taking a three-day Positive Image Building seminar at Northern Montana College in Havre, learning techniques on anger management. Now she keeps self-help notes posted on her refrigerator and bathroom mirror: "I love to coach." "Relax." "I respond well to pressure." "I am a positive person."

She checks her watch again. One minute to nine. She's been in Hardin long enough not to be surprised by Crow behavior. She knows all about Crow Time and how Crows rarely call to say they'll be late or absent. Still, she doesn't expect Sharon to miss the first day of practice. Nobody on this team, or any other team she's coached, loves basketball more than Sharon.

The last time she saw Sharon was in June at the team camp at Montana State in Bozeman. That was a special week. Out of twenty-four participating schools, including teams from the big AA schools in Billings, Missoula, Butte, and Bozeman, Hardin finished second. And out of all the players there, including several girls who'd already been offered scholarships, Sharon was chosen the camp's MVP, an award Coach Mac figured was not lost on the Montana State coaches.

But where is Sharon now?

It must be because of Crow Fair, assumes Coach Mac,

aware of the family pressure on Crow players to attend the tribe's biggest cultural event of the year. She has always tried to accommodate, scheduling practices early in the day so they don't conflict with fair events, most of which take place in the afternoon and evening. But she feels compromised, caught between having her team unprepared for opening game just thirteen days away, and being accused of being insensitive to Crow culture. She hates having to tiptoe through the minefield of political correctness. It has reached the point, she believes, that whenever a white coach or teacher looks cross-eyed at an Indian, some militant on the rez is ready to scream racism. To her, the complaint about practicing during Crow Fair seems hypocritical considering that Crows usually rank basketball right up there with oxygen in importance.

The clock strikes nine. No Sharon.

Coach Mac gathers the team around her. Rah-rah speeches have never worked for her. She just wants to keep it short, to the point.

"Remember how lousy we felt after losing in Divisionals last year?" she says. "Well, let's make sure we don't have to feel that way again this year."

Okay, I can see her working, starting the year off with a bit of negative reinforcement. I've had a coach or six try that strategy. I've even tried it a few times as a dad.

She blows her whistle, and thirty-four varsity hopefuls—nineteen Crows and fifteen whites—circle the gym, their Reeboks and Nikes squeaking against the shiny hardwood floor.

Leading the pack is the team's other co-captain, 5'10" senior Tiffany Hopfauf, her long, tan legs gobbling up the court. Like Coach Mac, Tiffany is used to Crows showing up at their own speed, and she resents it.

*   *   *

After practice, I hang around the gym, waiting for Coach Mac. We are going to lunch back at the Chat and Chew for a get-acquainted interview. As I wait, Tiffany and the other white girl slated to be a starter, Anita Dewald, stay in the gym, casually shooting free throws and rehashing the opening day of practice. Clearly, they are ticked off about Sharon's not showing up, suspicious about the legitimacy of her absence.

Eavesdropping, I take mental notes, not wanting to intrude. I haven't even met these two girls yet, and at this point, I'm still thinking I'm here to write a book about the boys' team. I am, however, seeing another story emerge. Is that a little racial hostility I detect? I edge closer.

To gather my story, whether it's about the boys or girls, I know I'll have to become something between an honorary seventeen-year-old and an invisible man, invited to witness the lives of these people close up, often as if I am not there. I must respect their privacy, and if I miss a cat-fight in the locker room, a place I'll never go, then I must depose the combatants and compare their accounts, even if it's a week later.

Gathering a story in this way is not new to me. In the same genetic way that I could throw a ball harder than others on the playground, I can take little credit for my ability to gain people's trust. My writing career has included a strange mix of experiences: traveling with an NBA team, hanging out with a weird sex cult, tailing the FBI. These weren't gonzo Plimptonesque type assignments where I actually snared rebounds, or did a group grope, or shot it out with fugitives. I just hung out with these people, made buddies, and when it was all over, found I had a story.

That is my MO here, and if it should turn out that it is the girls' team I will follow, then an honorary seventeen-year-old girl I'll become. Having taught high school and raised two daughters should help. Besides, acting like a kid has always come easy for me.

I don't know yet, but the confidences and revelations that will be given to me by the people I'm soon to encounter will go far beyond what I could expect. It's as if these people, Indians and whites, feel like talking just at the moment I happen by, much in the same way someone lost will flag down a stranger.

"You guys looked good out there today," I offer.

"Thanks," replies Tiffany with a who-the-hell-is-this-guy glance.

Over burgers, Coach Mac tells me she's heard Sharon has been doing some hard partying over the summer, which surprises her because she doesn't think of Sharon as the partying type. The rumor has come from her assistant coach, Dave Oswald, who's heard it from his daughter, Maria, a tenth grader on the junior varsity.

"Is this the best burger in town?" I ask, wondering how a restaurant in the middle of cattle country can serve such a bad burger.

"Afraid so," she answers.

My first impression of Coach Mac is good—a straightforward woman who takes her job seriously, maybe a little too seriously, and doesn't object to the idea of a writer hanging around. So far, anyway.

I ask why it is that these excellent Crow athletes never get a look from the colleges, no scholarships. Her explanation echoes the company line: college coaches are afraid to take a chance of wasting a scholarship on an Indian who most likely won't survive academically, socially, or athletically on a college campus. "They don't have the discipline," she says. Other than Jim Thorpe, I'm hard pressed to name a nationally notable Indian athlete, pro or college.

"Could Sharon be the exception?"

"Not likely," answers Coach Mac.

It's not that she doesn't think Sharon isn't talented enough or doesn't care about basketball. In fact, Coach Mac has never had a player take a loss harder than Sharon did after the team's loss in Divisionals last season. "The memory of her in our locker room after that game has haunted me for nine months," she says.

She tells it this way. In the double-elimination divisional playoffs to go to State, Hardin came into the tournament the hottest team in the league, riding a nine-game win streak after an erratic, contentious first half of the year in which the team nearly disintegrated. At the center of that disarray had been Roberta Yarlott, Sharon's second cousin, a talented but temperamental player whose outbursts in practices and games against her own teammates had fractured the team's harmony. The white girls on the team felt intimidated by Roberta and threatened to quit after she fired a ball at one of them from point-blank range in practice. But a team meeting to air their grievances, plus the nine wins in a row, helped smooth the ruffled feelings. In the double-elimination tournament's first round, however, they lost in triple overtime.

Facing elimination in the consolation bracket, their game against dreaded archrival Billings Central came down to the last minute. With Hardin trailing by one, Roberta, the team's only senior, fouled out on a disputed call. She protested vehemently, then as she left the court, the Central fans pelted her with boos and racial epithets. "Go back to the rez, squaw!" Coach Mac appealed to the refs to slap a technical on the Central fans for their unsportsmanlike behavior, but the refs refused. In the Hardin huddle, Sharon started to cry, not because of the crowd's racial insults—that was nothing new—but because her cousin was out of the game. Roberta had been the one who'd taught

26

her to be tough and aggressive, but now she was gone, her career at Hardin High over unless the team could pull it out in the last second. Sharon felt it was up to her.

It all came down to the last shot, and Sharon's desperation, off-balance attempt fell short, ending the season, as well as Roberta's career and the team's chance to go to State. On the way to the locker room, Roberta chased after the ref and blindsided him with a right cross to the kidney. She had to be pulled off, and was later banned from any further high school competition.

In the postgame locker room, Sharon sat in front of her locker, head buried in her hands, inconsolable, her plaintive wailing penetrating the walls. A tearful Coach Mac tried to console her, assuring her that she'd played a great game and that she'd learn from this and come back stronger next season. But Sharon didn't want to hear about next year. All that counted was the moment. She wept, not for one minute, or two, or four . . . at ten minutes she was still in full sob.

Coach Mac had never heard such wailing. She knew that Crow grieving was intense, and that funeral services often last an entire day with unrestrained sobbing. But this seemed unnatural, almost scary. She opened the locker room door and allowed the players' mothers, aunts, and grandmothers to enter, hoping they would bring calm. Instead, they brought more tears. Sharon's mother, Karna, entered, reeking of alcohol, as usual. Sharon turned her back, then spotted her grandmother, Danetta Fallsdown, who was also crying. That triggered more tears. Sharon began to struggle for air, her breath now coming in short, fitful gasps. The more she struggled, the harder it was to breathe. She started to hyperventilate. Her face turned pale.

Coach Mac rushed to her side and handed her a paper bag, instructing her to breathe into it. Sharon did as instructed, and slowly the air returned to her lungs, the color to her face.

In time the locker room emptied and only Sharon and Coach Mac were left. Eyes still rimmed with tears, Sharon put on her letterman's jacket and headed out into the cold, next season an eternity away.

Now, the start of next season has finally arrived . . . but Sharon hasn't. She is still partying at Crow Fair.

CHAPTER THREE

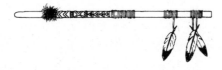

Slowly, Sharon awakes. It's almost noon. In bed next to her, her best friend, Holly Johnson, also begins to stir.

Sleeping in the same bed is nothing new for Sharon and Holly. They've been doing it since the seventh grade, Sharon spending as many nights at Holly's house in Hardin as she does with her grandmother in Crow Agency. In many ways, Holly's family is her closest link to stability, her refuge from the chaos of her own family. Holly's mother, Hjordis, has been more of a mother to her than her real mom, which doesn't take much; and Holly's dad, Ron, the best white player ever to come out of Hardin High, is the only male in her life ever to provide any discipline, regularly including her in his fatherly lectures and scoldings. Her own father is a wisp.

Sharon glances at the clock. "I missed practice," she mutters.

"Big deal," says Holly. "What are they gonna do, kick you off the team? Besides, this is our last day to party."

Tomorrow, Holly and her mom are moving to Bozeman, two hundred miles away, a messy divorce taking away Sharon's truest sanctuary and best friend.

Holly rolls out of bed, then struts in front of her Andre Agassi poster, the one she bought because she thinks he's some kind of naughty rebel. Seventeen and pretty, with brown eyes, milk white skin, pouty lips, and reddish brown hair, she takes pride in her body, not afraid to flaunt it, although sometimes she prefers to hide it under baggy sweatshirts to keep the cowboys at Hardin High from talking to her breasts. Sharon, on the other hand, has been taught, like all young Crow women, to be modest with her body.

Sharon rises out of bed, yawning, stretching, slyly keeping one hand on her neck to hide her new hickey. It's not that Holly, who lost her virginity in the seventh grade, is a prude. Hardly. She's known as "The Dictionary," a good source for questions about sex. Most of what Sharon knows about sex, which isn't much, she learned from Holly. Still, she doesn't want Holly to see the hickey and start asking questions about her and Randy Not Afraid again. Especially not on their last day together. Talking about Randy always ends in an argument. Holly won't even say his name, referring to him only as "The Asshole."

Holly watches Sharon head to the bathroom to check herself in the mirror. To her, Sharon is beautiful, her face soft and opaque. In a certain light Sharon's presence is so fragile it seems almost possible to walk right through her. But whenever Holly tells her she is pretty or sexy, Sharon discounts it, never good at accepting compliments. Whenever she looks at herself in the mirror, she senses nothing out of the ordinary—no makeup, no lipstick, no perfume. Once, Holly tried to get her to wear makeup, but she refused. Another time, her grandmother asked her if she wanted to try some perfume, and Sharon thought it must be because she stank.

"What's the plan today?" she asks.

As usual, Holly is set on finding trouble. First, they'll bootleg a bottle of peppermint schnapps from her dad's liquor cabinet and go check out Crow Fair, then later that night, probably around midnight, they'll go to a 49, a notoriously ribald tribal party. These are adult parties, with lots of booze and usually a few fistfights. Neither Holly nor Sharon has ever been to one.

"You gotta promise me that if you see The Asshole you won't take off with him," says Holly. "This is our last day together, remember?"

Sharon shrugs.

Strolling through the teepee area at Crow Fair, Holly watches Sharon's eyes glance left and right, much like she does dribbling the ball upcourt, eyes seemingly in the back of her head. "You're looking for The Asshole, aren't you?" she asks.

"No," replies Sharon.

"Liar."

Holly has heard all the rumors about Randy. Who hasn't? A twenty-four-year-old rodeo roper, he's notorious on the rez, known as a hard-drinking, macho kind of guy. The way Holly hears it, he's already been married, fathered a child, left them both, and cheated on every girlfriend he's had. It bugs her the way Sharon always drops everything, including her, whenever he calls. She's repeatedly warned Sharon that this is a guy with a dark side, but Sharon just shrugs it off. Besides, who is Holly to talk, all the losers and abusers she's been with? Isn't it true?

Certainly nobody knows Sharon better than Holly. For five years they've been inseparable, close as sisters, their friendship a racial anomaly in Big Horn County. When they first met on the seventh grade basketball team, Holly noticed that when other kids' parents came to pick them up after practice, Sharon had no mom or dad coming for her and always looked like a lost soul. So Holly started inviting her home with her, and pretty soon Sharon was part of the

Johnson family, going on vacations, getting an allowance, sleeping over. In the evenings, Hjordis gave her backrubs and Ron talked basketball with her, always amazed at her intuitive understanding of the game. For her part, Holly enjoyed the cachet that went with being best friends with the best athlete in the school. They gained a reputation as tough girls, not because they got into fights or bullied other kids, but because of Sharon's fierce presence on the basketball court. Holly knew, however, that Sharon wasn't so fierce on the inside. She couldn't count the times she'd seen Sharon cry in private, usually over her mom's binge drinking.

Because of Sharon, Holly felt socially comfortable with Indians, not threatened like so many of her white classmates at Hardin High. Or maybe it was because she never quite fit with any of the white cliques—the cheerleaders, the cowboys, the 4-H'ers, the jocks. It didn't seem to matter to these kids that she was smart, athletic, shapely, the daughter of attractive, well-educated, well-respected parents. What counted was that she dated mostly Indian boys. They called her names: *wannabe, easy, white trash, Indian lover.* She always felt like an outsider.

The girls continue meandering through the teepees and pickup trucks, Sharon's eyes still scanning. For her, Crow Fair has always been the centerpiece of her fondest childhood memories: wearing the beautiful new elks tooth dresses her grandmother sewed her . . . parading into the arbor for the traditional dancing . . . riding bareback through the campgrounds on her chestnut mare . . . sleeping in a teepee next to her mom. But this year's Crow Fair is none of that, especially the part about sleeping next to her mom. Sharon hasn't seen her mother in five months. The last she heard, she was in jail.

Suddenly, Holly stops and points at Sharon's neck. "You've got a hickey necklace," she exclaims.

Again, Sharon shrugs.

"How could you let The Asshole kiss you." Holly scowls, examining the hickeys closer. "Disgusting! He's branded you."

"Shut up!"

Sharon leads them toward the rodeo arena. Holly follows, knowing the purpose of this excursion, but by her calculations, it's better that Sharon runs into Randy now, while it is still daylight, than after dark, especially after dark at the 49.

Heading around the grandstand, Sharon tries not to think about tomorrow and Holly's moving to Bozeman. Who will be there for her during her senior year? Who will be her confidant? Who will make her laugh? It doesn't seem fair.

Memories flood her mind. Like the time in the eighth grade when she got suspended for three days after refusing to snitch after a schoolwide locker search uncovered two joints in her locker, joints she'd gotten from Holly. As part of her suspension she had to talk to a drug and alcohol counselor, which she actually liked because it gave her a chance to talk about her feelings about her mom. The counseling sessions did nothing to stop her smoking pot, however. In her junior year there was the time she and Holly left school at lunchtime and got stoned behind the wall at the car wash, returning to fifth period band class giggling like fools. Mr. Boggio must have suspected something, because he made them stand up in front of the class and play solos, Holly on the sax, Sharon on the clarinet.

Sharon scans the rodeo crowd but doesn't see Randy. "What a shame," sneers Holly.

"I mean it, Holly," says Sharon. "Stop bugging me about Randy."

* * *

33

It's after midnight when Sharon and Holly leave the fair-grounds and head to the 49. According to one legend, the term 49 originated with tribes in Oklahoma after 49 women got pregnant the night of a big powwow. Another legend has it that 49 men from a tribe in Oklahoma went off in World War II and all 49 returned. In any case, this 49 is on the banks of the Big Horn River at Two Leggings, a clearing named after one of the last Crow warriors to count coup for his bravery in battle.

Arriving at Two Leggings, Sharon parks her Mercury Cougar, a gift from her grandmother three months earlier, next to a picket of cottonwoods. She and Holly survey the jam-packed scene, cars and pickups everywhere. It is dark, noisy, bacchanalian, the night filled with hundreds of Indians. They hear the chanting and drumming, a drumming not of the traditional style, but a rhythmic pounding on the hoods of cars and pickups. The sound is intense, beautiful, part Jamaican oil drum band, part African tribal music. It's a 49 classic: "I'll Take You Home in My One-Eyed Ford."

Holly takes a quick swig of peppermint schnapps to bolster her courage. She feels uneasy, out of place. This is different from the parties she's been to with her Indian friends at school. Those were small gatherings or school activities, teenagers, situations she could control, places she felt safe, protected. This is different, large and unruly, unlit, remote, a place where conventional rules no longer govern. The people are older, drunker. She eyes a man weaving through the crowd, trying to grope every woman who dares into his path. She holds tight to Sharon's arm.

"Don't desert me," she urges. Sharon nods. Behind them, the steady drumming on hoods and fenders grows louder, like thunder rolling through the night.

Moving cautiously around the edge of the crowd, they stop, distracted by a commotion behind them—people pushing, shoving, cursing. Holly circles back to get a better view, but Sharon moves in the other direction, quickly vanishing into the throng.

"Sharon!" yells Holly.

No answer.

Holly retreats to the car, locking the door, bolstering her courage again with another shot of schnapps. How could Sharon do this to her? How could she abandon her on their last night together?

She knows that Randy is out there in the crowd, and whenever Sharon finds him, or he finds her, all the ingredients for disaster are present: alcohol, no rules, jealousy. Especially jealousy.

It's ironic that Holly is the one feeling abandoned. In the past, Sharon was the third wheel while Holly chased after her latest flame. Until Randy, Sharon had never dated, never had a real boyfriend. There was the Northern Cheyenne boy she'd lost her virginity to, but that was a regrettable one-nighter. There was also the boy who asked her to the prom, but that was a date she broke, choosing to go off to play in an all-Indian tournament in Denver instead.

But now there's Randy Not Afraid—first love, real love.

A shot rings out, the echo vibrating down the river and through the trees. The 49 falls eerily silent. Everything stops . . . the singing, chanting, drumming. Even the drinking. Even the crickets.

Holly, whose father is a serious hunter, knows enough about guns to recognize the shot comes from a high-powered rifle. Staying inside the car, she double-checks the locks. Minutes pass, then more minutes, until at last the 49 is in full revel again, word spreading that the shot was just a drunk firing his gun into the air.

Finally, after what seems like hours to Holly, Sharon's silhouette appears, Randy at her side. Holly steps out of the Cougar, watching them approach, studying Randy with a wicked glare, wondering again what is the attraction. How can Sharon think he is so good-looking? Can't she see his ugly teeth? That he is only an inch taller? That he swaggers like a rooster? That's he's too old for her?

That's not what Sharon sees, of course. To her he's perfect. She likes it that he's older, more mature than the high school guys she knows. She also likes it that he's a rodeo roper. In her book, rodeo guys are the rock stars. She also appreciates it that he has a job working construction for Crow Tribal Housing and a steady paycheck. But what she likes best about him are his looks. For reasons she can't explain, she's always imagined her ideal man would have dark curly hair and green eyes, hardly standard traits in an Indian. But that's what Randy has, his green eyes coming from his mother, who is half white, half Cherokee.

Sharon and Randy stop next to the car. Holly bends at the waist and sticks two fingers down her throat, pretending to vomit.

"Randy is riding back to town with us," declares Sharon, ignoring the theatrics.

Holly fumes, but not wanting to walk the seven miles to Hardin, she climbs into the back seat behind Randy.

"How come you're such a dickhead?" she asks, pressing her feet against the back of his seat.

He ignores her.

"How come you cheat on Sharon?" she asks, pressing harder.

Still no response, but she can see his shoulders tighten.

"How come you were with Rona Hugs the other day?" she continues. "And don't say you weren't because I saw you."

"Shut up, Holly!" demands Sharon.

"Whatever," says Holly, slumping back into her seat, deciding she's pushed enough.

They ride in awkward silence back into Hardin. As they pass the high school gym, where Sharon is supposed to be in four hours for the second day of practice, the first rays of sunlight are already inching over the eastern shelf of the Big Horn Valley. The Cougar pulls to a stop in front of Holly's house. "Good riddance," snarls Randy as Holly steps from the car. He motions for Sharon to drive away.

She glances at Holly, then at him. Then she drives off down the street, no teary goodbye, no fond farewell to her best friend moving to Bozeman.

Standing on the curb, Holly fights back tears, the taillights of Sharon's car disappearing around the corner.

CHAPTER FOUR

I'm just a small-town girl, you know, like the one Tanya Tucker sings about," says Tiffany. "You know that song, don't you?"

"Sure," I fib.

It's ten minutes before the start of the third day of practice and I'm standing under a side basket, retrieving shots for co-captain Tiffany, slated to be the point guard. On first impression, she seems bright and personable, maybe a little full of herself. She is also full of braces and gangly arms and legs, a good-looking teenager destined to get even better looking as she grows into herself, although from what I hear, the boys at Hardin High think she's pretty hot already.

"How was your summer?" I inquire, trying to break the ice.

She tells me she earned money for clothes by baby-sitting and working part-time at the Radio Shack on Center Street, but she didn't have much success in socking away any of it for college. Her plan is to get a degree in elementary education, maybe at Montana State in Bozeman, hopefully on an athletic scholarship, then come back to Hardin and teach. She's already had feelers for both basketball and volleyball.

Coach Mac enters, smiling. She's just spotted Sharon, her

AWOL post player, in the locker room. "Sharon's here," she announces.

Tiffany doesn't smile. The consensus among the players is that Coach Mac won't discipline Sharon for missing the first two days of practice.

Coach Mac glances at her clipboard, reviewing the day's drills, her schedule timed to the minute. She blows her whistle, motioning everybody to gather under the basket. As the team forms a circle, a side door opens, and in walks Sharon, yawning, looking as if she'd slept in her car—untucked jersey, untied sneakers, droopy socks, bloodshot eyes. Coach Mac surveys her but says nothing, continuing to address the squad.

"You're going to run your butts off again today, ladies," she instructs. "Lots of work on the zone press."

Sharon stands alone at the back of the circle, shoulders slumped, head down, almost an outcast. Against the wall behind her waits the heavy medicine ball, a tool used by Coach Mac to punish girls for tardiness or other infractions. The previous day, Christina Chavez, a fifteen-year-old sophomore guard with a reputation as a party girl, had to carry it for five extra laps, her punishment for missing the first day of practice. She'd been in the Crow Agency jail, picked up leaving Crow Fair the night before for being a minor in possession, not the first time she'd gotten in trouble because of alcohol. She told Coach Mac she overslept.

Sharon expects punishment, and if Coach Mac asks why she missed the first two days, she won't lie. To her, missing practice for Crow Fair, a cultural happening, is a legitimate excuse. So is her reason for missing the second day: she felt so bad about the way she and Holly parted, that she called to apologize, and when Holly asked her to drive to Bozeman with her, she did, skipping practice again. She spent last night with Holly and her mom in Bozeman, then got up before dawn to drive two hundred miles so she could make the 9 A.M. practice, coming straight to the gym, no breakfast, no juice. She's operating on four hours' sleep in two nights.

"Everybody give me five laps!" orders Coach Mac.

Sharon falls into step with the pack, circling the gym, the medicine ball sitting against the wall.

Tiffany shakes her head. But she's not surprised. The way she sees it, the teachers and coaches at Hardin High use a different yardstick when disciplining Indians, especially the good athletes. All the white kids know it. Indians never get punished. Coach Mac has a different take. On this day, she doesn't want to waste precious minutes waiting for Sharon to run extra laps. It's more important that the whole team works on the zone press. Besides . . . it's not like she doesn't know a double standard is bad for morale.

After the five laps, the team runs its line drills, a wicked conditioning exercise, players sprinting from end line to free throw line and back . . . then to midcourt and back . . . then to the other free throw line and back . . . and then to the other end line and back. Then they do it all over again, only this time backward. Then sideways. A total of ten times. Without stopping. A respiratory hell.

Sharon is the first to finish. She bends at the waist and gasps for air, her lungs paying the price for too many Marlboro Lights over the summer. Still, she's glad to be back on the court.

"Way to work!" encourages Coach Mac.

All things considered, Tiffany is happy to have Sharon back on the court. They haven't seen each other since the team camp in Bozeman in June, but Tiffany is hopeful that last season's hostility and resentment between them will be gone.

Theirs is a fragile alliance, a relationship dating back to

junior high when they first played together on the seventh grade basketball team, the two best players. Everybody who's watched them on the court together talks about their chemistry, an anticipation of each other's moves acquired over countless hours of playing together. Off the court, however, they mirror the way whites and Indians co-exist in Big Horn County—distant and suspicious. As juniors they barely talked.

Tiffany, whose great-grandparents immigrated to Montana from Germany in the early 1900s, has always sensed that Sharon resents her. She isn't sure why. Maybe it's because she is in the Honor Society and Sharon isn't, or because she lives in a nice house and has responsible parents and Sharon doesn't. Or because she is more popular with the boys. Or maybe it's because they are both so competitive and want to be the best player on the team. Or maybe it's because their personalities are from different galaxies, Sharon inward and laconic, Tiffany outgoing and gabby. So many possibilities. Whatever the cause, they've never sat down and talked about it.

There was a time when Tiffany thought the tension between them might be racial. But that didn't make sense. Sharon's two best friends, Holly Johnson and Amy Hanson, are white, and Tiffany's best friend, Geri Stewart, is Crow. No, Tiffany now thinks she's finally got it figured out—the problem is Holly.

The way she sees it, Holly is a foul-mouthed slut who poisoned Sharon against her. Back in the seventh grade, everybody on the basketball team was tight, Holly included. They all ate lunch together, shared birthday parties, gossiped about boys. Then in the ninth grade, for reasons Tiffany didn't understand, Holly and Sharon pulled away from the group and formed their own clique. It got so bad that during volleyball season the coach had to tell Sharon and Holly to sit with the other players or they couldn't play.

It didn't help when Tiffany heard that Holly was calling her names—*stuck-up, bitch, phony*—behind her back. Then, when word got around that Holly was moving to Bozeman, Tiffany hoped that with her gone, the tension with Sharon would disappear for their senior year.

Ten seconds of watching Sharon in the zone press drill is all it takes. The boys' story I've come in search of will not be the story I will follow. Her presence has charged the atmosphere of practice, bringing an animation and intensity missing the first two days. It isn't that she physically looks different from the other players. Like every other girl on the court, she wears her hair in a ponytail; like every other girl she wears black sneakers and a reversible black and white practice jersey. She has no special features to set her apart, and at 5'8", she isn't the tallest player on the squad. Or strongest.

But she has a presence, that special gift possessed by outstanding athletes. She brings a new energy to the building. The second unit tries to move the ball upcourt, and intuitively she cuts off the passing lane, trapping the dribbler along the sideline.

"Move up, move up!" she exhorts, directing traffic.

The other players quicken their pace, their eyes awaiting her cue. A six-cylinder hatchback is now an eight-cylinder roadster. The platoon has its sergeant. Tiffany is directing traffic, too, but her voice doesn't carry the authority.

The first unit switches to offense and Tiffany flips an overhead pass to Sharon, who in a flash feeds it back to her with a nifty touch pass. Tiffany starts to penetrate the middle but hesitates, losing her step advantage on her defender. Momentarily confused, she passes it back to Sharon, who drives the baseline hard and scores on a reverse layup . . . lefthanded.

I am drop-jawed astounded. A skinny seventeen-year-old Indian girl just can't be this good. She is throwing moves I never saw in any boys' game I played in back in the late 1950s. She dribbles the ball between her legs as smooth as soft chocolate. Nobody did that back then.

But I also notice something else. A paradox. She is intense, yet detached, at the heart of the action, then miles away. Coach Mac stops play to position two confused sophomores, and Sharon's shoulders sag and her head droops. Then the whistle blows and she turns and lopes down the court, passing every girl in front of her. A minute later she stands shoulder to shoulder with sophomore Kassi Elk Shoulder, smiling, then turns her head and looks as if she doesn't have a friend in the world. Then again, maybe I am just disposed by liberal guilt to read 140 years of suffering in the bleary eyes of a teen who's simply been up most of the night. Or maybe it isn't my imagination. Maybe this young woman is being torn in half, and consequently, hurts like hell.

At the end of practice, the girls spread around the gym to shoot free throws, two and three to a basket. Except Sharon. At a side basket she shoots alone, fetching the ball herself after every shot. Slowly, I ease toward her. Without saying anything, I position myself under the basket, flicking the ball back to her after each attempt.

She doesn't acknowledge me, her eyes zeroed in on the target. Coach Mac had introduced me to the team the previous day, but from Sharon's indifference, I can't tell if she thinks I'm a new freshman coach or an automated ball retriever.

I want to say something. But what? That I'd seen her at the court in Crow Agency? That I'd been told that despite her talent she didn't have a buffalo's chance on the

Pasadena Freeway of winning a scholarship? She swishes another shot, her sixth in a row.

"How do you think the team will do this season?" I ask rather feebly.

She shrugs, offering no verbal response, only a stop-bothering-me glance.

She swishes her ninth in a row.

"I got a quarter says you can't make it ten," I say, rolling the ball back five feet to her left, making her leave her spot on the line.

She picks up the ball with that same tricky little flick of the foot I'd seen at the court in Crow Agency and peers in my direction, expressionless. Returning to her spot, she toes the line, then cool as Larry Bird drains her tenth in a row. Then she turns and heads for the locker room, no glance back, no adieu, no request for her quarter.

Chapter Five

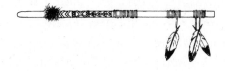

"Hi, Sharon," I say as she hustles past me on the sidewalk in front of the school.

She mumbles something in response, but with her head turned to the parking lot, I can't tell what it is. Whatever it is, I get the feeling I've just been demoted from automated ball retriever to truant officer. It's mid-morning and she's leaving school.

She hurries across the parking lot and slides into the passenger seat of a long Lincoln Continental with "Jr. Boss" vanity plates. A large Indian woman is behind the wheel.

Tomorrow is the season opener and school has been in session for a week. With the exception of the faculty's hostility toward the Hardin school board for its "insulting offer" of a 2 percent pay raise, Hardin High is off to a smooth start. Enrollment is slightly above the forecast—395 total students with 49 percent Indians—which is good for getting more federal dollars for educating Indians. The campus has been calm, with no major student incidents, not that any are expected. There's been the normal posturing in the hallways and racial slurs behind backs, of course, but nothing Ed "Awful" Aucker, the vice principal in charge of gruff, can't handle.

Things have gone smoothly with the Lady Bulldogs, too,

notwithstanding Sharon's disappearing act the first two days. So far, team harmony is good and expectations remain high. I'm convinced that three players—Sharon, Tiffany, and Anita Dewald—could make any team in America. I'm also convinced that two sophomores, 6'1" Stacie Greenwalt, the best pure athlete on the team, and guard Christina Chavez, the best ball-handler, should be starting, although Coach Mac doesn't see it that way, choosing to start sophomore Owena Spotted Horse and junior Rhea Beatty. The rest of the team doesn't figure to be much help, however, often running around like village idiots against the first team's full-court pressure.

In the parking lot, the long Lincoln Continental slowly exits and heads in the direction of I-90. As I watch it disappear around the corner, I smell something fishy, and it's not the big rainbows and German browns in the nearby Big Horn River. But I don't know what.

"I've got a secret weapon today," I say, flipping a ball to junior guard Anita Dewald.

"Doubt it," she answers.

As usual, she's the first one out of the locker room and I'm waiting for her, eager for our daily game of H-O-R-S-E before practice. Considering Hardin's limited entertainment options, our contests have become a highlight of my day. The series is tied, but she's on a three-game winning streak, killing me with long bombs from the corner. On this day, I've come to the gym early, practicing a little junior skyhook.

She hits her first two shots, jumpers from the key, and I miss, picking up a quick H-O.

"Now I'm ready," I warn.

Anita is America's perfect daughter—polite, good-looking, and very bright, a straight-A student with an eye on medical school. Of all the players on the team, she is the friend-liest, the most accessible, the most intellectually curious. She asks me questions. *Do I know much about Crow cul-ture?* No, but I'm learning. *Did I vote for Clinton?* Yes.

She frowns.

I battle back, tying the game at H-O-R-S with an under-hand free throw. As I set myself to administer my little baby skyhook coup de grâce, Coach Mac exits the locker room looking like a time bomb one tick short of flying debris. "Where's Sharon?" she demands.

Tiffany, who learned yesterday that she and Sharon had been nominated for homecoming queen, says that she sat next to her in first period government class, but hasn't seen her since. I think about telling Coach Mac about seeing Sharon leaving school earlier, but figure I'm not here to be a stool pigeon.

A degree of trust is starting to build between me and the players, although I'm not ready to declare myself an hon-orary seventeen-year-old. I'm blending in, a regular at prac-tice, a worthy opponent for a game of H-O-R-S-E. A couple girls have even asked for my help on homework. But not Sharon. I still haven't dented her veneer.

It's not surprising. By repute, Crows are suspicious of strangers, usually slow to open up, and Sharon certainly fits the stereotype. Yesterday, I saw her in front of the office and offered my congratulations on her being one of the four nominees for homecoming queen, but judging from her response, she must have been nominated on the Deaf and Mute ticket.

"Go over to Sharon's house and see if she's there," or-ders Coach Mac, pointing at senior Geri Stewart, a second-string forward and the team's third queen nominee.

Geri looks as if she's just been asked to go fetch. "No way she'd send somebody to look for me," she mutters, heading toward the door.

47

Coach Mac blows her whistle, and as the players take off on their laps, she stands against the wall, arms tightly crossed. She knows her own rule—miss practice without an excuse and you miss a game. This is an aggravation she doesn't need on the eve of the first game. She scowls.

I don't ask if Anita and I can go for the tiebreaker.

"Damnit, Rhea!" yells Coach Mac. "You gotta move!"

For the second time in practice, Rhea Beatty, a 5'7" starting forward, has been lead-footed getting into position on the press, allowing the second team to score an easy layin.

"Let's try the two-three press again," orders Coach Mac. "And Rhea, see if you can get it right this time. It's not that tough."

Rhea, a Crow, looks on the edge of tears. Easy to figure. I'm no shrink, but it looks as if Coach Mac is misdirecting her anger at Sharon's unexplained absence on the other players, especially Rhea, a quiet girl who dreams of becoming a photographer.

I'm still trying to figure out Coach Mac's discipline code. I've yet to hear her yell at Sharon, Tiffany, or Anita, her three stars, but she regularly zeroes in on Rhea and other players. Sharon skips two days of practice and nothing happens; Rhea doesn't rotate on the press and it's as if she threw cow pies all over the gym.

One explanation is that Coach Mac, who is bending over backward to accommodate me, is up to her eyeballs in pressure—pressure not just to have a winning season, but to capture a championship. She's been at the helm for five years now, and her teams have gotten better each year, but there are still no trophies in the showcase, still no trips to State. With the team's talent this year, anything less than State and her job might be in jeopardy.

The pressure to win isn't reserved for just the pro and

48

college coaches, and Coach Mac is reminded of this every day when she walks into the faculty lounge and sees Luke Gerber, the boys' coach who lost his job despite a better winning percentage than hers. At the end of last season, he came under fire from critics on the rez who didn't appreciate his deliberate style of play. They put pressure on the school board to can him and hire an Indian. ("He never lets the kids shoot so we might as well just take down the baskets.") A week after their complaints, he was fired as varsity coach, and John Whiteman, an Indian, was hired over assistant coach for the boys' and girls' teams Dave Oswald, a white with more coaching experience. "Basketball is the tail that wags the dog around here," vented Gerber.

"Rhea!" yells Coach Mac. "How do you expect to do it right in the game tomorrow night when you don't have a clue here today?"

"I thought I . . ." begins Rhea.

"Never mind. Let's take a water break. Maybe when we come back, Rhea will have remembered where she's supposed to be."

After the break, Rhea gets it right, but when practice is finally over—with no sign of Sharon—Coach Mac is still in a barking mood. She gathers the team around her. "I hope we play better tomorrow than we practiced today," she scolds.

Before heading to the locker room, the players join hands in a circle, then shout in unison as they break the huddle. "Unity!"

For Linda McClanahan, some days it feels as if her whole life has been stress and pressure, just one long courtship with her ulcers. Even as a child growing up in Judith Gap, Montana, population two hundred, a windswept dot in the middle of wheat county, halfway between the Big Snowy and the Little Belt mountain ranges, she knew stress. The youngest of eight children, she was only three when her parents divorced, her father walking out on the family. Probably just as well; he was an alcoholic with a reputation for slapping around his wife and kids. After he left, Linda's mother waited tables at the local cafe until poor health forced her to quit and go on welfare. It was a hand-to-mouth childhood for Linda, eight kids squeezed together in a small three-bedroom house.

As angry as she is at Sharon for missing practice, the absence doesn't surprise her. Sharon's ambivalent approach to the game is typical of the players she's coached from the reservation—a consuming passion on the one hand, and a disinclination to discipline themselves on the other. In games and practices, Sharon has always fought for every rebound, dived for every loose ball, but rarely arrives early or stays late, never runs extra laps, never lifts weights. Over the summer, she did no work on the skills that will help her to a scholarship, her ball-handling or outside shooting. At 5'8", her chances of making it in college, even a small college, are at guard, not as the post player she is for Hardin.

Coach Mac understands the reality. She and Sharon are both native Montanans who know at some separate but instinctual level that basketball to Indians is a war fought for spiritual rather than material terrain, including scholarships.

Coach Mac can't allow herself to think about where Sharon might be today or why she missed practice. Over the years, she's heard hundreds of sad stories from Crow players and students about why they're absent or late—they had to take Uncle Billy to the detox center; they had to spend the night in the back seat of grandma's Ford; they can't afford an alarm clock; they went to a powwow in Pine Ridge and ran out of gas on the way home. Sometimes these stories make it difficult to distinguish between cultural differences and ordinary dysfunction and irresponsibility. For survival, Coach Mac has learned to stay at arm's distance from the personal lives of her students and players, many of whom go home after school to total chaos. Maintaining this distance is her defense against burnout.

She knows little of Sharon's home life other than that there is no dad in the picture and an alcoholic mom. Beyond that, she thinks Sharon to be quiet, shy, vulnerable, a girl unlikely to come to her with her problems, a stalwart young woman surviving on her own, basically raising herself, staying free of drugs, alcohol, and sex. She has met her grandmother, but really doesn't know much about her other than that she wears lots of jewelry, perfume, and garish outfits, and drives a big Lincoln Continental. Somebody has told her Sharon recently moved in with an aunt in Hardin, but she really doesn't know where. Or worry about it. Housing is a fluid situation with the Crows, kids bouncing from house to house within the extended family, sleeping with an aunt one night, a grandma the next, always somewhere to go. On the rez, there is no homelessness. She has never probed Sharon about the intimate details of her life. She knows nothing of Randy Not Afraid, or the joints, or the Marlboro Lights.

She is confident Sharon will show up tomorrow night. One thing she knows for sure about the Crows . . . they take their games very seriously.

Part II

THE TIP-OFF
TOURNEY

CHAPTER SIX

Seated in front of her locker, Tiffany puts on her uniform in the same order she always has: shorts first, then the shirt, and finally the socks and shoes, right foot first. Next to her, Sharon follows her own superstitious routine, sprinkling a pinch of sage into the bottom of her black Reeboks, a tribal ritual she's learned from her aunt to ward off evil spirits and bring good luck. Earlier, Coach Mac accepted her story—that she had to drive her grandmother to the VA Hospital in Sheridan, Wyoming, for an emergency visit with her great-uncle dying of cancer. What was she supposed to do . . . call the hospital?

The Lady Bulldogs' opponents, the Sidney Lady Eagles, are already out on the court warming up. As co-captains Tiffany and Sharon lead their teammates toward the door leading to the gym, they are accompanied by Queen's "We Will Rock You," the decibels on the locker room boom box cranked high. Inside the gym, the Hardin pep band is even louder. I'm already hoarse trying to talk over the clamor.

Dressed in their brand-new orange and black warmups, the team assembles at the door, ready for their grand entrance. On the other side awaits that exalted moment in a high school athlete's life, the thrill of bursting out into the spotlight with the band blaring, the cheerleaders leaping, the crowd cheering.

Unrehearsed, Tiffany motions the other four seniors to join her in a small circle off to one side. She feels a lump gathering in the back of her throat, tears forming in her eyes. It is the sudden realization that a final chapter in her high school career is about to begin, her senior season in basketball, a time that will never come again. She has been through it all with these girls, teammates since the seventh grade—the victories, defeats, jealousies—Sharon LaForge, Geri Stewart, DyAnna Three Irons, Tiffany Hopfauf, Amy Hanson. Three Indians and two whites. Three homecoming queen nominees. She wants to freeze the moment.

Tightening the circle, the five seniors drape their arms around each other and pull closer. A tear rolls down Tiffany's cheek. She glances around the circle, surprised to see everyone else has tears, too, including Sharon. That really surprises her. She's seen Sharon cry before, once in the locker room after the loss to Billings Central in last year's Divisionals, and once when her mother showed up drunk at a volleyball game. But those times were somehow understandable. This is different, a sentimental moment, an unexpected display of emotion. This can't be Sharon. Warriors don't cry.

Tiffany brushes back her tears, then pushes open the door and gallops out onto the court in front of the cheering crowd. Sharon follows close behind, head down, embarrassed by her tears.

Hardin's opponent, the Lady Eagles of Sidney, an agricultural town on the Yellowstone River five miles from the North Dakota border, has lost all five starters off last year's team that finished second at State. Despite this lack of experience, they're picked in the Billings Gazette coaches' poll to finish third in the conference, just ahead of the Lady Bulldogs, a ranking that rankles Coach Mac, who's always believed that the rest of the league doesn't respect her program. This adds more proof. Sharon hasn't seen the poll, a daily newspaper not part of her life.

Although the games in the Tip-Off Tournament, a preseason competition between teams in the Eastern Conference, won't count in league standings, Coach Mac considers tonight and tomorrow night's games crucial to her team's psyche. She worries that a bad start will disrupt its fragile chemistry. This is a team capable of going south in a hurry. With tip-off a minute away, she checks to make sure her bottle of Mylanta is next to the bench.

The starting five take the court. Tiffany, looking like she's strolling into Dandy Tom's Ice Cream Parlor down on Center Street, smiles and shakes hands with two opponents, both blondes, just like all the Sidney starters. Sharon glowers, her face pulled tighter than rawhide. She surveys an opponent's extended hand, hesitates, then shakes it, no smile, no pretense of chummy fraternization.

With the near capacity crowd on its feet, Anita controls the opening tap, tipping it to a wide-open Sharon, who dribbles twice, then casts off from 15 feet. Swish. The season is four seconds old.

Against Hardin's full-court pressure, Sidney inbounds the ball, their panicked guards looking as if they've never seen a press before. Or an Indian. Sharon intercepts a crosscourt pass, then rifles the ball to Tiffany for an easy score. Five seconds later, Tiffany intercepts another lame pass and feeds it to Sharon, who drains a jumper from 17 feet. Six points in 18 seconds. Sidney still hasn't gotten the ball to midcourt. Rhea is right where she is supposed to be.

Midway through the first quarter, with Hardin cruising 13–3, Coach Mac pulls the starting five and inserts the second unit. She takes a deep breath. Her bench has looked relentlessly confused in practices, clueless as to where to be in the zone press . . . and in her fast-break, pressure-defense style of play, the zone press is everything. Stacie Greenwalt and Christina Chavez, the two sophomores I think should be starting despite their inexperience, aren't even in uniform. Coach Mac wants them to play several games with the junior varsity before getting minutes with the varsity. The rule is that a player can play in a junior varsity and varsity game in the same day, but for no more than a total of four quarters. She worries that the three senior subs will pitch a fit if she leapfrogs these sophomores over them too soon.

"Relax!" she instructs as senior Geri Stewart turns it over.

It takes Sidney just 50 seconds to score seven straight points. The scrubeanies have flunked their first test.

"Horrible!" yells Coach Mac, waving the first team back into the game.

Coach Mac has always dreamed of that rare moment when everything comes together on the court—offensively, defensively, emotionally—that elusive circumstance when pure basketball synchronism happens and all five athletes enter a zone, everybody working in perfect union, a controlled frenzy. And for the next six minutes, that's exactly what she witnesses, something truly remarkable.

Sharon triggers it with a jump shot, then swipes a pass at midcourt and hits Anita with a look-left-dish-it-right pass for an easy two. Then she shanghaies another errant pass and fires a pass between two dazed defenders to Tiffany, who cashes in. Six points in 30 seconds. The crowd goes nuts.

Over the summer, Coach Mac decided to take the first string's two tallest starters, Tiffany, 5'10", and Anita, 5'9", and make them guards. It will be their job to hound the ball in the backcourt and use their quickness and long arms to pressure opponents into bad passes and turnovers. Now, just eight minutes into the season, the experiment is working. Six straight times the Sidney guards, confronted with a whirlwind of arms and elbows, turn it over, the Lady Bulldogs converting it into easy baskets, each score raising the crowd noise to a higher, more deafening level. After 14 unanswered points, the Sidney coach calls a timeout.

"Switch to a diamond zone," orders Coach Mac.

Sidney inbounds the ball and Sharon deflects it, diving sideways into the bleachers to save it. With a flick of the wrist, she flips it backward over her head as she crashes through the pep band. Tiffany gathers it in and drives the baseline, swooping beneath the basket like a giant bird of prey, releasing the ball softly over her head like an egg, kissing it off the backboard through the hoop.

It's bedlam in the stands, everybody standing and roaring, me included. I notice that Crows and whites, folks not likely to offer a glass of water to each other in a fire, are standing shoulder to shoulder, cheering themselves hoarse.

The Sidney coach frantically signals another timeout, but by now the run is up to 23, breathtaking in its energy and execution. Before Coach Mac finally calls off the attack dogs and puts the second string back in, the first unit has reeled off 26 unanswered points. *Twenty-six.*

At halftime Hardin leads 42–15, only three of Sidney's points coming against the first team. Coach Mac can't remember a better streak by any team she's ever seen. Who cares if Sharon cut practice?

In the second half, the Lady Bulldogs let up, big-time, a total swoon, physically and mentally, playing with no purpose, no intensity. Despite the hemorrhaging, they hang on to win 62–50, Tiffany leading the scoring with 23 points and 11 steals. Sharon, who left the game in the fourth quarter with a bloody lip, isn't happy. Part of it has to do with the fat lip, a result of a wild elbow under the basket. She is also disappointed with her own performance: 12 points, four rebounds, eight assists. But mostly she is irked at Tiffany. How can she sit there with such a big cheesy postgame grin on her face? How can she not be concerned about the team's abysmal collapse in the second half? Does she only care about how many points she scores?

"Girls," Coach Mac scowls, "that second half was embarrassing. Play like that tomorrow night against Miles City and you'll get buried."

Then she walks around the corner and takes a big swig of her Mylanta.

CHAPTER SEVEN

After the game, I drive down Center Street and see two Indians stagger out of the Wagon Wheel. Big surprise. Drinking around here, especially among the men, is beyond out of control. Forty percent of the adult population is hopelessly alcoholic, and it goes a lot deeper than just not being able to find a job. For one thing, these are the boonies, mostly dirt and Budweiser for a hundred miles around. The sun's gone down, the basketball game is over, so what are the options? Go back home and watch *The Simpsons*? Hey, why not go to the Wagon Wheel, drink ten beers, play Pac-Man, flirt incompetently with the curvy bartender, get in an argument, maybe even a fistfight, climb back in the car, and drive around the county at a million miles an hour until the car's in a ditch? Nothing folks around here haven't been doing for years . . . and they've got the white crosses next to the road as proof.

I go home and check the answering machine. There's a message from Sarah, my younger daughter. She says it's urgent and I need to call her "the second" I get in. Urgent to Sarah, however, is not necessarily urgent to an ER doctor. I check the clock. It's 10:30, which makes it 9:30 back in Eugene where she's starting her second year at the University of Oregon. Let's see, what are the chances of her being home on a Friday night? After all, this is a kid who thought I was a fuddy-duddy for making her be home before dawn on Wednesday nights. But a great kid, nonetheless.

Surprise. She's home. "What's up?" I ask, half expecting her to tell me she had to spend $3,000 more on books than she budgeted and could I please help her out. I'm sort of correct.

The problem, she explains, is that the sorority she wants to de-pledge won't give her a refund on the $900 check I wrote for initiation fees. And now she has no money for a deposit on the apartment she wants. Enter the father. Luckily I'm currently in the chips, so I agree to send her the money. She thanks me profusely. I hang up, wondering how many kids on the rez could squeeze nine hundred big ones out of their old man. In fact, I wonder how many of them could even find their old man to give any kind of a squeeze. Sharon couldn't.

Next, I call Marcie, my girlfriend. We've been living together for, what, seven years now. This separation, however, is not easy. So far, we've talked on the phone every night since I left home. She's planning on a visit; I'm planning a trip home.

For a guy used to living in a crowd, this expedition to the prairie frontier is a big change. I can't help but wonder about the locals' reaction. Because I'm always coming and going by myself, do these people around here think I'm some sort of eunuch loner? Or maybe because I'm focused on a bunch of high school girls, they have me pegged as a voyeur. Yesterday, I walked out of the school in the middle of the day and a sheriff's deputy slowed down to check me out. I stopped to put a camera in my trunk, and out of the corner of my eye, I saw him turn around. I figured, nah, this isn't about me. I got in my car and drove to the IGA—about five blocks—and he was in my rearview mirror the whole time. I was still thinking, nah. But when I pulled into the parking lot, he was right behind me, his lights now flashing. He approached the car. "What's the problem, Officer?" I asked. He said he saw me coming out of the school, and he noticed the out-of-state plates, and he was just wondering what I was doing around these parts. My first inclination was to tell him it's none of his damn business. But I tried that with a cop in Portland once and it didn't get very good results, so my second inclination was to show him pictures of my girlfriend and daughters, and if that didn't impress him that I was a square shooter, well, maybe we could go to the Chat and Chew and I could tell him about my stint as a Big Brother. "I'm a writer," I explained, "and I'm here to research a book on the Crows and basketball and what goes on around here." He pondered the information, then replied. "Well, I don't know why anybody would want to read about that, but . . . good luck."

In the second quarter at home against the Miles City Cowgirls, another all-blond team, Sharon puts a move on her defender, rough and tough Joleyn Wambolt, a shoulder dip that nearly sends the girl into the tuba section. To my left, three very substantial men with long ponytails and satin jackets from a long-forgotten Indian basketball tournament emit substantially loud war whoops, so loud that a shiver runs down my back. These guys haven't sat down the whole game. Fine by me.

A few plays later, Sharon steps into the lane on defense, and Wambolt, who outweighs her by thirty-five pounds, charges into her, knocking her flat on her skinny ass. The ref calls the foul on Sharon. Along with everyone else, I shout my disapproval, forgetting for the moment that I'm supposed to be an impartial observer.

A minute later, with the score tied, Owena Spotted Horse fires up an air ball. "Come on, Owena!" I yell.

I hear the words rush off my lips. Okay, I need to settle down. I mean, what am I doing angrily yelling at a fifteen-year-old high school girl, and a member of an oppressed minority at that? All I can think of is . . . she shouldn't have taken the shot.

At halftime, Hardin leads by one.

In the lobby outside the gym I spot the woman who was driving the big Lincoln in which Sharon left school. My hunch is that she's Sharon's grandmother, Danetta Falls-down, an infamous character on the rez, a flamboyant woman known for her garish outfits and outspoken involvement in Crow politics. On her sweater, she's wearing a plastic button with Sharon's picture in a basketball uniform emblazoned on it. She's also wearing enough perfume to choke a cosmetics clerk. I introduce myself.

"Sharon's mentioned you," she says.

That's a shock. I was still under the assumption I was invisible to Sharon.

Standing by the nachos dispenser, we talk, or rather she talks. A shy, taciturn Indian she's not, her words flying at me like bullets. Out of nowhere she asks if I'd like to come to the house next week for a special dinner with family and clan members to honor Sharon before the start of conference play. "I'd be honored," I reply. There will be prayers to the Great Spirit in a tradition handed down through the generations, a ritual to connect Sharon with tribal history and bring her good luck.

"There'll be a medicine man there," she adds.

I picture a guy gyrating around in feathers and buckskin, waving rattlesnake tails and sprinkling peyote dust as he chants voodoo songs.

"You can take a sweat, too," she says.

"Great," I lie, picturing buzzards swooping down to pick the last strips of carrion from my toasted carcass. I've been warned that there are jokesters on the rez who like to crank up the heat to about 900 degrees whenever a white rookie ventures into their sweat lodge. But what the heck. It's not that I think I need to go on some kind of vision quest to gather my story, but if I have to work up a little sweat to gain a reservation stamp of approval, I'm game. I just hope I don't have to crawl in there naked with a bunch of grandmas.

As we head back to the gym, she offers her first-half analysis. "That Tiffany girl needs to stop hoggin' the ball," she says.

A check of the first-half stats shows Sharon taking eight shots, Tiffany four.

This isn't Anita Dewald's night. At the end of the third quarter, she has nine turnovers, the last one allowing Miles City to close the gap to five. On the way back to the bench, she hangs her head, looking like she's ready to cry. Sharon eases alongside and throws a comforting arm around her shoulder. Anita seems surprised.

Anita has never been sure what to think of Sharon. Sharon has always been cordial enough toward her—saying hello in the hallways, greeting her before practice—but they aren't close, never connecting on a personal level, their relationship strictly sports. Anita knows nothing about Randy, not even that he exists. She knows that Sharon's home life is unstable, but on the reservation, isn't everybody's?

Anita respects, even reveres Sharon's athletic talents, meeting for the first time as preteens on the Hardin Community Center swim team. Sharon had never swum competitively and had missed the first month of the season, but after only three days of practice, she took third in the statewide Big Sky Games in the backstroke. Anita, who holds several county records, is convinced Sharon could've been a state champion if she'd stuck with it.

But she questions the depth of Sharon's athletic dedication, much of her suspicion the result of an incident that happened between them over the summer. They were driving to the Big Sky Games basketball tournament in Miles City in Sharon's car. For Anita, the two-hour drive would be a chance to get to know Sharon better. Riding with them were sophomore teammates Kassi Elk Shoulder and Owena.

On the way out of Hardin that day, Sharon pulled off the road and asked Anita to drive. Anita said okay and Sharon climbed into the back seat. A few miles down the road, Anita glanced over her shoulder and was shocked to see Sharon lighting up a joint. Anita, a girl who'd never kissed a boy or missed a Sunday in church, freaked. She'd never seen dope before, let alone been in a car when someone was smoking it.

With Sharon getting high in the back seat, Anita's first reaction was to stop the car and get out and walk back home. But she kept driving. Pretty soon a State Trooper pulled in behind them. Nervously, Sharon told her to slow down. Anita checked the speedometer. She was under the speed limit. She remembered from her *Just Say No* training that dope skewed people's perception of time and space, and figured that's what was happening to Sharon.

The trooper followed them for a couple miles, then turned off on a county road. But for Anita, the damage was done. If Sharon wanted to smoke dope, that was her business, but how could she put others at risk? In Miles City, Anita called her parents, who came and picked her up after the game, refusing to let her ride home with Sharon. They won the game.

For Anita, the incident left a sour taste. It wasn't helped when Sharon didn't show up the first two days of practice.

Returning to the court for the fourth quarter, Sharon still has her arm around Anita's shoulder. "Hang in there," she encourages.

With 1:27 left in the game, Hardin is up by seven, the crowd acting like the Lady Bulldogs are about to win the World Cup. And this is a preseason game.

Despite the lead, Sharon looks frustrated. She hasn't played particularly well, scoring only seven points, although she has 12 rebounds. She's gone to the floor three times after loose balls, each time because a teammate has thrown a careless pass, then stood flatfooted while Sharon gets the floorburn.

She also looks exhausted. So do the other starters. Tiffany, Rhea, and Anita have played the whole game, and Sharon has been out for less than a minute, and only then because she had a leg cramp. Is Coach Mac nuts? This is the second game of the year.

Miles City scores, steals the ball and scores again, then gets it right back and scores again. A seven-point lead is vaporized to one. There are 45 seconds still left.

Waiting for the inbounds pass, Sharon and Wambolt jostle for position, trading elbows. They're well acquainted, having competed against each other since the ninth grade. Once, as freshmen, they wrestled on the floor after a loose ball, and when they got up, Sharon accidentally on purpose stepped on Wambolt's fingers, not to hurt her, but just to give her a little Charles Barkley intimidation move, letting her know she was tough, too.

"Protect the ball!" yells Coach Mac.

Anita promptly dribbles it off her foot and out of bounds, her 12th turnover of the night. As Miles City prepares to in-bound the ball, their coach, Gary Vels, jumps up and down, waving his arms like a madman, signaling his girls to call a timeout.

"Goddamnit!" he rages. "Pay attention to me!"

It's not the first time in the game that he's gone ballistic at his players, berating them in front of the stands, a man who evidently thinks coaching is an act of intimidation.

Play resumes with 23 seconds left and Miles City works it to Wambolt, who misses a shot but is fouled by Rhea, sending her to the line for two. Now there's only 12 seconds left.

As Wambolt steps to the line, everybody in the gym is stomping and screaming. Wall-to-wall noise. The three large men with ponytails and satin jackets all reach behind their backs and pull imaginary arrows out of imaginary quivers, then load them into imaginary bows and aim right at Wambolt. They let the arrows fly just as she shoots.

Swish.

So much for the arrows. The game is tied.

"Time out!" calls Coach Mac.

If it's noise that's going to fluster Wambolt, it's right there in her ear, the decibel level peeling the paint. Then, calm as dawn, Wambolt returns to the line, eyes the basket, and arches the ball skyward.

Swish again.

Hardin trails by one. Nine seconds left.

With no timeouts left, Anita quickly flips it to Tiffany, who dribbles upcourt along the sideline, a defender right on her hip. Cut off, she passes ahead to Rhea. Five seconds left.

Rhea dribbles once, then spots Sharon cutting down the

middle, wide open. The pass is perfect, Sharon getting it at the top of the key—exactly as Coach Mac diagrammed earlier in the huddle—but Sharon momentarily hesitates and Wambolt slides in front of her, blocking her lane to the hoop.

Then, in a move she's practiced a thousand times on the baked dirt in her grandma's yard next to Custer Battlefield, Sharon takes one step and launches a jump shot. Wambolt jumps, too, and as Sharon releases the ball, it skims over the defender's outstretched fingers.

All eyes turn toward the rim, all voices hush. Then the ball kisses the front of the rim and slides down through the net as the horn sounds. The Lady Bulldogs are 2-0.

PART III

CONFERENCE PLAY
(First Half)

CHAPTER EIGHT

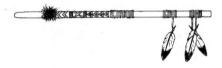

I exit the freeway, turning toward Custer Battlefield. Just down the hill and across the road stands Danetta and Blaine Fallsdown's weatherbeaten and weary three-bedroom house, Sharon's home for most of her life. As a child she rode her horse through the coulees of the battlefield, walked to the Custer Trading Post, arched jump shots at the family's backyard basket.

The house stands alone in a barren field, surrounded by parched dirt and buffalo grass. I approach on a gravel road as the autumn sun starts to disappear in the west behind the benchtop across the valley of the Little Big Horn, its hills cast in beautiful hues of crimson, orange, and yellow. Off to my right I see the sweat lodge, Grandpa Blaine standing in front of it, stirring a pile of red-hot rocks with a pitchfork.

Normally, the hardened dirt next to the house serves as the family's basketball court, but on this evening it is a parking lot for relatives and friends who've come to honor Sharon. Off to the side sit the Fallsdowns' two main contributions to the tribe's junkyarding of its sacred land. One is a '76 Jeep station wagon, inert, hopeless, and corroded, with broken windows, flat tires, and an interior crammed to the ceiling with mildewed junk. A set of antlers sits on the hood. In its better days, Sharon's mother drove it, but then she forgot it needed oil and water, so the engine blew and now it's just a big pile of crap. Behind it, an unsightly house trailer adds a second scar to the landscape. Propped up on cinder blocks, its windows are boarded shut and its turquoise paint is peeling like dead rattlesnake skin.

I park next to Danetta's Mark IV with its "Jr. Boss" vanity plates. Walking across the decaying gray planks that lead to the decaying gray steps of the front porch, I can't figure out which needs a paint job worse, the house or the doghouse. Two huge chained dogs—I guess them to be part Saint Bernard, part malamute, part buffalo—greet my arrival with bored yawns. Neither looks as if they've had a bath since, well, ever.

I knock on the door but nobody answers. I can hear voices inside, so I knock again. Still no answer. Cautiously, I open the door and ease inside, apprehensive, remembering the fate of other whites who tried sneaking up on Indians around here a long time ago. I walk past an old water heater, then into the kitchen, where Danetta is stirring a broth on the stove. Sharon, the one to be honored, has not yet arrived. Danetta, a stout woman, light-skinned, with oval face, permed black hair, and dark-framed glasses, offers a warm greeting.

"I knocked but nobody answered," I apologize.

She laughs. "I see we're gonna have to teach you a few things about life here on the rez," she replies, explaining that nobody around here locks their doors and everybody just walks in. "That door has never been knocked on . . . except for when the sheriff came here causing trouble."

The house, I soon learn, was built by HUD in 1975, and was Danetta's Xanadu. Brand-new when she and Blaine moved in, it had been a reservation showcase, with expensive oak furniture, wall-to-wall carpeting, and a Charles

Russell original. Danetta brags that it was once "just like a white man's house." She even hired an interior decorator.

Now the house is tired and cluttered: faded yellow sheets drape the windows; frayed blankets cover the couches; cat litter spreads across the bathroom floor; dirty ashtrays stink up the dining room. There is enough bric-a-brac and trinkets to supply a swap meet.

Despite the clutter and disrepair, to Danetta's family and friends the house is a gathering place, welcoming. For Sharon, who moved in with her aunt Marlene a block from school for her senior year, it continues to be the one place she always feels safe, secure, and surrounded by family. She can count on Danetta for cookies, gas money, love.

"Who's that?" I ask, pointing to a watercolor portrait in the living room of a handsome, long-haired young man.

"That's my son, Blaine Junior," replies Danetta, her voice dropping. She moves to the portrait, gently touching the face, explaining that the red banner draped over one edge of the frame is a Crow symbol for mourning, and that the hand-carved coup stick resting across the top is the tribal symbol of respect and honor. Then she sits down at the dining room table, pulls a package of tissues from her purse, lights up a Benson & Hedges menthol and tells me the story of her son's murder, a brutal crime that still echoes through the lives of her family, including Sharon, two decades later, a murder that shapes who they are, their anger, their sadness, their sense of loss.

Nicknamed "Junior Boss" because he helped his dad on their ranch, Blaine Junior was a tall, gangly kid who wanted to be a cowboy. Back then, life was good for Danetta and Blaine—regular trips to Vegas, a credit line at the bank, a cattle ranch with four hundred head, and lots of deeded land they sold and leased by the acre to fund the good life. They were envied by many in the tribe, and everyone liked their son, a boy known for his politeness and sense of humor.

As the youngest child and only son, Junior Boss, Sharon's uncle, was the pride of the family, and like most boys on the reservation, spoiled. Whatever Junior Boss wanted, Danetta and Blaine bought him—car, pool table, motor scooter, racehorses, snowmobile, rifles. He rarely left the house with less than a hundred bucks in his pocket; once when he complained he didn't have anyone to play with, Danetta let two cousins move in; when he saw a silver streamlined horse trailer he thought he needed, she paid $2,900 for it on the spot. By the time he turned sixteen, she had already bought fourteen buckskin and ten elks tooth dresses for his future wife, even though he didn't even have a girlfriend. When friends warned her that she was smothering him, she scoffed.

On the Friday night he disappeared, Danetta and Blaine had already gone to bed, but when she awoke in the middle of the night and realized her son hadn't come home, she instinctively knew something was wrong. It wasn't like him to stay out all night—he never spent the night with friends and always called home whenever he was going to be late.

Unable to go back to sleep that night, Danetta and Blaine searched the streets of Crow Agency until dawn, then called the police. Because Junior Boss had disappeared on an Indian reservation, which is under federal jurisdiction, the FBI joined the search. At first, agents suspected kidnapping, figuring that somebody had seen Danetta flashing her money and thought she'd be a good target for a ransom.

For two days, dozens of searchers combed the reservation, then Danetta received a call from Terry Bullis, the mortician in Hardin. The body of a young man with his head caved in had been found by hunters on a remote road on the Northern Cheyenne Reservation. Bullis doubted it was Junior Boss because the corpse had long hair, a 1970s style of the Northern Cheyenne but not the Crows. But just in case, he asked Danetta to come to the mortuary to check the body.

When she first viewed the corpse, her screams could be heard a block away. Three days later, a son and nephew of Austin Two Moons, a respected Northern Cheyenne medicine man and religious leader, turned themselves in to the police. According to the FBI's report, Junior Boss went to Bair's Truck Stop and Cafe in Hardin after a high school football game. In the parking lot he encountered two teenagers who knew he usually carried big money. On this night, he'd gotten $100 from his dad, another $100 from his mother. The two boys overpowered him and dragged him into their car. On a deserted road they robbed and beat him with a baseball bat, crushing his skull with seventeen blows to the head.

The murder touched a raw nerve with the Crows, reigniting the tribe's long hostility toward the Northern Cheyenne that dated back to the buffalo days when the Northern Cheyenne and Crows were mortal enemies, fighting for territory. Lawyers for the accused boys argued to have them tried as juveniles. Danetta vowed to sell every inch of her land to keep them behind bars, but because they were minors, and because the crime happened on an Indian reservation, the case fell under the jurisdiction of the Bureau of Indian Affairs. The boys were released when they turned twenty-one.

Danetta had never been a drinker, but after the tragedy, she turned to alcohol. Blaine, already battling a drinking problem, slid deeper. When sober, he was a quiet, stoic man; on alcohol, however, he turned belligerent and abusive. He and Danetta became regulars in the Hardin bars,

Danetta learning to hide her bruises and black eyes with heavy makeup.

Junior Boss's death also rearranged the lives of his two older sisters, Marlene and Karna, Sharon's mom. At the time, Marlene was a junior at Hardin High and a star on the track team, but after the murder, she dropped out of school and, like her parents, found comfort in booze. Her sister, Karna, was nineteen, divorced and living back at home, trying to cope with being a parent to her two-year-old daughter, Sharon. Already hooked on whiskey, Karna fell further into drink and despair, but unlike her sister and parents, who eventually returned to sobriety, Karna remained an alcoholic.

"Not a day has gone by since the murder that I haven't questioned myself," says Danetta, dabbing at a tear and lighting another Benson & Hedges. "What if I hadn't been so flashy with my own money? Lately, people have been warning me that I'm repeating the same mistakes with Sharon, you know, giving her a car, spoiling her, making her the center of my life. They say I'm smothering her just like I did with Junior Boss. But I say the hell with 'em. To me, love means providing, giving, sharing. Is that wrong?"

She slowly rises from the table and pulls back the faded sheet covering the window, pointing to a rusted Ski-Doo snowmobile parked on a nearby slope behind the doghouse. Partially hidden in the shadows of the gathering dusk, it sits in the exact spot where Junior Boss parked it the night before his murder. For two decades, she and Blaine have left it right there, untouched except by the buffalo grass in the spring and the snow in winter.

"Before your sweat, I got something I want to show you," says Danetta, disappearing into a back bedroom. When she reappears, she carries a long aquamarine and silver strapless evening gown that looks suited for a mermaids' ball. "Isn't it beautiful?" she asks. "Sharon's going to wear it at the homecoming coronation."

"Nice."

"I drove Sharon up to Billings last Thursday afternoon and we looked at lots of dresses," she says. "This was the best. Cost $375."

Guess Sharon didn't go visit her dying great-uncle as reported.

In preparation for my sweat, I had read up on the ritual, learning that the purpose of the sweat lodge is to take a person through pain, beyond his or her physical being into another realm. It is in this indefinable space, the Crows believe, that wisdom, healing, and spiritual strength are found, and prayers are heard. A sweat is "good medicine," which is defined as anything improving one's connection to the Great Mystery and to all life. Sacrificing one's physical comfort is somehow supposed to bring healing and good fortune to family, friends, and fellow creatures. The medicine from this sweat is for Sharon.

In the twilight, Blaine and two other men, both built like bears, each with a jet black ponytail down to his waist, are stripping naked. I haven't met any of them. Saying nothing, Blaine nods in my direction, gesturing for me to take off my clothes and put them on a nearby bench. But shouldn't we get to know each other first?

For Blaine, a fifty-nine-year-old, barrel-chested ex-rodeo roper, a sweat is a communion taken at the end of each day to relax and pray. He's spent most of his adult life working on ranches, including his own, but now he is retired, spending his days in relative calm, driving to the store for supplies, repairing what needs to be fixed, reading the paper, watching TV, dabbling in tribal politics. He is a superstar in hand games, a spirited Indian team contest in which a player from one team attempts to confuse the guesser on the other team as to which hand holds a small white bone. It's a game of legerdemain like button-button-who's-got-the-button, and Blaine set the all-time record with twenty-seven consecutive guesses, shattering the old mark by thirteen, making him the Babe Ruth of hand games.

His real passion, however, is watching his granddaughter play basketball. More than anything in his life, he wants her to excel on the basketball court, to bring honor and dignity to the family, to *count coup* in the ways of his ancestors . . . and to help ease the sadness he's carried with him since the day his only son was murdered.

It has been eight years since his last drink, his sobriety coming not through AA or a treatment center, but by the aid of a major spiritual resource—the sweat lodge. He had concluded that unless he quit drinking, he would lose his marriage; Danetta had already stopped. To help in his recovery, he built a sweat lodge, not only to share with family and friends, but to retreat to every day in search of a higher voice. For years, he was a deacon in the Crow Baptist Church, a regular on Sunday mornings, but a falling out with the minister during his drinking days drove him from the church. Now the sweat lodge is his place for prayer. And this particular sweat is extra special, not because he is joined by a white guy he's never met before, but because this sweat is to ensure success in the season ahead for Sharon, his pride and joy. He's as anxious as she is for the conference season to begin.

I survey the four-foot-tall lodge. Instead of the animal skin coverings used in the warrior days, heavy old blankets and tarps stretch over the arched willow branches. I know the lodge's round shape is a metaphor for the earth's womb, and the painful ceremony is a symbol for birth. The small opening faces east, toward the sunrise and the symbolic dawning of a new day, or in this case, a corroded turquoise trailer. I've also learned that in Crow culture sweats are not coed, unless it is husband and wife. Sharon and her grandma will take their sweat later in the evening.

Blaine nods for me to enter first. On my hands and knees, naked, I crawl into the lodge, turning right just inside the flap. In the warrior days, it was unusual for Crows, modest people by nature, to be naked around others; even in sweat lodges men wore G-strings. Not anymore. As soon as I make my right turn, the bear of a man behind me slaps me hard on the butt, scaring the bejeebers out of me. Somehow, I don't remember reading about that part of the ritual.

"Enter to the left," he sternly instructs.

Oh yeah, now I remember my readings, clockwise to the left, like the direction of the Earth around the sun. Sorry, rookie mistake.

After we're all inside, we sit cross-legged in a semicircle around the hot rocks piled in a small pit in the middle of the lodge. The entrance flap is still open, and I can see the faces of the other men. They look like they mean business.

The other two men are Gilbert Birdinground, thirty-nine, and Oliver Half, forty. Blaine has invited them because of the good medicine they can bestow on Sharon for the start of conference play. It is a tribal custom passed down through the generations to enlist the prayers of somebody with good medicine, a person of supposedly strong character and accomplishment who can provide a hedge against leaving anything to chance. In the pre-reservation days, a person of good medicine prayed for a successful hunt or war party. Now it's basketball.

Blaine reaches into a small pouch and pulls out a package of Tops rolling papers and a little Baggie of what in the dim light looks to be pot. Or maybe it is a pinch of the tribe's sacred tobacco seed, considered by the Crows to be the most valuable of all medicines. I can't be sure.

After rolling it up, Blaine takes four drags—four being the mystic number in Crow culture—then passes it to Gilbert to his left, who also takes four big puffs. Suddenly it dawns on me . . . they will pass this thing to me and I will be expected to take the traditional four hits as some sort of modern peace pipe ceremony. Normally, that would be very cool, but years ago I vowed *never ever* to allow any tobacco or pot to enter my body ever again. Not even a puff. It is a vow I take seriously. I've had nightmares in which I have a cigarette dangling from my lips as I make an important speech. And now here I am, about to be handed the object of my nightmares. Maybe I can just fake it, pull a Clinton and not inhale.

Oliver hands it to me. I hesitate, then slowly raise it toward my face. As it nears my lips, I still don't know what it is. What if it is some sort of peyote and I never come back from the far side?

I can't back down. Cautiously, I put it to my lips and take a little baby hit. It is tobacco, Bull Durham tobacco, and as soon as I inhale, once, twice, thrice, four times, just like I'm supposed to, I feel a buzz. I pass it back to Blaine, already hoping it will make it back around the circle again.

Blaine starts telling about his visit earlier that day to his youngest grandson's Head Start classroom. "It was cute," he says. "They all lined up to sing me a song. I was expecting something like 'Mary Had a Little Lamb,' but do you know what it was?"

"What?"

"'Achy Breaky Heart,'" he answers.

Simultaneously, as if conducted by the Great Spirit, the three men break into a pitifully out-of-tune chorus of "Achy Breaky Heart," a song that under normal circumstances I consider the worst song of all time.

Wait a second. I'm sitting here cross-legged, buck naked, about to get sizzled like bacon, and these three big hitters from the rez have me smoking stuff I wouldn't even touch in my nightmares, not to mention their wretched singing.

Blaine flicks the remaining ashes into the burning rocks, then sprinkles cedar needles on top to provide a sweet incense. Then he closes the flap and throws the lodge into total darkness. I can't see the hand in front of my face. Hell is about to begin.

It starts with Blaine, the firekeeper, dipping a ladle into a bucket of cold water and pouring it onto the white-hot rocks. Instantly, a blast of sizzling heat shoots through the lodge. It's as if I'm caught in a tunnel and a GI is blasting his flamethrower right down the chute.

Blaine pauses, then pours another dipperful over the rocks, then two more, making a total of four. All right already, I get the point. But I know it has to be four, one to represent each season. I also know that this is only the first of four rounds, the second round with seven pourings, the third with ten, the fourth with . . . I can't remember. What difference does it make? I'm already scorched.

Blaine sets down the ladle after the fourth pour. It is time for the first round of prayers, which after all, is why we're here. He speaks in Crow, his voice low and controlled. I have no idea what he's saying. But I know he is supposed to be praying for the well-being of those present in the sweat lodge. I hear my name. Unfortunately, the prayer drones on and on. A smothering blanket of heat chokes the air. My only thought is . . . get me out of here. Maybe I can tell them I just remembered I promised to help Danetta fix dinner.

It is the custom that the man who is pouring has control over how hot the sweat gets. He's the minister of pain. He can control it by how full he fills the ladle, or whether or not he allows the flap to be opened between rounds. I'd been warned that several reservation firekeepers take a perverse pride in turning up the heat to an insufferable level. Fortunately, Blaine isn't one of them. He opens the flap, and a thimbleful of fresh air wafts in, offering if not relief, then hope. We pass a large eagle feather, fanning ourselves, supposedly to sweep away evil spirits. I don't know about the other dudes, but I'm using it to get cool.

The flap closes quickly and it is back to the blast furnace. The second round is seven pourings, one for each day of the week, each pouring adding another degree to hell. My skin is on fire, my lungs scream.

It is said that the bravest warriors remain seated in an upright position for the duration of a sweat, while the weak lie down on the ground, down where the only pocket of breathable air exists. Surprisingly, I hear the other men drop to their sides, curling up low. I am down in a flash as well, hugging the ground, trying to suck whatever oxygen I can right out of the earth. It is hopeless. My head is now bumped up smack dab against Oliver's butt, which happens to be about the size of a sea lion. I don't care.

I am trying to get one with the process, or with the earth, or wherever it is I'm supposed to be transported to. I try to go contemplative, be transcendental, blissful, thoughtless, serene. But it isn't working. The pain is too much.

Oliver is the next to pray. The importance of his presence at this sweat is considerable. He is Sharon's clan uncle, a father of three and a construction foreman for Crow Tribal Housing. But it is his position as a respected medicine man and Sun Dance leader—one of four in the tribe—that provides him his prominent role in Crow spiritual life. The medicine man (*Bache Baaxpe*) is still an important figure on the reservation, indispensable, a person engaged in the business of healing and problem solving. Oliver's training period was longer than medical school. He'd spent a decade learning what herbs to prescribe for toothaches or snakebites or whatever the ailment. He now uses this knowledge and experience, combined with a holy communion with the Great Power, to help people in sickness and distress, as well as to dispense wisdom. Getting him to offer a prayer on Sharon's behalf is like having the pope show up to bless your birthday party. I just want him to pray fast.

He doesn't. His focus is on Sharon's good health and good fortune in the season ahead, but because he is speaking in Crow, he could be praying for me to get my head off his butt for all I know. But finally, mercifully, he finishes. Blaine opens the flap again, and once more, hope flickers through hell.

The third round is ten pourings. It might as well be 640, because I am out of it after the second one. I'm not alone. In the darkness I hear the other men moaning. It is almost sexual in nature, as if they are passing through to a higher state. I join the moaning, but it is more of a deathbed groan.

Gilbert Birdinground, the son of Blaine's stepmother, leads the next round of prayers. An All-State forward at Hardin High in the 1970s, he is the only Crow ever to play in a Division I college game, seeing limited action in his sophomore year at Montana State before dropping out of school because, in his words, the coach was prejudiced. He worked ten years as a truck driver and drag line operator at Sarpy Mine, then five years with the tribe's Department of Fish and Game, assisting in the tribe's unsuccessful battle with the state over who controls the riverbed of the Big Horn River and its lucrative fishing and access rights. But now he's unemployed. It is his duty in the sweat to offer a prayer that gives away a condition or state of mind no longer needed. He'll be offering Sharon his formerly impressive skills as an All-State basketball player.

Again, I don't know what he is saying, but on and on he prays. Then the flap opens up, and I momentarily return to Montana from another excursion to purgatory. I want desperately to crawl up and over Oliver's big rump and leave, but for reasons I cannot begin to understand, I stay for the fourth and final round.

"Would you like to say the last prayer?" asks Blaine just before closing the flap again.

I look around, hoping he isn't talking to me. With the exception of my weddings, I haven't been to church since the Eisenhower administration, and the only prayer I can think of is *God is great, God is good, and we thank Him for all this food.* I suspect these guys are looking for something a little more profound than that. After all, this whole clambake is to bless Sharon with all the good fortune necessary to win State and bring glory to the tribe. But how can I be expected to utter any kind of rational prayer when my entire being has been reduced to a little bowl of ashes? All I need is an urn and the cremation will be complete.

"I'd be honored," I answer.

Somehow, and I have no idea how, I manage to cough out a minute or two of supplication, something about good health, good fortune, and good sportsmanship . . . basic Christian Athlete stuff.

And then my long sweaty nightmare is over. Up goes the flap, and I nearly crawl up Oliver's colon to get out of there.

On the outside, it is a warm evening, but as the four of us sit on a bench next to the lodge, steam rises off our bodies and heads like it does off of those big ugly linemen in Green Bay in the dead of winter. Slowly, I towel off, a slight breeze coming in from the east, fanning my body as sweetly as if it is a call from the Publishers Clearing House

Prize Patrol. Suddenly I feel great, the toxins of the world drained away. I have journeyed to the center of hell for fifty minutes and lived. No doubt Sharon will be impressed.

Sharon is leaning against the dining room table. I smile, feeling rather proud for having survived my ordeal by fire, maybe even a little smug. She looks back at me with all the recognition of a rock. Earlier in the day we had our first sit-down interview, and she was polite, friendly, even talkative, rambling on about zone traps and how great her grandma is and how she hasn't yet signed up to take her SAT but plans to "soon." But now she is preoccupied, maybe even feeling a little pressured. The house is filled with people, including a Sun Dance leader and tribal basketball legend, all here to honor her and share in a feast for her success, to pat her on the back, to tell her how good she is. They are here because she carries their hopes on her bony shoulders. It is up to her to live up to all the dreams and reveries they've never accomplished.

I sit down to await dinner, surrounded by Indians, all of them smoking, all of them speaking Crow, all of them making no effort to include me in their conversation. A thick cloud of cigarette smoke chokes the room. The only person paying any attention to me is Sharon's rambunctious four-year-old cousin Evon Little Light. He pulls a nylon stocking over his head and invites me to play a home version of Rob the 7-Eleven. I'm the clerk.

In time I escape into the kitchen to chat with Danetta. She lights up another Benson & Hedges menthol, not bothering to put out the one still smoldering in the ashtray. "If you think this is a big gathering, wait'll you see the one I have when we win State," she boasts. "I'm going to throw the biggest powwow this tribe's ever seen."

More pressure on Sharon. Conference play hasn't even

started and grandma's already got the catering trucks circling the ranch. And this for a team that has never even been to State and is picked by the other coaches in the league to finish no higher than fourth.

Hosting big gatherings is Danetta's specialty. As the family matriarch, she loves to entertain, and going overboard is part of it. When visitors come, expected or not, she considers it her duty to feed them and make them feel welcome, even if it's just a cup of Instant Folgers. A believer in the Crow concept of sharing, she holds to the proposition that as long as she has adequate food, clothing, and shelter, it is her responsibility to provide for her relatives' welfare.

Glancing at all the people in the living room, I'm not sure who is family and who has just wandered in off the prairie. I overhear Danetta refer to a couple of women as her daughters, yet I know they aren't. Then I hear her refer to these same two women as her sisters. I've read all about the Crow concepts of extended family and clan, and I'm beginning to wonder if maybe this is a case of tribal eugenics gone awry.

At dinner I sit next to Blaine, finally formally introducing myself, which seems a bit odd having just hung out naked with the guy. His handshake is soft, his greeting barely audible. On first impression, he is as stolid and phlegmatic as Danetta is flamboyant and verbose.

The men all seat themselves at the dining room table while all the women relegate themselves to eating on the couches and chairs in the living room. It reminds me of the Thanksgiving family dinners of my youth when all the kids had to eat at card tables.

Smiling like a charming Southern hostess, Danetta serves the dinner, men first. The main dish is a bowlful of chunks of beefsteak, its well-done, leathery texture insuring that nobody at this gathering will get *E. coli*. To go with the beefsteak, there is macaroni in a broth and enough fry bread to feed Billings. To drink, we have our choice between Instant Folgers and a nice kelly green Kool-Aid. For dessert, it is powdered sugar donuts.

I'm not sitting in the no-smoking section. Whatever purity attained in the sweat is now ancient history, my lungs clogged, my clothes smelling like a Philip Morris test center. By the time I lick the last speckle of powdered sugar from my lips, I have a raging, secondhand headache.

After the women clear the dishes, Sharon is summoned to the dining room table. She moves gingerly, favoring her lower back, which has been bothering her for several days. She looks uncomfortable. The room draws suddenly quiet.

She stations herself next to Oliver, the medicine man who is also her clan uncle. A key member in Crow family structure, the clan uncle is responsible for offering praise, prayer, and protection to special family members. In the warrior days, clan uncles addressed young warriors about to leave for battle; now they speak to young Crows about to leave for military duty, or an important basketball game. In the past, the custom was reserved for young men. Sharon's being honored is a sign of the gradually rising status of women in Crow society. For rendering his praise and prayer, the clan uncle will be rewarded with gifts and the family's respect.

Dressed in jeans and flannel shirt, Oliver speaks in Crow, his voice controlled and deliberate, the moment taking on an air of solemnity. With my new buddy from the sweat lodge, Mr. Birdinground, serving as my interpreter, I can understand that Oliver's advice focuses on what Sharon needs to do to succeed in the season ahead: she should conduct herself in an admirable manner, avoid outside distractions, beware of jealousies, stay within her abilities, remain focused, and ignore the pressures.

Arms at her side, Sharon stands at attention, her normally

slouched posture straightened except for a slight lean to the left to ease the pain in her lower back. Saying nothing, she listens intently, respectfully, and tranquilly, in sharp contrast to her demeanor during a short address by Coach Mac at the end of practice when she stood at the rear of the circle, fidgeting, spinning a ball on her finger, eyes darting all over the gym.

Oliver finishes dispensing his wisdom, then Danetta quietly presents him with a new western shirt, Pendleton blanket, and $100 in cash. He stuffs the money in his pocket, then disappears into the night, his service delivered. Danetta beams, her granddaughter now blessed by the words and wisdom of the medicine man. Conference play starts tomorrow.

CHAPTER NINE

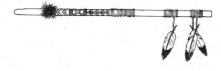

Waking up beneath her Michael Jordan poster, Sharon throws back the covers and stretches her limbs, trying to get the circulation going. It is 7:55, only five minutes until the warning bell for Mr. Nesovic's first period American Government class, her only class before boarding the team bus, *Bulldog I,* for the two-hundred-mile drive to Glendive and the conference opener.

Her basement bedroom at Aunt Marlene's is dank and messy, its only window covered by a black and green velvet tapestry, its floor hidden beneath empty pop cans and piles of discarded clothes. The room has no magazines or books, not even schoolbooks—those are stuffed in her locker at school. The only artwork is the Jordan poster and three framed photographs atop her dresser: a studio portrait of Holly, a team photo of the Lady Bulldogs, and a posed shot of her in her uniform. There is no picture of Randy Not Afraid. Her framed MVP certificate that she won at team camp in June is at her grandma's, along with all the other ribbons and trophies she's accumulated in her athletic career.

Basketball isn't the only sport at which Sharon excels. But in her other athletic endeavors, there's a pattern. In the sixth grade she was the only girl on her Crow Agency Little League team, playing first base and batting cleanup. But the team couldn't come up with a sponsor the next year and folded. So much for her baseball career. In swimming she took third as an eighth grader in the statewide Big Sky Games, showing great promise. Then her coach left town under a cloud of suspicion for sleeping with one of his high school swimmers, leaving Sharon with nobody to push her. So she quit. Her tennis career ended quickly, too. In the tenth grade she turned out for the team, mainly because Holly talked her into it, and despite never having played the game, she won her first three matches. Then she was ruled ineligible because of too many classroom absences, and never came back. She'd also shown great promise as a horsewoman, learning to ride almost before she could walk. She rode her chestnut mare every day over the hills and past the ravines around her grandparents' house. By the time she was thirteen, she'd gained a reputation as one of the best barrel racers and horse trainers on the reservation. But then she injured her hip falling off the back of a pickup and quit riding, deciding she should focus her talents on volleyball and basketball. In volleyball, she's lettered twice, making All-Conference her junior year. But when she really thought about it, volleyball wasn't all that important to her either. Now she's considering not turning out for her senior year. Basketball is all that really matters.

Nearing the bathroom, she stops to flex her knee, the one she'd strained the last day at team camp. As it is most mornings, it's stiff, but on this day, it's her back that bothers her more. She slept with a hot water bottle held in place with an Ace bandage. The doctor told her that if the pain persisted, he'd give her muscle relaxants, and if that didn't do the trick, then she'd have to sit out a couple of games to let it heal. For her, sitting out is not an option.

She hobbles up the stairs, greeted by four-year-old Evon

Junior, her buzzsaw of a cousin, a kid with raven black hair that's never been cut and hangs to the middle of his back. He's traded in his nylon stocking mask from his game of Rob the 7-Eleven for a Nerf basketball. He begs Sharon for a quick game, but she turns him down, explaining that she has to get to school. Seeing his sad face, she reaches down and hugs him, her long slender arms cradling him to her chest. In the Crow way of extended family, she is more of a mother to him than cousin. Most nights she is the one who tucks him into bed.

From the kitchen, Marlene motions her to the table. "Here's some toast," she offers.

Sharon doesn't reply.

"Aren't you going to eat nothing?" Marlene asks, concerned about her niece's recent eating habits.

Sharon shakes her head and heads for the door.

Marlene heaves a motherly sigh, then follows her niece to the door, handing Sharon a sprinkling of sage to put in her basketball shoes for the conference opener. "Promise you'll eat something before the game," she orders.

Sharon nods, then she's gone.

For Sharon's senior year, Marlene will be the adult most responsible for her well-being, the person to sign her report cards, make her doctor's appointments, set her curfew. But Marlene has more to worry about than Sharon.

A heavyset woman with a friendly, lived-in face, thirty-five-year-old Marlene Fallsdown has a deadbeat husband, three children of her own, and Sharon living under her roof. Financially, she is barely getting by on welfare, tribal per capita, and small contributions from Danetta and Blaine. Her husband of fourteen years, Evon Little Light, is no help. She hasn't seen him in almost a week. For most of their marriage, he's been drunk and unemployed, often disappearing for days at a time. Usually, Marlene doesn't ask where he's been, afraid he'll dish out another black eye. Recently, Sharon asked why she is still with him . . . and Marlene couldn't come up with a good answer. He had just been laid off again, this time for failing to show up to work three days in a row at his job mending fences for a corporate farm. It doesn't help that Marlene recently lost her job, too, laid off from her position as a teacher's aide with Head Start in Crow Agency. Her boss told her it was because of budget cuts, but she didn't buy the story. The real reason, she knows, is political. In the spring, her father, Blaine, ran for tribal chairperson against the incumbent, Clara Nomee, and in the dirty world of Crow political patronage, much like the dirty political world of, say, Chicago, it is commonplace for family members of political opponents to lose their tribal jobs.

Despite the hard times, Marlene remains positive. A spiritual woman, she has an abiding faith her family will endure. To her, poverty is just another obstacle to overcome, like alcohol, the disease she's battled since her brother was murdered when she was sixteen. Her recovery hasn't been easy. When she was seventeen she spent a month in a treatment center in Winnebago, Nebraska, and then for the next fifteen years she's been in and out of sobriety, busted twice for drunk driving. But now she's two years clean and sober, shouldering responsibility.

Marlene credits her recovery to the Sun Dance, a rigorous four-day religious ceremony of dancing, drumming, and fasting. Originally, the ritual included self-torture, with warriors piercing their chests and stringing sinew through it, staking themselves to a tree under the blazing sun. Now, piercing is allowed only in the upper arm area and participants who pass out can recuperate in the shade. Marlene has invited Sharon to take part in the ceremony next summer, an offer Sharon says she'll think about.

It has been three months since Sharon moved into Marlene's house on Choteau Street, a block from the school. It's a drab $350-a-month rental with three bedrooms, faded yellow siding, dead grass, and a cracked foundation. The move was Sharon's idea, partly because she knew Marlene wouldn't be watching her like a hawk the way Danetta did. Marlene has set curfews—10:00 P.M. on school nights, midnight on weekends—but so far she hasn't enforced them. She doesn't think she needs to. In her book, Sharon's a good girl, never sassy, never coming home drunk. Lately, however, she's noticed changes—mood swings, loss of appetite, staying out late. She suspects it may be connected to Randy. But she doesn't ask.

Marlene still hasn't met Randy. Most of what she knows about him has come from rumors . . . that he fancies himself a ladies' man, that he drinks too much, that he hit his ex-wife. But those are just rumors. Sharon has promised to bring him by the house to introduce him, but so far it hasn't happened. To Marlene, he's a mystery man.

Like everyone in the family, she is proud of her niece, nursing the hope that Sharon will be the Crow to finally put it all together and earn a basketball scholarship. But she worries about her, too, especially in recent weeks. She's afraid Sharon might be headed down the same dead-end road she and Sharon's mom took while they were at Hardin High—smoking dope, getting pregnant, dropping out, continuing the cycle.

It bothers Marlene that her sister has been such a lousy mother to Sharon, and now she's heard a rumor that Karna was spotted down at the Wagon Wheel, sucking down the booze. She prays it isn't true, that Karna isn't back in town. Over the past couple years, every time Karna tries to reappear in Sharon's life, Sharon gets reeled in by the hope that Karna will sober up and become a real mom, only to be let down again.

*   *   *

Sliding behind the wheel of her Cougar, Sharon wishes she could just skip school altogether and head straight for the game. But the rules say she has to be in class on game days.

One block, barely one hundred yards from her front door to school, not even enough time to light up a Marlboro Light. But driving to school in her new car is a must, never mind that she can get there faster on foot.

The yellow buses have already come and gone, delivering Indian kids from Crow Agency and sons and daughters of third-generation German immigrant farmers from as far away as Fort Smith forty-five miles to the south. Sharon parks on the north side of the student parking lot, the side where all the white kids park. It isn't an act of political defiance, but a matter of convenience. It's closer to the school's entrance. The tardy bell has already rung.

She trudges into the school, a low-slung one-story brick and stucco structure built in 1960. In front of the office she encounters vice principal Ed "Awful" Aucker, the last person she wants to see. He is an imposing man, with a full beard, bolo tie, cowboy boots, turquoise belt buckle, and gray slacks with raised seams. He is the bad cop of the school, the gnarly disciplinarian, a former English teacher who thinks every kid on a tractor should be able to quote *Beowulf.*

"You must not want to play in the game today," he snaps.

Sharon just keeps walking, head down, saying nothing. He lets her go. She turns the corner and heads down the main hallway, her pace to the classroom slow and unhurried. Over the summer, she hoped that somehow, magically, her attitude toward school would improve once she started her senior year. But it hasn't. Her schedule of classes bores her, especially Government, English, and

Health. In essays and term papers she is a better than average writer, able to construct logical and grammatically correct paragraphs, but she doesn't like to do it, doing only what is required, sometimes less. Like most Crow students, she's never been a serious discipline problem, content to sit passively in class, uninvolved, unchallenged by her teachers, basically sleepwalking to her 2.8 GPA. In her freshman and sophomore years, Holly sometimes did her homework for her. The only classes remotely stirring her modest intellectual appetite are Algebra 2 and Computers. She's always done well in math, a subject that is black and white, straightforward, no gray areas of interpretation or analysis as required in history or English, no deep thought. She's even thought about a career as a bookkeeper or accountant. But so far, that's all it is—thought.

Sharon's spiritless attitude toward academics is typical of Indians at Hardin High. The absentee and tardy rate for Crows is seven times higher than that for whites. Militants on the reservation blame this inferior performance on the Hardin school board and the administration, claiming the school district loves to use politically correct words such as *equality* and *color-blind,* but when it comes down to reality, the board's real heart is demonstrated by conduct not words. These critics trot out statistics to prove their point: in a school with a 49 percent Indian population, the certified staff at Hardin High includes *no* Native Americans, and the curriculum offers *no* classes in Native American studies—*nothing* in Crow culture, language, or history. I asked history teacher Luke Gerber, the fired basketball coach, if he teaches the Indians' side of the story, and he replied, "I get so tired of all this political correctness. Those people on the reservation seem to forget about a little thing called the Louisiana Purchase."

Quietly, Sharon opens the door to her Government class and eases her way across the back of the classroom, hoping to go unnoticed. But the class is small, only twelve students, a hard place to blend into the woodwork

"Morning, Sharon," greets Mr. Nesovic, smiling. He likes Sharon.

Sharon slides into her seat behind Tiffany. Mr. Nesovic, 6'5", 240, with a walrus mustache and a degree from Northwestern, is the most liberal member of the faculty, its loudest voice in the bitter fight between the teachers and the school board over a salary increase. He waits until Sharon settles into her seat, then continues reading the bulletin. Next week is homecoming, he announces, and students will vote on Monday for the queen to be crowned at next Friday night's football game.

Sharon wishes now she'd declined her nomination. It all seems a big hassle: wearing a gown, riding in the parade, trying to persuade Randy to go to the dance, competing against Tiffany. Especially competing against Tiffany. She hates the idea of losing to her, and the way she figures it, she will. Tiffany is more popular, more likely to smile in the hallway for votes.

As Mr. Nesovic starts his lecture on the three branches of the federal government, Sharon yawns, her mind wandering to tonight's game. In her estimation, Glendive will be Hardin's toughest opponent in the conference, fast and strong. Last year they devoured the Hardin press, and if they do it again tonight, she's afraid Coach Mac won't switch to a man-to-man. To her, Coach Mac is too rigid in her strategy, sticking with a game plan no matter how badly it's going.

Mr. Nesovic continues to ramble on about the branches of government. Sharon vaguely hears his voice, but the words sail right on by her, too unconnected to her life. What does checks and balances have to do with her life on the rez? It isn't that she doesn't like Mr. Nesovic. She thinks he's one of the few Hardin High teachers who isn't prejudiced; she likes the way he gets things riled up in class with interesting discussions—date rape, gambling on the reservation, abortion. She's even spoken up herself—something she rarely does in class—not worried that he'll put her down in front of the other students the way she feels other teachers do. But on this morning, her mind is on basketball.

Finally, the bell rings, ending first period. Sharon exits the classroom, avoiding eye contact with Mr. Nesovic. She came to class knowing nothing about the three branches of government, and she still doesn't.

CHAPTER TEN

From my seat on *Bulldog I,* I say hello to Sharon as she climbs aboard. I assume my presence at her honoring ceremony last night will grant me a friendly nod. Not so.

At the rear of the bus, she stretches out across the back seat, cashing in on an entitlement of her senior status. Anita scoots over, giving her berth. Toward the front, freshman and junior varsity players scrunch two to a seat. On the sidewalk next to the bus, the cheerleaders wave their pom-poms, giving the team a send-off.

"I can't stand those idiots," announces Sharon.

"Did anybody else bring any cassettes?" asks Tiffany, wearing a New York Mets T-shirt and holding up a Reba McEntire tape. Nobody has. "Guess Reba's all we got," she says, popping the tape into the boom box.

"You a Mets fan?" I ask.

"I don't know anything about 'em," she replies. "My new boyfriend gave it to me."

Her new boyfriend, Kent Bullis, is the son of the town's mortician, a member of Hardin High's pitiful football and golf teams, and according to Holly, a "little boy." Tiffany first hooked up with him at a spring barn dance, and they've been inseparable ever since. For her, it's a rebound romance, of sorts. In her sophomore and junior years she was tight with handsome Deano Yarlott, an Indian boy two years older, her first sexual experience. Her parents thought Deano was "a nice young man, polite and responsible," but they weren't upset that the relationship came to a screeching halt when Tiffany found out he'd been two-timing her. They never felt comfortable with her going to visit him on the reservation and, in fact, never let her. They didn't think that was being racist; they just thought the reservation wasn't safe after dark. They also believed that life for Tiffany would be easier down the road if she married somebody from her own race.

"Let's go, Louie," instructs Coach Mac.

With a grinding of the gears, Louie Landrie, the fifty-five-year-old bus driver, heads out of town. For thirty years, Louie has been driving *Bulldog I.* He is an institution in the community, a man whose gruff, curmudgeonly facade fools nobody. He can recite the names and family histories of every athlete, Indian or white, who has ever stepped on his bus. By his estimate, he's watched over ten thousand Hardin High varsity, JV, and freshman games, and logged over two million accident-free miles transporting "his" teams to the games. The round-trip to Glendive will add another four hundred miles to his odometer, a journey across the flat, arid expanses of eastern Montana, mile after tedious mile of alkaline-caked creek beds and sandstone outcroppings, with only a few scattered brush pines and the Yellowstone River winding its way alongside the highway to break the monotony.

And mile after mile of Reba entertaining the troops.

Riding shotgun in the front seat, Coach Mac studies notes she's taken watching Glendive's games in the Tip-Off Tournament. The Lady Red Devils lost a game, but she still considers them the team to beat in conference. She puts down her notes and picks up a copy of the *Billings Gazette,* turning to the first prep rankings of the season. The Lady Bulldogs are ranked sixth, their highest ranking ever. "This is bullshit," she mutters. "How can Glendive be rated fourth, ahead of us? They lost a game."

In the back, as Reba rewinds and starts again, Sharon shifts in her seat, trying to get comfortable, her back even stiffer than when she awoke. Anita slides across the seat and slowly begins to massage the sore area, saying nothing, just rubbing.

To Sharon, Anita seems almost too pure to be real—perfect smile, perfect grades, perfect attendance. She's never seen Anita get mad or raise her voice or say a bad word about anybody, not even after the summer dope-smoking incident. How can anybody be so relentlessly nice, so unfailingly polite? Anita is as nice to Indians as she is to whites. Sometimes Sharon wonders if it's all a big act.

Just as Reba is coming on for the third time, Coach Mac instructs Louie to stop for lunch at the Hardee's in Miles City. Sharon and Anita are the last off the bus, walking into the restaurant side by side, smiling, looking like the best of buddies. For Sharon, this will be her first food since her powdered donut dinner the night before. They approach the two tables where their varsity teammates are already seated, Indians at one table, whites at another. Two empty seats are available at each table. They pause, then instinctively part to their separate tables, just as Indians and whites from Big Horn County have always done. For lunch, Sharon eats half an order of fries.

Considering all the factors—her slender frame, her all-out style of play, her poor eating habits—it seems safe to assume that this is a girl who somewhere down the line will hit the wall.

Located thirty-five miles from the North Dakota border, Glendive, population 4,500, sits on the east bank of the

Yellowstone River. Its pleasant, tree-lined residential streets have two-story, older homes with more architectural character than the flat, listless homes in Hardin. When Shell's discovery of oil in eastern Montana generated economic euphoria, the experts predicted the town would quadruple in size. But the boom fizzled—just like in Hardin—and the area went back to proclaiming itself "the center of the rich inland agricultural empire of eastern Montana."

At the Chamber of Commerce is a picture of an archaeological dig with a caption telling how dinosaurs once roamed the nearby canyons and crags, an area the Sioux named *Makoshika*—the Badlands. Another picture shows a cowboy standing next to a fish as big as a shark that he'd caught in the Yellowstone, a hideous, homely prehistoric-looking thing with a long narrow bill that looks like grandpa's old rusted blade saw. The caption reads: "Glendive, the paddlefish capital of America."

"What'ya use for bait to catch these things?" I ask the clerk, a kindly volunteer wearing an American Legion cap.

"Them suckers is so stupid they'll bite on D-cell batteries," he advises.

The team changes out of their bus-riding shorts and T-shirts into fashion statements. Tiffany emerges first out of the locker room, looking like a long-legged country-western star, with a bright rainbow-colored western shirt and ultratight raspberry red Rocke jeans. Next, Sharon exits, her skintight brown and white polka dot dress accentuating her sharp angles and corners and her bony hips. Still, she looks beautiful, a young woman rather than a gangly kid.

During the freshman and junior varsity games, the varsity sits high up in the bleachers, braiding one another's hair and jabbering like it's a slumber party. Tiffany is holding court, telling about the time her oldest sister got the family car hung up on some bushes and rocks at a kegger out in the boondocks, then got caught lying about it. "My dad listened to her story," Tiffany says, "then grounded her for three months, one month for each lie."

"Must've been a bad liar," observes Stacie Greenwalt.

Tiffany starts another story, this one about a summer trip to Phoenix to play with a Montana all-star team in a tournament against teams from other Western states. Sharon wasn't selected for the team, an omission her grandmother claimed was racist. "I met all these girls down there who've never been around Indians," explains Tiffany. "It was weird. They all had heard a lot of bad stuff about Indians, like you know, all they do is steal, carry knives, beat people up, stuff like that. I told them it wasn't like that, and how Indians had gotten a bad deal being put on the reservation and all that, and how it's all working out for them now."

If games are decided in pregame warmups, then the Lady Bulldogs should climb back on *Bulldog I* and go home and admit defeat. It's almost comical, players bumping into each other, missing shots from two feet, dribbling off their shoes. Sharon looks as if she should be in traction. Anita stands and watches Glendive's layup drill, mouth agape as if it's Jordan and the Bulls.

On Glendive's first possession, the Lady Red Devils' guard blows by Tiffany and Anita, then dishes off to a forward for an easy score. "You gotta stop the dribbler if she gets by the press," Sharon barks at Rhea. On Hardin's first possession, Sharon threads a perfect bounce pass to Anita, who is wide open at the free throw line. But Anita doesn't even glance toward the basket, passing it back outside to Tiffany like the ball is contaminated.

"Shoot it, damnit!" yells Sharon.

Despite Hardin's shaky start, they hold the lead midway through the first quarter 12–11, thanks to Sharon's eight points. Her back is still killing her.

Then things turn ugly. Glendive reels off 10 straight points, shredding the Hardin press with crisp passes up-court. At the end of the quarter, Hardin trails 21–12.

"Ladies, you're standing around!" roars Coach Mac.

In the second quarter, things get even uglier. Glendive has figured out they can rush the ball upcourt with crisp passes and beat the press for easy scores, especially when Rhea and Owena don't rotate forward from the back line to stop the ball-handler before she penetrates too deeply. And when Hardin's press does slow Glendive and force them into a half-court game, the Lady Red Devils zip the ball around the perimeter for wide-open shots for talented guard Michelle Frenzel. Owena is moving slower than winter.

"Move, Owena!" yells Sharon, glancing over at Coach Mac, hoping she'll sub for Owena or switch to a man-to-man. Coach Mac does neither.

The hemorrhaging continues. Glendive scores 16 unanswered points, a blitz lasting eight minutes. At halftime, Hardin trails by 17. Sharon, Tiffany, and Anita have played the entire half.

In the locker room, Coach Mac surprisingly keeps her calm. "Be patient," she advises. "There's no 17-point play. Just get back in it one basket at a time."

Sharon isn't so calm. She wants Coach Mac to get in somebody's face, shake things up, yell, bench someone, in particular Owena and Rhea. It seems like they've given up.

*   *   *

Late in the third quarter, Hardin still trails by 17 and only divine intervention from a top medicine man can save them. Under the basket, Anita holds her ground on a Glendive fast break and takes the charge, getting knocked over backward for her effort. The ref calls the foul on her.

"Good call!" yells Richy Powell, the Glendive coach.

"Sit down, you idiot!" hollers Anita's dad, Bob Dewald, part of the vocal contingent of four hundred Hardin families and fans—mostly Indian—who have made the two-hundred-mile trek to cheer for the team.

"Come down here and make me!" retorts Powell, feet planted, finger pointing.

Dewald points back.

For Bob Dewald, forty-nine, the postmaster of the Hardin Post Office and a deacon at the Church of the Open Bible, this is out of character. A family man, he's never been a jock or a fighter, not even back in his days at Hardin High. But watching his daughter's team getting crushed, and then to have Anita knocked on her keister, has momentarily short-circuited his fuse box.

"What's keepin' you?" shouts Powell. "Right now, right here!"

Donna Dewald, Anita's mom, tugs on her husband's elbow, urging him to abandon the cause. He glares at Powell, then sits back down, ending the embarrassment.

With a minute left in the game, Coach Mac finally pulls Sharon, Tiffany, and Anita, all having played the whole game despite the blowout. On her way to the bench, Sharon looks like a war refugee, holding her back. She reaggravated it diving after a loose ball.

Despite the pain and the drubbing, she's played her best game of the young season, 24 points and nine rebounds, her hustle the only thing keeping the final score respectable, 65–57. Tiffany's another story, playing her worst game, scoring only nine. The bench isn't any help, contributing only three points and no rebounds. And Coach Mac isn't going to win any Coach of the Week awards on this one, showing no imagination, sticking with the press to the bitter end.

On the bright side, somebody lost the Reba tape.

During the long bus ride home, the girls curl up and sleep, their dreams of an undefeated season already down the tubes. They're now 0-1 in conference play.

I try to sleep but can't, staring out the window at a zillion stars up in the Montana night sky. I think about last night's sweat and feast to honor Sharon, and wonder if it's too much pressure.

Louie and I are the only ones awake. He puts in his own tape, *Poland's Greatest Polkas,* turning the volume down so only he and I can hear it.

"Polka music keeps me awake," he explains.

"Me, too," I reply.

On into the night we travel, *Bulldog I* chugging west on I-94 in two-quarter polka time. I hear a noise from the back seat. Sharon stirs, a hot water bottle taped to her back. She rises from her seat and wraps her Indian blanket tightly around her, then lies down in the aisle between the rows of seats, squirming, trying again to get comfortable, but failing.

It's 3:00 A.M. when the bus finally pulls into Hardin. She is still awake. As she climbs off the bus and retrieves her bag from the baggage compartment underneath, she can barely stand up straight, shuffling along like an old woman. It's painful to watch.

CHAPTER ELEVEN

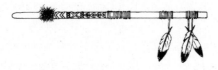

It's early on the Saturday of the Lodge Grass game and all is quiet in Crow Agency. Except at Danetta's house. A major shouting match shatters the morning calm. Danetta and her daughter Karna, Sharon's mother, are nose to nose, fists about to fly. Karna reeks of booze. Blaine stands behind her.

"Get out of my house!" demands Danetta.

Karna doesn't budge.

Bloated by whiskey, she looks fifteen years older than her thirty-four years, with bags under her eyes, lines in her face, and fingertips yellowed by years of cigarettes. This latest binge started in the dive bars of the south side of Billings, the underbelly of Montana's biggest city. But as she often does when her booze money runs out, she comes back to the reservation, back to her parents' house. And as usual, it's warfare. It started this time when she accused Danetta and Blaine of being lousy parents; they countered by telling her what a worthless drunk she is.

"How can you come here and have the nerve to stand there and tell me what a bad parent I've been," shouts Danetta. "Look at you! You're so drunk you can barely stand up."

Karna sways, trying to focus. She knew that coming to

the house would ignite a family riot . . . but what choice does she have? She is out of money, nowhere else to stay.

"Where's Sharon?" she asks.

"None of your damn business," says Danetta.

"Fine, then don't tell me. I'll just talk to her at the game tonight."

"No you won't. You're not going to that game. I won't allow it. I won't let you embarrass her again."

"You can't stop me. She's my daughter."

"No she's not. She doesn't want anything to do with you."

Karna steps forward and tries to push her way past Danetta, but her foot catches on the edge of the couch and she stumbles, falling to the floor on one knee. Danetta turns and picks up the phone, dialing the BIA police.

Karna grew up with much the same promise Sharon now has—smart, good-looking, athletic. She remembers a happy childhood—horseback riding on sunny days, going to the Baptist Church on Sunday mornings, playing the piano in the living room. She was a pretty girl, tall and wiry. As a child she often complained that her brother, Junior Boss, was spoiled, but she always wore the prettiest dresses, rode the fastest horse for barrel racing at Crow Fair, took piano lessons from the best teacher in Hardin, attended the most expensive church camp in the state. As a freshman at Hardin High in 1974, she was a starter on the school's first girls' basketball team, its leading scorer. When she got pregnant with Sharon at the end of her sophomore year, the coach offered to adopt the baby. Karna declined, convinced she was ready for the responsibility of parenting. She was fifteen.

Her history of bad relationships with men started with Michael LaForge, Sharon's father, a high school dropout five years older. When Karna got pregnant, they married, but by the time Sharon was born, they had already split. She remarried when Sharon was three. Her new husband was handsome, possessive, a wife beater. On several occasions, Karna gathered up Sharon in the middle of the night and escaped to her parents' house, but each time, she returned and the cycle started again. Eventually, she divorced husband number two, but then they married each other again, and for a while, life got better. She stopped drinking, got her GED, and gave birth to two sons, Clarence and George. The family, including Sharon, moved to Billings, where her husband got a job in a rendering plant grinding horses into dog food while Karna enrolled at Rocky Mountain College. For the first time as an adult, she displayed her talents and intelligence, getting As in her classes, playing in the school band, taking care of her children. Danetta and Blaine were so encouraged they sold some land and bought her a house in Billings. She was happier than she'd ever been.

But soon her husband lost his job and hit the skids. She joined him in drink, and the beatings resumed, sometimes in front of Sharon, who would crawl up on her mother's lap and cry for the fighting to stop. Karna fled to a battered women's shelter in Billings, a place she returned to so often that she was appointed to its advisory board. Later, after she finally left him for good and returned to the reservation, she was asked to help start a women's shelter in Crow Agency. Domestic abuse was epidemic on the reservation—even worse than reported by the authorities—but she concluded that working in a shelter for battered women on a reservation filled with so many jealous men would not be safe. She declined the offer.

On the Crow Reservation, suicide is the fourth leading cause of death behind cirrhosis, drunk driving, and heart failure. Karna tried it three times. Her first attempt was when she commandeered her dad's pickup and drove it sixty miles an hour off an embankment next to the Big Horn River, the same place where Sharon attended her first 49. The second time was by pills, gulping down painkillers she was taking for the back injury suffered in her first failed attempt. This time she chickened out halfway through the bottle, driving herself to the hospital to get her stomach pumped. The third time was by knife. She started by carving her wrist, but as the blood began to trickle out, she decided slashing her wrists was a bad idea because if somehow she survived, she'd have scars she'd have to explain. So she decided to slash her stomach instead. But just as she was starting to cut, Danetta and Blaine walked in on her. Blaine quickly bear-hugged her from behind. He wasn't in the shape he'd been back in his days as a rodeo roper, but with the adrenaline rushing, he lifted all 195 pounds of her off the ground, then body-slammed her to the floor, the knife flying loose. Zero for three.

Karna was taken to the Rimrock Psychiatric Center in Billings and locked up under a suicide watch in a padded room for a week, then transferred to the treatment side of the center for counseling. Already a veteran of therapy, now she got more, going for treatment at the state hospital in Galen, the expenses paid for by the federally funded Indian Health Services. Over the next decade, she was in and out of treatment six times, staying an average of a month per visit at a total cost of $84,000, all of it paid by IHS. She sampled twelve-step, Antabuse, group sessions, hypnotism—and each time she came out proclaiming she was cured. She knew all the buzzwords—dysfunctional, co-dependency, enabling, recovery, one day at a time. What she didn't know was how to stay sober. Or how to be a mother.

She liked to joke that she'd been in so many programs that she could open her own treatment center. In one program, a counselor had her reenact her brother's funeral, an experience that led her to conclude she had never properly taken the time to grieve or say goodbye to Junior Boss because she was too busy trying to be emotionally strong for her distraught parents. In another program the therapist worked with her on repressed memory, and she recovered a memory of being raped when she was nine. But when her inpatient care was over, she sought no further counseling on the matter.

All this therapy merely provided rationalizations for why she drank. One rationale was that it was genetic, an answer that included scientific data about Indians missing an enzyme in the pancreas that helps in the absorption of alcohol. But on this day, as Danetta waits for the police to come and take her away, Karna has a different explanation.

"Maybe I wouldn't be a drunk if you didn't always treat me like shit," she says.

"Stop making excuses," counters Danetta. "You drink 'cause you won't take responsibility for your own life."

Ten minutes after Danetta's call to the BIA police, Chester Headdress, the chief of the tribal police, arrives at the house. "Karna's drunk and out of control again," explains Danetta. "She tried to hit me. I want her put in jail."

Calmly, Chief Headdress moves to the bedroom where Karna sits on the edge of Sharon's bed. A large man with two decades of experience in tribal law enforcement, Headdress has been summoned to domestic disputes hundreds of times and knows when to get tough, when to use diplomacy. In a slow, deliberate voice he informs Karna that he is taking her down to the station.

"Can I take a shower first?" she asks. She'd been tossed in the Crow jail a dozen times to sober up and knows it is a sweatbox, with no air conditioning or water fountains.

Chief Headdress agrees, but Danetta fidgets. "Make it

quick," she implores, worried that Sharon will show up and see her mom being taken away in handcuffs, a sight she's determined to spare her granddaughter on this game day.

As Karna showers, Danetta paces, stopping only to pour Chief Headdress a cup of instant coffee. "You coming to see my granddaughter play against Lodge Grass tonight?" she asks. Of course he's coming.

After finishing her shower, Karna puts on her nightgown and slippers, then follows Chief Headdress outside to his police car. With his hand on her head, he eases her into the back seat. Danetta watches from the porch, relieved that Sharon has not arrived yet.

At the BIA police station, Karna waits on a bench while Chief Headdress fills out the paperwork. She feels the room start to spin. Her stomach churns. Lowering her head, she vomits on the concrete floor.

"We need to get you over to the hospital to see a doctor," says Chief Headdress, summoning a deputy to escort her.

The conflict between Karna and her parents started in adolescence when she began experimenting with alcohol and pot. She'd sneak out of the house to meet friends and get high, then Blaine would track her down, throwing her into the back of the car and embarrassing her in front of her friends. Years later the situation reversed, Danetta sending Karna into Hardin to retrieve Blaine from the bars. Once, when she was bringing him back to Crow Agency on the freeway at one hundred miles an hour, he ordered her to slow down, and when she refused, he hit her on the side of the head, drawing blood. She pressed charges, but later bowed to family pressure and dropped the complaint. Their relationship reached its nadir when he imprisoned her in a room for two days, and despite her pleas, refused to bring her an inhaler to combat an asthma attack.

Karna's relationship with Danetta is equally scarred. From Karna's viewpoint, it is because Danetta consistently disapproves of her behavior, especially with men, once calling her a "fucking whore" in front of Sharon. On another occasion, when she was off on another binge in Billings, Danetta tracked her down at a friend's apartment and found her sitting on the couch with a black man. Danetta summoned her to a back bedroom and told her she was taking her home because "no daughter of mine is going to be with a nigger." Karna refused to go. "If you weren't my mother," she said, "I'd beat the shit out of you right here."

Karna doesn't care what color a man's skin is—she has slept with more men than she can remember, white, black, brown—"but no Chinese"—mostly guys she meets in seedy bars on the south side of Billings. All that really matters is that they buy her a drink. Sometimes she goes to the bars by herself, or sometimes with friends, and when the bars close, she either crashes with friends for the night or with the last person to buy her a drink. Normally, her drinking routine includes a couple of wake-up shots of Seagram's 7, her favorite, then two or three beers in the afternoon to keep the buzz, then back to the Seagram's at night. Sometimes, during her side trips off the bottle, she buys pot with her welfare check, money that is supposed to go for food and clothes for her kids. Initially, she tried to hide her dope habit, going into the bathroom to get high, blowing the smoke out the window, covering the smell with perfume, getting the red out with Visine. But after a while she quit trying to hide it. Sometimes she and Marlene got high together, and when

Sharon was around, they'd have her roll the joints for them. At the time, Sharon was ten.

Part of Danetta's frustration with Karna is that when sober she is a bright woman, caring, a mother who wants to do right by her kids. Karna has tried to make the therapy work for herself, even reading self-help books. But nothing has worked. She is diseased, addicted. During her last trip to rehab, a physician examined her and informed her that her liver is a mess and if she continues to drink she'll be dead of cirrhosis within two years. Once again she promised to stop, then disappeared into the south side of Billings, not resurfacing in Crow Agency again until the morning of her daughter's game against Lodge Grass. Wasted.

At the hospital down the street from the jail, Karna takes a seat in the crowded waiting room, the deputy right next to her. She is not handcuffed. Five minutes pass, then ten. Growing impatient, the deputy whispers to her that he needs to return to the station to take care of business. "If you get examined before I get back," he says, "call me and I'll come back and get you." That's the way it is on the rez—not enough officers to handle all the drunks.

Karna continues to sit and wait. Ten more minutes pass and still she sits, no sign of being called. She feels horrible—from the booze, from her fight with her parents, from the poison in her system. Her kidneys hurt. She throws up again.

Then it hits her. What's to keep her from getting up and strolling right out that side door over there? Wearing only her nightgown and slippers, she quickly checks to make sure the deputy isn't coming, then shuffles down the hallway, her slippers flopping against the shiny floor. In the time it takes to pour a shot of Seagram's 7, she's out the side door and into daylight. Short of breath, she lumbers across the street, past the court in Crow Agency in the center of town, then to a friend's house around the block, her escape a success. She convinces her friend that the place to be tonight is the Lodge Grass gym. Then she falls asleep.

Chapter Twelve

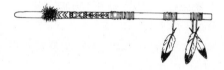

Before heading to the game at Lodge Grass, I make my daily visit to the market for a quick slice of Hardin life, always on display at the IGA. In the parking lot, my Honda is dwarfed next to the huge four-door Chevy pickup with a bumper sticker warning that "Seven Days Without Beef Makes One Weak."

In the meat section, there's certainly no shortage of prime cuts, which helps to compensate for no fresh fish and a lack of quality produce, which is surprising considering the abundance of rich agricultural land nearby. "Indians just don't eat a lot of vegetables," is how store owner Gary Stevenson explains it.

On this day I've come to pick up a couple of gallons of bottled water. I've also been surprised to learn that Hardin's tap water, which I figure would flow straight and pure from one of Montana's pristine alpine rivers, tastes like Valvoline.

Approaching the checkout line, I bump into Marlene. In her shopping cart she's got all the reservation pre-diabetic food groups: ice cream, Oreos, Lucky Charms, Ding Dongs, and generic pop. We walk outside together and she invites me back to her house. There, over Oreos and commodity powdered milk, she talks of her sister's failed attempt at motherhood, of Sharon's resentment.

According to Marlene, Karna's self-destruction is a sorrow Sharon tries to block from her thoughts, but can't. It's been that way for as long as she can remember. Sharon's "who cares" attitude is the way she's learned to deal with Karna, but sometimes in private moments her indifference turns to anger—anger at her mom for the years of pain and neglect, anger at herself for letting herself care.

For the past three months, Sharon has worked hard at not thinking about her mom. It's her defense against being burned like she was after Karna's stay last spring at Thunderchild, a treatment center in Sheridan, Wyoming, where Karna spent a month drying out. This was the first time Sharon felt a part of her mom's treatment, getting to visit during family week, staying overnight on the grounds, sleeping in the bed next to her mom, participating in family counseling sessions. She sensed a breakthrough in communication and an honesty between her and her mom she hadn't been able to express before. She told Karna how angry she was, how helpless she felt watching her destroy herself . . . the booze, the deadbeat men, the constant battles with Blaine and Danetta. She confessed her loneliness and depression, and how there'd even been times when she'd thought about suicide, maybe not seriously, but enough that there were days when all she could think about was how rotten she felt. She told the therapist about the confusion she felt shuffling between Marlene, Danetta, and Karna, and about the time at a family gathering when she asked them which one was her mother, and all three raised their hands. She also told the therapist about the time Blaine and Karna were fighting over her, both of them drunk, both of them holding on to one of her arms, pulling in opposite directions, each thinking they were rescuing her. Danetta also came to a session at Thunderchild, and the therapist had the three of them—grandmother, mother, daughter—draw pictures of themselves as children. The therapist arranged the finished drawings with Sharon's in the middle, slightly on top. "This is the adult of the group, the most mature," the therapist concluded.

Marlene is adamant about her sister not showing up in Lodge Grass. The last time Karna showed up at one of Sharon's athletic contests was at the state volleyball tournament in Livingston in March and it was a total catastrophe, not only reducing Sharon to tears, but costing the team the State Championship as well. Hardin had won the first game of the final match against Lewistown and was leading in the second 14–7, with Sharon serving for the title. One point and the trophy was theirs. The opposing coach called a timeout, and while the Lady Bulldogs huddled, Karna decided to head for the nearest bar to celebrate—the pint of Seagram's she'd used during the match to spike her Coke was empty. On her way out, she stopped next to the Hardin huddle and waved her arms, catching Sharon's attention, as well as everybody else in the gym. "I gotta go, babycakes," she slurred. Then she staggered out the gymnasium doors. Mortified, Sharon returned to the court and dinked her serve into the net. Side out. Then disaster. Lewistown ran off nine consecutive points to win the game and send the match into a third and deciding game. With the state title on the line, Sharon and her teammates, including Tiffany and Anita, fell apart, losing 15–3. After that, Karna disappeared into the dark side of Billings again.

The mood on the bus to Lodge Grass is somber, matching the ominous thunderclouds moving in from the west. Although it's only the second conference game of the season, it is big. A second loss will put them down two in the standings, a hole probably too deep to escape, physically or mentally. Also, it's big because it's against Lodge Grass, the reservation rival.

On the rez, a battle on the hardwood between Hardin and Lodge Grass is second only to Crow Fair in terms of tribal spirit and support. Although the schools are not in the same conference or classification, games between them count in their respective conference standings. The rivalry is intense, especially for the smaller, Class B Lodge Grass, a school with a 95 percent Indian population. They take a special pride in knocking off the bigger, whiter, Class A Hardin High.

The rivalry borders on racial. To the whites in Hardin, Lodge Grass High is a school with underachieving students and an inferior academic program, an assertion that tribal leaders dismiss as standard racism from the white establishment. They point out that in recent years Lodge Grass students have scored almost as high on standardized tests as Hardin students.

Whites also accuse Lodge Grass High of being a basketball factory, a school where players regularly receive special treatment, especially in the boys' program, which has won four Class B state titles in the last decade. A lot of the ridicule is directed at the boys' coach, Gordon Real Bird. A few years earlier, Elvis Old Bull, the star player on three consecutive championship teams and a reservation legend, dropped out of school after his last game, admitting that he was a phantom student and rarely attended classes. Real Bird, who has achieved legendary fame and power himself on the reservation for his coaching prowess, was blamed. He came under even more flak a couple years later over another incident. The school's athletic director, a white, pulled two players off the team bus just as it was leaving for the first game of divisional playoffs—these two players had skipped classes earlier in the week, making themselves academically ineligible. But Real Bird interceded and overruled the athletic director. Not only did the players get back on the bus and compete in the playoffs, the athletic director was fired. This reaffirmed the belief in Hardin that basketball, not academics, rules at Lodge Grass High.

To the people of Lodge Grass, the town of Hardin is seen as headquarters of the Evil Empire, home of the county jail, white merchants, and bankers who won't give them loans. To these Crows, Crow Agency may be the cultural and political center of the reservation, but Lodge Grass is its true heart. To them, the ultimate test of tribal loyalty for their brothers and sisters who live in Crow Agency is where they send their children to school—Hardin or Lodge Grass— they have the choice. A choice of Hardin makes you an apple—red on the outside, white in the center.

Sharon has no confusion about her ethnic center. If they want to resent her for going to Hardin High, that's their problem. Nearing Lodge Grass, she watches a car speed around the bus and honk. She can't be sure, but the woman in the back seat looks like her mom. She prays it's not.

While the players head for the gym, I walk through the town of Lodge Grass. It feels somehow more intimidating than Crow Agency. Maybe it's the scary black storm clouds and the swirling winds picking up litter and blowing it down the streets. Or maybe it's because in Crow Agency I feel emboldened by the presence of the community college and the national park at Custer Battlefield. Here, there are no white tourists in Winnebagos. What there is . . . is visible, crushing poverty.

At first glance, Lodge Grass looks cozy, a community nestled in the bucolic serenity of the surrounding landscape—rolling hills, cottonwoods, meadows, the Little Big Horn River. But on closer examination, the picture changes. There is the usual reservation blight: run-down houses, littered yards, abandoned cars, boarded storefronts.

On the main street leading to the high school, the potholes are cavernous. Small battalions of scroungy dogs wander loose, looking for food.

Lodge Grass is a town on the verge of bankruptcy, its unemployment rate at 85 percent. Its primary source of revenue comes from payments for water and sewer services, but with 200 of the town's 291 water service accounts delinquent on their bill, public services have been drastically reduced, including garbage collection. The odor proves it.

Law enforcement has been cut, too. The previous week, a large crop of marijuana was discovered on the edge of town, but because of budget cuts, the officer who would have staked it out was laid off, so the pot growers went free. An even bigger problem is the town's water pipes. Two years earlier, new pipes were installed beneath the streets, but not deep enough below the frostline to keep them from bursting in the frigid Montana winter, leaving entire sections of the town with no water. With winter coming and no money for repairs, the problem is urgent. With the rain starting to fall, I head back to the gym.

The reservation big shots are here: state senator Bill Yellowtail; president of Little Big Horn College Janine Windy Boy; tribal chairwoman Clara Nomee; BIA police chief Chester Headdress; county sheriff Larson Medicine Horse. And, of course, Danetta, who works the pregame crowd like a politician, shaking hands, reminding anyone who'll listen that her granddaughter is a superstar. Few listen. On her sweater she wears the big plastic button emblazoned with Sharon's picture in her basketball uniform. It is the first accessory she puts on, not just on game days, but *every* day.

So far, no sign of Karna.

The trophy case is filled with pictures and trophies of the boys' teams' many triumphs. There's even a picture of the great Elvis Old Bull. Evidently the showcase committee didn't pull a Pete Rose on him and deny him his place of honor for his transgressions off the court. I study the picture knowing that someday I will be able to tell my grandkids I actually saw Elvis leave the building. Here's how it happened.

Shortly after arriving in Montana, I traveled to Billings to watch a Native American basketball tournament with teams from around the country. On the Crow team were two of the reservation's greatest players ever, Jonathon Takes Enemy and Elvis, both of whom were in their mid-twenties and past their prime. Each had seen the promise of a college career cut short by excess booze and women. Despite being out of shape, it was clear they possessed extraordinary gifts, the Magic Johnson and Michael Jordan of tribal basketball. That they were out of shape was evident when Elvis finished a fast break by opening the rear door of the gym, and while the rest of the players ran back down the court, stepped outside and barfed. Elvis had left the building.

Late in the first quarter, the menacing black clouds turn into a violent thunderstorm sweeping through Little Big Horn Valley, with fifty-mile-an-hour winds snapping limbs off trees and knocking out power in parts of Lodge Grass. But in the small, cramped gym at the high school, there's no shortage of electricity. The Lodge Grass Indians are leading by eight.

Coach Mac calls a timeout. Walking back to the huddle, Sharon grimaces, her hand pressed to her back.

"What's wrong?" inquires Coach Mac.

"It hurts to run," Sharon answers, easing herself down on

the bench. Coach Mac signals for DyAnna Three Irons to check in.

Sharon is mad—at herself for having to come out, at her teammates for playing so timidly. Anita looks as if she expects an Indian to come flying out of the Lodge Grass stands with a tomahawk; Tiffany looks distracted, as if she wishes she was back in Hardin with her boyfriend, Kent. Both girls hate playing at Lodge Grass, intimidated by the cramped gym filled with screaming Indians. They know the fear is irrational—they've been playing in front of Indians their whole lives, and besides, half the crowd is rooting for Hardin. They also know they aren't in any physical danger. There hasn't been a fight or a racial incident at a Lodge Grass basketball game in years.

"I'm ready to go back in," Sharon advises less than a minute after sitting down. Coach Mac obliges.

To Sharon, playing against Lodge Grass is not a hate thing like Hardin's rivalry against Billings Central, but rather a tribal pride thing. She knows the Lodge Grass players, girls she's played hoops with at the court in Crow Agency for years. She has dozens of relatives and family friends in the stands, clan aunts and uncles, all of them convinced she's the best player in the state.

Seconds after reentering the game, she dives after a loose ball, skidding headfirst into a bottom bleacher. Unfazed, she scrambles to her feet, catches a pass from Tiffany, and with two defenders draped all over her, eases up a soft hook with her left hand. The shot is good and she is fouled. She makes the free throw, then 20 seconds later scores again on a power move to the hoop. I'm not sure I've ever seen such a determined look. It's almost possessed. At halftime, thanks to Sharon's hustle, Hardin leads 30–26, then in the third quarter they widen it to a dozen. But it isn't pretty. Aside from Sharon and Tiffany, the team is out of sync. Lazy defense, sloppy passes, no half-court offense, no intensity. During a timeout, Sharon notices several teammates scanning the stands.

"Come on!" she snaps. "We should be killing this team."

Despite her admonition, the Lady Bulldogs plod listlessly through the final quarter. But at the final buzzer, they lead on the scoreboard, 65–53, a victory attributable to Sharon's grit.

After the game, Sharon and Tiffany, two of the four homecoming queen candidates, exit the locker room together, athletic bags in hand, hair soaked. Between them they accounted for 46 of the team's 65 points—24 for Tiffany, who played the whole game, and 22 for Sharon, who played all but that one minute. Crossing the gym, they dodge a pack of Crow youngsters running wild on the court, shooting baskets with a wadded-up sock, their game ending when the sock hangs up on the rim. Near the exit, a small crowd of relatives and friends engulf Sharon. Tiffany veers off to join Anita. Next to the door leading outside to the bus, Coach Oswald stops them.

"Make sure you stay together," he warns, sounding like a platoon sergeant behind enemy lines. "It can get weird around here."

Sharon edges away from her admirers. She is twice relieved—at winning the game, and at her mom's not showing up. Karna is back in Billings, killing herself a drink at a time.

CHAPTER THIRTEEN

After practice, starting forward Rhea Beatty waits for a ride in front of school. She looks impatient, impertinent. Coach Mac drives from the parking lot and waves goodbye. Rhea pretends she doesn't see her. A minute later, a Ford Taurus pulls to the curb and Rhea gets in, unsmiling. It's her dad.

They ride in silence down Center Street, Rhea glaring out the window. She has been in a bad mood since getting grounded again—this time for missing curfew, a grounding that includes no use of the Taurus and no TV.

They stop for gas at Jay's Auto Service, and as Fred Beatty fills the tank, Rhea continues to glare out the window. She spots Paul Little Light driving by, and scoots down in her seat. Paul's the school heartthrob, the one who dreams of being a movie star, and Rhea's got a mini-crush on him. But now isn't the time to see him. Not when she's riding with her father, not when she's in such a lousy frame of mind.

Her sour mood is out of character. Normally, she is polite and thoughtful, attentive at practice and in her classes, respectful of her parents, an above-average student. In July she participated in the Academic Challenge, an annual educational competition for Indians held at Northern Montana

College in Havre. She took second in the speech competition, a surprise to most of her teachers, who thought of her as too shy for public speaking. Also over the summer she worked as a records clerk at Crow Hospital, a job that piqued her interest in a possible career in the health science field. But that's not her dream career. That would be photojournalism. Mr. Alvarado, her art teacher, says she has the best eye for photography of any student he's ever had.

Mr. Beatty, who's worked ten years for the city of Hardin in road maintenance, pays for the gas and continues the silent treatment on the drive home. Rhea has inherited his light complexion, Anglo features, and smooth release on her jumper. A handsome light-skinned Cato Indian with teeth as white as sugar cubes, he was an All-City guard back in his high school days in Oklahoma City, averaging 20 a game. From her mom, a full-blooded Crow employed as a cook at Crow Elementary, she's inherited her soft-spoken disposition. On this day, however, she feels like spitting, irritated at her father's strict ways and silent treatment. Lately, it seems his sole mission is to make her life miserable. She doesn't know anyone who's been grounded more than she has, or has an 11:00 P.M. curfew on weekends, or isn't allowed out on school nights.

"It's not fair," she says.

He keeps driving, saying nothing.

This latest grounding is the result of her coming home fifteen minutes past curfew on Saturday night. She'd been to a party and met a guy from Colorado. He is twenty-five and drives a Harley. What was she going to do . . . say, *Excuse me, it's nice talking with you but my daddy wants me home by 11?*

They approach their house, a government prefab hidden at the end of a long dirt road five miles south of town. The rutted dirt road is surrounded by cottonwoods. At the gate, they are greeted by the family's aging pit bull and Rhea's younger sister. Rhea grabs her books and heads for the house, glancing back over her shoulder at her father. He motions for her to set down the books, then he bends down and scoops a worn basketball off the dirt.

"There's still some daylight," he says. "Let's do a little work."

Rhea sighs, then obeys his instructions. He tosses her the ball and she takes a halfhearted shot, the ball caroming off the flimsy rim bolted to a broken telephone pole.

"Come on!" he asserts. "You're not going to get nothing out of this unless you put something into it."

She sighs again.

Working on her shooting is something they've done before. Many times. Over the summer, he pushed her hard, and it shows in her shooting touch in practices. Next to Anita, she is the best shot on the team, especially deadly from the right baseline. That's because their family court has a rickety corral fence bisecting the left side, leaving only the right side for practice. On the afternoon before the Lodge Grass game, she and her father spent two solid hours working on her quick release and follow-through, him feeding her pass after pass. By his estimate, she took five hundred shots that day, hitting 80 percent. In the game, however, she took only four shots and missed them all, scoring no points.

Rhea started the season with high hopes. In her sophomore year she started every game, and although she averaged only six points, she still has dreams of a scholarship. Realistically, she knows her speed and defensive skills aren't good enough to make it at a big college, but she thinks she might have a chance at a smaller, NAIA (National Association of Intercollegiate Athletics) school like Rocky Mountain College in Billings. Last year she'd been hesitant to assert herself, afraid of the upperclassmen, including Sharon. But this year was supposed to be different. All summer her father drummed it into her that if she works hard in practice and stays out of trouble, good things will happen. So far, they haven't. In the team's first two conference games, she scored a grand total of six points, with three rebounds, no assists, and six turnovers.

She loves basketball—and not just because her father pushes her. She loves everything about it: the kids talking about the games in the hallway, the fans blowing off the roof, the running up and down the court. On game days, she thinks of nothing else. During Crow Fair, it never dawned on her to cut practice. When Sharon didn't show up those first two days, it bugged her and showed a lack of commitment and leadership. It also bugged her that Coach Mac didn't punish Sharon. If that had been her cutting practice, she'd still be circling the gym with the medicine ball.

She continues to take passes from her father, drilling shot after shot, all from the right side. Finally, as darkness falls, he signals an end to the practice and they head inside.

"Just shoot like that tomorrow and you'll be all right," he says.

She doesn't reply, heading straight to her room.

Midway through the first quarter, Coach Mac flings down her towel in disgust after the Shepherd Lady Mustangs score 10 straight points and take an early lead. "Get it together, ladies!" she fumes. "This is our house."

The ref blows his whistle. Tiffany has committed her third careless foul in less than two minutes. Coach Mac calls a timeout, moving to greet Tiffany as she pouts off the court. "Hang in there," she encourages, patting her on the back.

Play resumes and the ref whistles another foul, a questionable call on Rhea, also her third. "Damnit, Rhea!" snaps Coach Mac, waving a sub into the game. "Pitiful."

To Coach Mac, Rhea seems preoccupied, as if something's bothering her. She's noticed subtle changes the last couple weeks—clothes worn a little tighter, hair teased a little higher, scowls in practice. It's probably boy-related, she thinks.

Rhea slumps down on the bench. That Tiffany got a pat on the back and she got yelled at doesn't go unnoticed.

Behind the Hardin bench, her father hustles down the bleacher stairs and approaches. He bends down and whispers in her ear, his voice loud enough for people close by to hear. "What are you thinking about out there?" he utters. "It's embarrassing!"

She slumps even lower.

Fathers. I've been thinking a lot about the position lately. In my case, I got lucky. I've never doubted my dad's love or support. When I was a kid growing up in L.A., he took me to the park and hit me grounders until he had blisters, never complaining, never pushing too hard. In Glendive, when Anita's father got into the testosterone shootout with the coach, I couldn't imagine my dad doing such a thing in a zillion years. Nor would he ever come down to the bench and berate me in front of others. He didn't even do it at home, alone. Not once.

I guess it isn't just my own daughters and father that have me thinking about fatherhood. Being on the rez, where involved fathers are as scarce as fresh halibut, I see kids being raised by moms, aunts, grandmas. But not dads. Not that Crow fathers have a corner on being deadbeats. There are bad dads in suburbia, too. But very few Father's Day cards get sold at the Crow Mercantile.

*　　*　　*

Coach Mac feels the familiar rumbling in her stomach. Relax, she reminds herself. It's not easy. Shepherd is a running team, with taller and stronger players, and more depth. It doesn't help that Tiffany and Rhea are now on the bench.

Seated high in the bleachers across the gym, Kathy Schick, the assistant coach from Montana State, scribbles notes in her scouting book. Everybody knows she's up there—there's not a Hardin player who wouldn't love to go to Bozeman on a ride—and if ever there's a night to shine, this is it.

"Come on, Anita!" shouts Bob Dewald, Anita's father.

Earlier in the week, he had talked to Anita at the dinner table, echoing what she'd heard from Coach Mac . . . that she needed to play more aggressively, look for her shot, stop deferring to Tiffany and Sharon. It wasn't the first time that she'd heard it, but this night she is resolved to do something about it. In practice this week she was unstoppable, dominating scrimmages; yesterday, after everyone else left the gym, she stayed and worked on her outside shooting, hitting 28 of 30 from the top of the key.

Of all the girls on the team, Anita is the best bet for a college scholarship. Maybe for basketball, probably volleyball, definitely academically, and if all those fail, then musically. But given her mediocre play in the team's first four games—9.5 a game and a lowly 53 percent from the free throw line—a ride for her talent on the saxophone and piano seems more likely than basketball.

On Hardin's first possession after Rhea's third foul, Anita hits a jumper from the top of the key, then steals the inbounds pass and scores again. Following two short jumpers by Sharon, she hits another outside shot, then a three-point bomb at the buzzer. From 10 down to a three-point lead at the end of the first quarter.

Anita starts the second quarter still hot, scoring on a fast break, then swishing a 15-footer. She's in—as they say—the zone, feeling a shooting touch she's known only in practice. She wants the ball and calls for it, something she's never done. For the first time in her varsity career, she feels she's on the same level with Sharon, an equal instead of a supporting player. At halftime she has 19 points, hitting a sizzling nine of 10 from the field, her shots coming from all over the court. Kathy Schick writes it all down.

In the second half, with Rhea and Tiffany on the bench with four fouls each, the Lady Bulldogs continue their swarming defense and up-tempo offense, building a 20-point lead. If Anita owned the second quarter, Sharon owns the third, scoring 10 points, twice skidding across the floor in pursuit of a loose ball, twice taking a charge and getting knocked on her butt.

Midway through the fourth quarter, Rhea fouls out, leaving the game with four points and two rebounds. As she walks off the court, Coach Mac doesn't say a word, turning her back as Rhea passes. In the stands, Fred Beatty gets up and exits the gym.

With two minutes left and Hardin up by 22, Coach Mac drifts toward the end of the bench, ready to finally substitute. Senior reserves Amy Hanson and Geri Stewart don't see her coming, too busy talking.

Coach Mac leans between them. "Excuse me if I'm interrupting," she says.

Both girls glare.

"If you can't even bother to watch the game, then you might as well turn in your uniforms," she says, turning to wave sophomores Christina Chavez and Stacie Greenwalt into the game.

"Bitch!" mutters Geri.

Coach Mac doesn't hear her.

Sharon and Anita exit the game to a standing ovation. They have played spectacularly, scoring 50 points between them, 27 for Anita (13 for 15 from the floor) and 23 for Sharon, her third straight game over 20. She also adds eight rebounds and seven assists. In conference play, she's now averaging 23 points a game, leading the league.

Fathers. One of those standing and applauding as Sharon exits the game is Michael LaForge, her father. He has had no contact with her ever, but this is the second game in a row he's attended. At Lodge Grass, Sharon spotted him at the end of the game, but it did nothing to change her feelings about him—she wanted nothing to do with him. He hadn't been there for her during her whole childhood, so why should she want him back in now? She wondered if his suddenly showing an interest in her games was so he could sit in the stands and say, *"That's my daughter down there scoring all those points."* Her only confusion is who she resents more: her mom or her dad?

Exhausted, she plops down on the bench, grimacing, trying to ease a spasm in her lower back. Seeing her discomfort, Anita slides in next to her like she did on the bus, and gently massages the sore spot, saying nothing, not stopping until the final buzzer.

The final score is 86–74. Hardin's overall record is now 4-1, 2-1 in conference. With Glendive losing to Colstrip, the Lady Bulldogs are now in a three-way tie for first place. But leaving the court, they look more like losers.

Geri and Amy are the first to reach the locker room, quickly changing, not bothering to shower. Tiffany follows, still pouting. She spent half the game on the bench, scoring only seven, all but ruining her chances for a ride to Montana State.

Sharon is next, holding her hand to her lower back and proclaiming there's no way she's going to take part in that "stupid homecoming" tomorrow night.

The last off the court is Rhea, head hung, looking like someone just ran over her pit bull. Anita stops and waits, putting an arm around her shoulder.

"I'm hurting the team," says Rhea. "We'd be better off if I quit."

"You can't quit," counsels Anita. "We need you."

They walk a few more feet, then Rhea says, "No, you don't need me. I'm quitting."

After all the players have left the locker room, Coach Mac exits. She's all smiles. Her team is in first place and just scored more points than any team in the state this year, proving to her what's she's believed from Day One—that nobody in the state can stay with them when they play like they did tonight. And based on Anita's great game, she now has three potential All-Staters.

Still, beneath her postgame high, trouble lurks. Tiffany is in a funk, Sharon can barely walk, Rhea wants to quit, and Geri and Amy hate her guts.

CHAPTER FOURTEEN

The Friday night lights of the Hardin High football field illuminate the cold, clear prairie sky. Fall's chill is sweeping across Montana. Shivering in the shadows of the end zone, Sharon stands next to the three other candidates, waiting to be summoned to center stage for the big halftime crowning of the queen. She feels conspicuous, uncomfortable in her tight-fitting mermaid gown.

"I'm freezing my butt off," says Tiffany, her turquoise off-the-shoulder gown exposing the goosebumps on her bare shoulders and long neck.

The four candidates giggle. In a couple minutes they will walk across the football field to the fifty-yard line in front of the grandstands, and a silver tiara will be placed on one of their heads. Everyone assumes, including the other two candidates, Geri Stewart and Kindra Melville, that the contest boils town to Tiffany vs. Sharon, the two best-known girls in school, the two biggest stars.

"I wish they'd hurry and get this over with," says Sharon, smacking her lips, unaccustomed to having them coated with lip gloss.

*   *   *

I want Sharon to win. It isn't that I don't like Geri or Tiffany—they are both friendly toward me, and Tiffany's pouting seems nothing more than the typical teenage snit I've seen come through my own front door a thousand times—but Sharon is the underdog, the anti-queen.

"Are you going to the dance?" asks Tiffany.

Sharon shakes her head. She hasn't pressed Randy to go—a high school dance isn't likely to be big on his social calendar. Evidently, neither are her games. He still hasn't seen her play.

Waiting with the candidates is a small circle of family and friends, including Tiffany's mom, Karen, a cheerleader back in her days at Hardin High, pre–Title IX. She probably would've been a homecoming queen candidate, too, but in her senior year she got pregnant with Tiffany's oldest sister and was asked to leave school. In those days, pregnant girls weren't allowed at Hardin High.

Sharon's aunt Marlene is also there. So is Holly, who's driven back from Bozeman to be with her best friend on this special night. "Sharon's gonna win," she predicts.

"What makes you say that?" asks Marlene.

"'Cause it's time an Indian finally wins something around here."

Tiffany paces. Holly's presence bothers her. Holly is the girl who bad-mouthed her for two years and helped drive a wedge between her and Sharon, and for her to pop back into the picture at zero hour of a major high school moment is not part of Tiffany's grand design for her senior year. And she definitely has a grand design: homecoming queen, honor roll, All-State, scholarship offers. She wishes Holly would butt out.

* * *

The wait is over. The royal court is escorted across the field to a spot in front of the grandstands, Sharon on the arm of Paul Little Light. In his white tails and hat, he looks like the movie star he dreams to be.

The crowd rises to greet them, including Rhea, who has decided not to quit after all. The candidates are introduced, then the public address announcer waits patiently for the applause to subside. Milking the moment, last year's queen walks slowly behind each candidate, holding the tiara high. Sharon braces for the phony shrieks and hugs.

"Ladies and gentlemen," intones the announcer, "this year's Hardin High homecoming queen is . . . Tiffany Hopfauf."

Four hours later, Sharon and Holly sit in Sharon's car in the darkened parking lot behind the Wagon Wheel Tavern. They've been sitting there for thirty minutes, staking out Randy's truck. He's inside the bar, but he's got somebody waiting in his truck. It's sixteen-year-old Raylene Pretty Elk, the sexy little number he assured Sharon he wasn't seeing.

"Come on, let's go!" demands Holly. "Don't you get it? He don't give a shit about you. He's in there getting drunk while his two dopey teenage girlfriends wait for him in the parking lot like fools."

"Shut up!" says Sharon.

The back door of the Wagon Wheel bangs open and Randy storms into the parking lot, followed closely by Don Young Buck, a guy under the impression that Raylene is *his* girlfriend. Randy just informed him otherwise, and now they're stepping outside to settle it Mike Tyson style. The bar crowd follows, including the manager.

It's dark and Sharon can't tell who throws the first punch,

but she can definitely see that they're both flailing wildly. They wrestle to the ground, Randy on top.

"Someone call the sheriff's office," yells the manager, trying to pull them apart. Randy struggles to his feet and looks in Sharon's direction.

"Randy! Randy!" she yells, waving him toward the car.

"He ain't gettin' in here!" says Holly, locking the doors.

Randy runs to his truck, and in a squeal of tires, backs up and peels out of the parking lot, Raylene right beside him. Sharon wastes no time, throwing the Cougar into gear and tearing out after him.

The chase is on. Randy turns onto the frontage road next to I-90 and floors it, heading south toward Crow Agency, Sharon ten car-lengths behind him.

"I don't wanna die 'cause of this asshole!" screams Holly.

Both cars continue south, Randy pulling away. He's not worried about the cops; the Montana Highway Patrol rarely patrol the reservation roads.

Reaching Crow Agency, Randy turns under the underpass and disappears down a side street. Sharon turns up one street, then down another. "There's his truck!" she exclaims. It's parked behind the house of Raylene's grandmother, and there's no sign of Randy. Or Raylene. "I'm gonna go see if they're in there."

"What if they are?" asks Holly.

"I just want to see if they're in there."

"No, you wait in the car," Holly orders. "I'll handle this."

Bolstered by the beers she'd drunk while on stakeout behind the Wagon Wheel, she hurries up the walkway to the pitch-black front porch. The front door lock clicks shut. She bangs on the door.

No answer.

She bangs again.

Still no answer.

"I know you're in there. Come to the door."

She peeks in a window and sees a shadow move. Then she hears a voice. It's Raylene's sister, Janette. "You wanna kick Raylene's ass, don't you?" Janette says.

"I just want to talk. That's all."

"Go away!"

"No."

"Then you're gonna have to spend the night out there 'cause I'm not opening the door."

"Chickenshit!"

Deciding that she doesn't want to spend the night on the porch, Holly returns to the car.

"Maybe he's not in there," suggests Sharon.

"Get real! He's probably already screwing his brains out with that little whore. When are you gonna get it into your head? He's a loser. Let's go!"

Reluctantly, Sharon drives away, heading back toward the freeway, but then turns around for one last cruise by the house. Turning the corner, she sees the taillights of Randy's truck pulling away. She follows, and when he parks in front of his uncle's house several blocks away, she pulls behind him. "Stay in the car," she tells Holly, then chases after him, catching up on the front porch. Holly watches them talk, too far to hear.

A minute later, Sharon returns to the car. "What'd he say?" asks Holly.

"He says that wasn't his truck behind Raylene's house."

"And you believed him?"

Sharon shrugs.

"The guy's scum. He cheats right in front of your face and then tells you he's not. Don't be stupid, Sharon."

"You don't know what he was doing. Besides, he's drunk."

"Oh, now I get it . . . being drunk makes it all right."

Sharon heads back toward the freeway again. "I don't want to talk about it anymore," she says.

"You're meeting him tomorrow, aren't you?"

Again, Sharon shrugs.

At Marlene's they tiptoe downstairs to Sharon's bedroom in the basement. With her homecoming gown piled in a corner, they finally fall asleep on her bed. The first fingers of dawn are already creeping through the darkness. In eight hours, Sharon will be on the bus heading for tonight's game at Laurel High.

Also that night . . .

Rhea sneaks up the dirt road leading to her house. It's four hours past her curfew, and there's a good chance she could be in the biggest trouble of her life. She needs a miracle. The dog barks.

"Shhhh," she instructs.

It's not like she planned to stay out this late. She started off with good intentions, going to homecoming just like she told her parents. But after the game she went to a party, the kind of party her father would call the "wrong crowd," with lots of gangsta rap and beer, of which Rhea imbibed a few. That was trouble enough, but the twenty-five-year-old guy from Colorado, the one with the Harley, was there again. His name, she learned, is Richard, and if the rumors are true, he's married, has a kid, and is a gangbanger. Maybe it's true, maybe it's not. All she knows for sure is that he's nice to her.

But as she creeps up the steps to the darkened house, she's expecting her father's wrath to come crashing down on her.

Slowly, she opens the door. It's not locked—it never is. Her plan is to sneak down the hall past her parents' room and into hers. Shoes in hand, she tiptoes through the living room, then stops, sensing eyes peering at her in the darkness. Across the room is a silhouette. It's her father. He's sitting at the kitchen table, arms folded. She doesn't need to see his face to know he's pissed.

"You ain't playing no basketball tonight," he states. "In fact, you ain't playing the rest of the year."

CHAPTER FIFTEEN

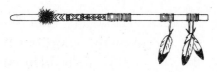

The doorbell startles Coach Mac. It's eight o'clock Saturday morning, the day after homecoming. She peeks through the curtain.

It's Rhea's father.

Puzzled, she ushers him inside. He's there to tell her that Rhea won't be traveling with the team to Laurel tonight. "She broke the rules," he explains. "Now she has to pay the consequences."

"How long will she be grounded?" she asks.

"Until she changes her attitude," he answers.

Despite the bad news, Coach Mac feels strangely encouraged. Learning of Rhea's troubles at home affirms her sense that something has been bothering the junior forward. She is also bolstered by Mr. Beatty's tough response to Rhea's breaking curfew. Hardin coaches have long complained that Indian athletes receive little or no parental control, leaving coaches to discipline in a vacuum. For an Indian father to come to her door and say he's putting his foot down is a positive sign. It helps that tonight's game is against winless Laurel, the worst team in the conference. Maybe this will be a good night to give sophomore Stacie Greenwalt more minutes.

* * *

Her gym bag thrown over her shoulder, fifteen-year-old Stacie bolts across her front porch and down the steps, heading for the car, nearly bowling over her strapping good-looking father in her haste. Doug Greenwalt got custody of Stacie and her older sister five years ago after he and their mother divorced, the mom moving to Helena. Stacie's new stepmom, youthful and spirited, has worked hard to fill the breach.

"Did you clean the barn?" he yells after Stacie.

"Tomorrow," she explains, throwing her bag across the front seat of the family pickup she'll drive into town. "The bus is leaving for Laurel in forty minutes. Gotta fly."

She rams it into reverse, then practically pops a wheelie zooming onto the highway. She's been driving since she was ten, first learning on one of dad's tractors, and now with her new driver's license—in Montana the driving age is fifteen—she's free to go charging around the county roads in a two-ton hunk of horsepower, a concept that is, in the words of Coach Mac, "a scary proposition."

Nicknamed "Spacey" by her teammates, Stacie is the team flake, nobody even close. She's ditzy, quick-witted, irreverent. Some days she comes to practice as Betty Boop. Other days it's Marilyn Monroe entertaining the troops in Korea. It's hard to tell if it's an act or if she is just naturally goofy. Either way, the boys at Hardin High eat it up. Some think she's the sexiest girl in school, although at 6'1", she towers over most.

She turns and waves goodbye to her dad, a successful wheat and beer barley grower. Recently, he built a large, rustic log cabin on the family property, complete with a large concrete slab and basketball hoop for Stacie to practice on, but so far, he's had no more luck persuading her to practice than he has getting her to clean the barn where she keeps her 4-H blue-ribbon Herefords.

Located thirty miles south of Hardin in an area the locals

call "The Deep South" because of its concentration of red-necks, the Greenwalt farm, like most in the area, is a patch-work collection of acreage, 30 percent of which Doug Greenwalt owns outright, the other 70 percent leased from Indians. Stacie loves the rural setting, although she likes the action in town, too, sometimes making two round-trips a day, 120 miles. Yesterday, I saw her on the road, stereo blasting, cigarette smoke billowing out the window.

Evidently, smoking hasn't stunted her growth. She's not only the tallest girl on the squad, but the strongest as well. Blessed with quick hands and quick feet, she can outrun and outjump everybody on the team and is far and away the best shot blocker. Sharon is convinced that Stacie, even as a sophomore, can be the best center in the conference, if not the whole state. Half of Sharon's battle wounds come from scrimmaging against her, a task she considers harder than actual games.

Stacie passes the abandoned brick missionary school in St. Xavier, once part of the white man's plan to educate the Indian children as to the ways of Christianity, or as the say-ing went, "to kill the Indian and save the man." She accel-erates, afraid she'll miss the bus. Ahead, a combine on the highway blocks most of the road, slowing her down. She floors it, swerving onto the shoulder to get around.

As talented as she is, she has two major flaws in Coach Mac's eyes. The first is her lack of varsity experience. The other, and the one that drives Coach Mac nuts, is her ten-dency to go brain dead on the court. For reasons science has yet to explain, even capable teenagers can go utterly stupid for minutes, even hours. Earlier in the week Coach Mac stopped practice to instruct Stacie how to shift her feet to cut off the baseline, then on the very first play, Sharon drove baseline on her through a gap as wide as one of her Herefords. In the zone trap, there are days she looks as if she isn't sure if she's supposed to be at midcourt or Missoula.

It's because of her mental lapses and occasional flights of goofiness that Coach Mac wants to bring her along slowly, play her mostly with the junior varsity and maybe a few minutes each game with the varsity, the theory being that by tournament time, she'll be ready to step up to bigger minutes. In the varsity's first five games, however, she has played only four minutes. Sharon wonders why Stacie isn't starting right now, convinced her pure athleticism will make up for her mental lapses. She and Stacie could play twin posts, or Stacie could play low post and she could move to forward in Owena's spot.

Passing cars like they are standing still, Stacie blows into Hardin with five minutes to spare. With a huge smile, she throws her bag on the bus, takes a seat toward the back, and declares, "Come on, girls, let's not waste this time together. Who's got the beer?"

Laurel, population 4,500, is ten miles west of Billings and is a strong union town, its biggest employer the Cenex Oil Refinery. The high school got its nickname—the Locomotives—because of the huge railroad shipping yard on the south side of town. At the end of the first quarter, it appears that it'll take a major train wreck to stop Hardin. They lead 26–8.

Anita is on fire again, scoring 14 points in the quarter. In her last five quarters, she is 20 of 23 (87 percent) from the field and attacking the basket. Sharon hasn't cooled down either, scoring eight first-quarter points. DyAnna Three Irons is playing in Rhea's place.

To start the second quarter, Coach Mac keeps the starting five in the game. "We want Stacie! We want Stacie!"

chant a group of boys right behind the bench. Coach Mac ignores them.

Coach Mac's substitution pattern worries me. She seems determined to stick with the first unit, no matter the physical toll on them or the psychic toll on the benchwarmers. In the team's first five games, Sharon has averaged 31 minutes out of 32 and has a swollen ankle, bruised arm, back spasms, and now a giant hematoma on her thigh. Anita is also averaging 31 minutes, and Tiffany is averaging a little less only because she ran into foul trouble against Shepherd. With the game against Laurel already a blowout, this seems a perfect time to give the scrubeanies playing time.

Coach Mac sees it differently. With four tough games coming up, she thinks it's important to keep the first team on the floor—they're playing great together now and she's afraid to disturb the chemistry. More playing time, she believes, will solidify them even more. It's especially important for Anita to keep playing; she's the hottest player in the state right now and Coach Mac wants to build her confidence even higher. She also wants the team to work on its half-court offense, and game action is better than practice.

"We want Stacie! We want Stacie!" the chanting continues.

Coach Mac continues to ignore the call, but Stacie turns from the end of the bench and issues a coquettish little wave to her fans.

With 1:47 left in the first half and Hardin up by 23, the big three still haven't come out of the game. Near midcourt, Tiffany deflects a pass toward Anita, who bends to scoop it up. To her left, an opponent trips and stumbles, heading out of control in her direction. They collide, the sickening sound of colliding flesh and bones audible all the way to the top row. Anita collapses to the floor, grabbing her left

knee, the same one she dislocated her freshman season and spent the year rehabbing, the same one she popped out of joint skiing her sophomore year, the same one that crumpled on her during team camp over the summer.

Without waiting for the ref to call time, Coach Mac races out onto the court. In the stands, Anita's mom buries her face in her hands, too horrified to look.

In the fickle balance of sport, one moment Anita is the hottest player in the state, then the next she is writhing in agony, her chances of an athletic scholarship blindsided, her team's chances for State devastated.

She rolls around the floor, her cries piercing the chilling silence of the gym. Finally, Coach Oswald carries her off the court to the locker room. There is no trainer or team doctor in the building to examine her.

Instead of taking her to the hospital for X-rays and immediate attention, Coach Oswald wraps her knee in ice and then she limps back out to the court to watch the second half, her leg propped up on the bench. She will wait until tomorrow to see a doctor and get X-rays. "I'm okay," she promises.

With two minutes left, Coach Mac finally puts Stacie into the game, much to the delight of her fan club. She quickly scores three baskets and blocks two shots, then with the clock winding down, she sprints the length of the court on a Laurel breakaway, catching up to the dribbler from five steps behind. Taking a giant leap, she launches herself, her long arm reaching over the girl's shoulder to block the shot with a monstrous swat, knocking the ball three rows deep into the bleachers. Her fan club goes into deep frenzy.

Hardin wins 81–48, improving their record to 5-1. Tiffany tops the scoring with 22, Sharon adding an easy 17. But as the team stops for burgers at a Hardee's on the way out of town, there is, if not a pall, a gloomy cloud of resignation.

Anita assures everyone that there's nothing broken or ripped, yet she has to be helped into the restaurant.

I'm the first to down my burger, then I sit back and wait for everyone else to finish. I feel a tap on my shoulder. I turn, surprised to see Sharon standing next to me. She extends an ice cream sundae toward me.

"I can't eat this," she says. "You want it?"

I see a peace pipe. The sundae doesn't stand a chance.

While everyone finishes eating, Stacie returns to the counter for a refill on her fries. Her ankles are taped and she's wearing an ultratight, black and white cowhide miniskirt that looks like it might have come right off the back of one of her dad's cows. Behind her, a slim-hipped teenage cowboy, wearing a black Stetson that makes him almost as tall as her, stares hard at her hind side. She watches his eyes in the reflection off the chrome plating behind the counter.

The clerk places her fries on a tray. "Excuse me," she says in a British accent, "but do you have any Grey Poupon?"

"Huh?" replies the clerk.

"My good man, do you mean to tell me you have no Grey Poupon?"

Another huh.

Feigning indignation, she grabs her tray and turns, her way blocked by the ogling cowboy behind her.

"Out of my way, Bug Eyes," she says, "or I'll break your bony little ass."

Sharon LaForge
COURTESY OF DENNIS SANDERS,
HARDIN PHOTO

Owena Spotted Horse
COURTESY OF DENNIS SANDERS,
HARDIN PHOTO

Rhea Beatty
COURTESY OF DENNIS SANDERS,
HARDIN PHOTO

Tiffany Hopfauf
COURTESY OF DENNIS SANDERS,
HARDIN PHOTO

Stacie Greenwalt
COURTESY OF DENNIS SANDERS,
HARDIN PHOTO

Anita Dewald
COURTESY OF DENNIS SANDERS,
HARDIN PHOTO

Hardin Lady Bulldogs. Back row: Coach Mac, DyAnna Three Irons, Anita Dewald, Stacie Greenwalt, Maria Oswald, Tiffany Hopfauf, Coach Oswald. Middle row: Bobbie Romine (mgr.), Sharon LaForge, Amy Hanson, Rhea Beatty, Owena Spotted Horse, Kim Schroeder (mgr.). Front row: Geri Stewart, Christina Chavez, Kassi Elk Shoulder, Monica Allendigs (mgr.).

Amylynn Adams
COURTESY OF DAVID MEBANE,
BIG HORN COUNTY NEWS

Sharon fires a
jumper against the
Colstrip Fillies in
another narrow
victory.
COURTESY OF DAVID
MEBANE, *BIG HORN
COUNTY NEWS*

Winner of a MacArthur "genius grant," Janine Pease Windy Boy stands in front of the school she established.
COURTESY OF CHIP SIMONS

Sharon sits on the front porch of her grandmother's home.
COURTESY OF DONNA LEE HOLMES

Just down the hill from Little Big Horn Battlefield, the Fallsdowns pose for a family portrait (Blaine, Aunt Marlene, Sharon, Danetta, and Junior).
COURTESY OF DONNA LEE HOLMES

On the basketball court in her grandmother's backyard, Sharon and Junior play.
COURTESY OF DONNA LEE HOLMES

Homecoming queen candidate and reserve forward Geri Stewart.

Homecoming queen candidate Sharon and her escort, Paul Little Light, at the big event.

CHAPTER SIXTEEN

Damnit!" barks Coach Mac, stopping practice. "Reverse the ball to the weak side. Quick passes. Come on, get serious!"

The focus all week has been the team's half-court offense, pitiful in every game, and not much better in practice. Whenever the opposition's defense stops the fast break and forces the offense into set plays and patterns, the wheels get wobbly. Lazy passes. Sluggish movement. Lack of attention. It's taken everything in Coach Mac's anger management arsenal, including repositioning the Post-it notes on the refrigerator door—to keep from exploding.

The week hasn't been a total loss, however. In fact, most of the news has been good. Anita's X-rays revealed her knee injury wasn't as serious as originally feared and she'll be in the lineup for tomorrow's showdown for first place against Colstrip. Rhea will be in the lineup, too, her father agreeing to let her play again, although she's still grounded indefinitely.

"I want at least six passes around the perimeter before you take it inside," orders Coach Mac.

Anita makes the initial pass to Rhea, who spots Sharon cutting to the basket and passes her the ball underneath.

"Goddamnit, Rhea!" explodes Coach Mac. "What did I just say? If you're not going to pay attention, why be here?"

Rhea's shoulders slump.

After everyone has left the gym, Coach Mac flips off the office light and heads outside to the darkened parking lot and her 4x4 Datsun pickup with its "L Mac" vanity plates. She tosses her grade books into the back, then slides behind the wheel and lights a cigarette. It's only four blocks to her house, hardly enough time for three puffs.

She parks in the garage behind her modest two-bedroom house and is wildly greeted at the back door by Spice, her hyper-mutt that's been home alone all day. The house is cold and dark, but Coach Mac is happy to be home. She feeds Spice, then turns on ESPN and plops down on the couch, exhausted, another twelve-hour day behind her.

There are times, she admits, that she thinks about having a partner to come home to, but when she really thinks about it, coaching and a relationship seem incompatible. Like on this night. She's too tired to do anything but veg out in front of the tube, catch the scores on the local sports news, and maybe watch a *Night Court* rerun. Lots of nights she falls asleep on the couch.

Coaching is Linda McClanahan's life and she doesn't want it any other way, but sometimes she wonders if people understand how demanding the job is. Not just the Xs and Os and lazy passes, but the other stuff, the unseen demands. Like on this day. She arrived at school at 7:00 A.M., an hour before classes begin, to correct exams from her health class, then plunged into her teaching day of six classes, skipping lunch to fill out disciplinary reports and call parents. After the final bell at 3:30, she had thirty minutes to prepare for the start of a two-hour practice. By the time she put away the balls and cleared the locker room, it was after 7:00 P.M. She'd planned on going to the school board meeting to voice her objection to the board's pitiful salary offer to teachers, but that needed energy she didn't have. So it's just a twelve-hour day.

She doesn't need to be a math whiz to figure out that her yearly $2,500 coaching stipend works out to be less than she could make flipping burgers at the new Dairy Queen. And that doesn't include all the time she spends thinking about the job, which is every waking hour, and a few sleeping ones, too. Last night she dreamed that she left the uniforms at home in her washer after the last game and the team had to play in their street clothes.

For her, the toughest part of the job isn't the long hours, or low pay, or washing the team's uniforms. It's the pressure. Coaching in a town that heaps so much attention on basketball puts her under the microscope; she's recognized everywhere she goes, always getting coaching advice. At the IGA last week, a clerk suggested she switch Sharon to point guard. She said thanks for the tip, paid for her groceries, and forgot about it.

I thought it sounded like a good idea.

But more than the pressure from the community it's the stress she puts on herself that knots her stomach. She desperately wants to prove she's worthy. Coaching is her calling, her way of rising above the austerity of her childhood and leaving a mark. This mark doesn't have to be a Coach of the Year trophy or a promotion to a big-time college job . . . it's simply about turning the Lady Bulldogs into the best they can be.

The team's inconsistency makes her nuts. They run off 26 unanswered points, then go scoreless for a quarter; they score more points than any team in the state, then look like candidates for clown school. It baffles her how Sharon can dive headfirst after a loose ball, then skip practice.

She is convinced that fans don't understand the com-

151

plexities of coaching girls' basketball. Yes, girls are more coachable than boys in some ways—better listeners, more eager to learn, less likely to think they know it all—but they're also more emotional, moodier. A fight with a boyfriend, a bad grade on a test, an argument at home . . . anything can trigger a funk. Rhea is a perfect example—she gets grounded at home and suddenly she's worthless on the court. Coach Mac also believes boys don't bring their problems onto the court the way girls do. Two years ago one of her starters got pregnant during the season and had an abortion four days before Divisionals; she played anyway, but performed terribly and the team lost. Coach Mac knew about the situation, but when asked to explain why the team lost, she certainly couldn't mention the abortion.

Finally, after the ten o'clock news, she falls asleep. It's not until morning that she realizes she forgot to eat dinner.

How can this be happening? In the team's last two games they averaged 83.5 points a game to move up to a number three ranking in the state, but after two quarters at home against the Colstrip Fillies, they trail 27–16. The half-court offense they worked on all week is nonexistent; the crowd is quieter than a Quaker meeting; Rhea is looking for the hook every time downcourt; Owena stinks; and Sharon has one point.

"It's mental, ladies," says Coach Mac.

It's physical, too. Anita isn't limping, but she looks nothing like the dominating player of the last two games. Tiffany has a head cold and looks as if she should be home in bed with a bowl of chicken soup and a vaporizer. And Sharon is a mess. In the second quarter she fell to the floor with a severe leg cramp, and when Coach Oswald rushed out to see if she was all right, she got up and hobbled off the court and right on out the exit, dragging her cramped leg behind her, stoically suffering in private. The cramp went away, but the pain in her lower back hasn't. It was so bad during the week that she slept on the floor; it was only after much cajoling by Aunt Marlene that she reluctantly went to the clinic in Crow Agency, where the doctor prescribed Motrin and Tylenol, but told her the only real cure is rest.

Waiting for the second half to start, Coach Mac closes her eyes and tries to relax. She knows that Colstrip, rated number four in the state, is a good team—they beat Glendive, the team that blew out Hardin—but how could this be happening, down by 11? She gathers the team around her.

"I've got just one word for you," she says. "Embarrassing."

Sharon opens the third quarter with a twisting lefthander from five feet, then steals the ball and drains a 15-foot jumper, cutting the deficit to seven. Suddenly, the gym rocks. By the end of the quarter, Hardin leads 39–38, paced by Sharon's 12 points. She's possessed. It's a complete reversal, precisely the inconsistency that pumps the acid in Coach Mac's stomach.

In the fourth quarter, the lead seesaws, then with 1:34 to go, DyAnna Three Irons, who replaced a disconsolate Rhea in the third quarter, scores on a layin off a football pass from Sharon to put Hardin up 48–45.

"Don't foul!" pleads Coach Mac.

DyAnna, who leads the league in hair, her braided black mane falling below her butt, fouls.

But the free throw is missed and Sharon grabs the rebound, her 12th. "Don't shoot unless it's a layin," yells Coach Mac, 58 seconds left.

DyAnna, who also leads the league in poor shooting technique, heaves a brick from 15 feet. Coach Mac stomps

and pirouettes like a broken gyro. Colstrip grabs the rebound.

The crowd wants Rhea back in there. Or Stacie. Or anybody but DyAnna, who's a really nice kid with great hair,
but not ready for crunch time. Not now, not ever.

Hardin leads by three, and everybody in Big Horn
County knows the Fillies' strategy: get the ball to Darcy
Jensen, their deadeye outside shooter, and let her shoot the
three for the tie.

Calmly, Colstrip works the ball around the perimeter, the
clock ticking down: 25 . . . 20 . . . 15. "Stay tight on Jensen!"
implores Coach Mac.

With five seconds left, Jensen gets the ball at the top of
the key just beyond the three-point line. She is disgustingly
wide open. How is this possible?

Swish. Tie game. Overtime.

"You guys look like somebody just shot your dog," says
Coach Mac. "Come on! It's not the end of the world. You
can come back."

Given the long faces, it seems unlikely.

Breaking the huddle, Tiffany takes another hit from her
inhaler. She looks embalmed.

On Hardin's first possession, with the place in Stage II
bedlam, Anita scores. Then it's Sharon for two. Then Anita
again. Colstrip can't regroup, and when the horn sounds,
Hardin wins 59–48, an 11–0 whitewash in overtime, Sharon
and Anita combining for nine of the 11 points. On the
night, Sharon leads all scorers with 19, all but one coming
in the second half. She also has 13 rebounds, a season
high.

The Lady Bulldogs are 6-1, and with Glendive losing to
Miles City, they are now all alone in first place.

* * *

Despite the overtime victory, it's still not all smiles exiting the locker room. Rhea walks with her head down, fighting back tears. She scored zero points and played zero minutes in the second half . . . and for the first time in her basketball career, her father was not at the game. He missed it on purpose, still angry at her. They haven't spoken in three days.

Sharon is happy the team won, but can't enjoy it. During the game, she was able to push the pain out of her mind, but now that it's over, she can feel the pain shoot from her lower back all the way down her leg. Maybe she'll double the Tylenol tonight.

Tiffany, who played the whole game, sounds like she has a clothespin on her nose. She doesn't look so hot either, combining an ugly nasal congestion with a significant pout. It's hard to tell if she's pouting because she's all clogged up, or because she played poorly, turning the ball over six times, scoring only 11 points, and making but one of six from the free throw line. In conference play, she is averaging 14.6. Sharon is averaging 21.

The last to exit, as always, is Coach Mac. She's finished her postgame chores: calling in the score to the *Billings Gazette* and the TV stations; entering the statistics into the computer; writing the refs' evaluations; checking bus and insurance forms for tomorrow night's game against Billings Central; gathering up the uniforms to take home and wash.

"Good game," I offer.

She exhales, catching her breath for the first time since leaving home fifteen hours ago. "Too bad I don't get paid for overtime," she says.

CHAPTER SEVENTEEN

My girlfriend, Marcie, has come to my little corner of Montana for a visit and we do the tourist thing—Custer Battlefield, Beartooth Mountains, Yellowstone, Glacier National Park. We return to Hardin and follow the Big Horn River south to Fort Smith, and then up to Yellowtail Lake in the foothills of the Big Horn Mountains. It's a man-made lake created by the construction of Yellowtail Dam in 1962, a government project that paid the tribe $10 million, the money dispersed equally among the 3,500 enrolled tribal members, most of whom blew their windfalls on pickups and TVs.

I'm looking forward to Marcie meeting Sharon and seeing the Lady Bulldogs in action. "I feel like I know these kids already," she says as we drive to Billings for the game against Billings Central in The Dungeon, the school's infamous gym.

From what I've heard, The Dungeon is small, dark, poorly ventilated, and home to the most unruly fans this side of Philadelphia. Allegedly, racial epithets fly out of the stands like spitballs. *Prairie Nigger . . . wagon burner . . . ugly squaw.* Sharon claims to have heard it all.

Arriving at the gym my first thought is claustrophobia. It's an old-fashioned crackerbox out of the 1950s. On one side of the court, there's no bleachers, just enough room for the players' benches. On the other side, bleachers extend down from the rafters to a ten-foot wall bordering the sideline. I envision players smashing into this wall, leaving behind splattered blood and broken bones. In the stands, spectators cram together, Central fans on one side of the aisle, Hardin on the other. At both ends of the court, portable bleachers reserved for Central fans extend to within an arm's length of the end line, the fans in the front row close enough to touch the players. It's menacing.

I introduce Marcie to Coach Mac and the players. I probably should say here that Marcie is an attractive woman, and I'm thinking her presence will validate me and dispel any lingering doubts, if there ever were any, that I might be some kind of predator posing as a reporter. I don't know if it's The Dungeon, pregame jitters, teenage indifference, or Marcie's urbane manner, but when I introduce her to several players, they lower their eyes and speak in mumbles. Sharon offers no hint of conviviality, responding only with a nod. Marcie later says she thinks it's because I've achieved insider status with these people and she is too much the outsider.

The exception is Amy Hanson, the third-string center. She is cordial and talkative to Marcie. She is also rapidly becoming one of my favorite members of the team, a real underdog. Not to mention she is a good source of information about Sharon.

Blond and stocky, Amy is a player with limited skills. She has been played only sparingly, and has yet to score her first point. Still, she diligently comes to practice every day, always works hard, and faithfully encourages her teammates during the games. I'm hard pressed to decide whether Coach Mac yells more at her or Rhea. In the class-room, she has learning disabilities and half her courses are in special ed.

Sharon and Amy have been friends since seventh grade, and in some ways, Sharon feels protective toward her. It bothers her the way other kids pick on Amy and sometimes make her the brunt of their jokes. In their sophomore year, Amy started dating Indian boys, and as usually happens when white girls date Crows in Big Horn County, she heard the names: *white trash . . . Indian lover.*

Amy's was a rough childhood—a father murdered when she was an infant, an alcoholic stepfather, verbal abuse. In her junior year, she attempted suicide, swallowing a hundred aspirin. After spending a month in Rivendell, an adolescent psychiatric treatment center in Billings, she was treated as an outpatient with antidepressants and counseling. Basketball became her escape, providing a whisper of recognition, if not self-esteem.

In the past, Amy traveled on the fringe of Sharon and Holly's clique, sometimes invited to tag along, yet never feeling an equal. Holly would make fun of her behind her back, calling her "the dork," but with Sharon there was the common thread of a screwed-up home life. Following Amy's suicide attempt, it was Sharon who provided a shoulder to lean on, offering her rides and loaning her money. In basketball it was Sharon who encouraged her not to quit; and during the summer, it was Sharon who invited her to a camp in the Wolf Mountains sponsored by the Baptist Church, a trip that turned sour and created a temporary barrier between them.

Initially, the camp was fun—swimming, basketball, group discussions, sharing a cabin—but on the last day, Amy started talking about how anxious she was to get home to her new boyfriend, Cody Ware, Sharon's twenty-year-old second cousin. Somehow the words got twisted and next thing Amy knew, Sharon was calling her a "ho." More insults flew, and the trip ended badly. The next day, Sharon stopped at Amy's house to retrieve a sleeping bag and was greeted at the door by Cody, a former center during his playing days at Lodge Grass High and a very substantial young man. He told her he didn't appreciate the way she talked to Amy. When she tried to force her way past him, he pushed her, knocking her backward down a small flight of stairs. She picked herself up, but in the weeks that followed, her relationship with Amy turned silent. In recent weeks, however, they had brushed the incident aside and moved forward. It was Amy who pushed to reconcile; it was Amy who now regularly invited Sharon to her house. For her part, Sharon still admitted no wrongdoing, but she was happy to have her friend back, especially with Holly now gone. Amy felt equally relieved, although she worried that Sharon was sometimes using her as a ploy. Sharon would tell her aunt and grandmother that she was going to Amy's house when she was really sneaking off to see Randy. When Sharon told her that Randy had not called as promised after she'd caught him with Raylene Pretty Elk, it came as no big surprise to Amy. She shared Holly's view of him: loser.

As the players head for the locker room, Coach Mac ominously motions Rhea toward her. Rhea steels herself.

"I'm starting DyAnna in your spot tonight."

Rhea chokes back tears. Coach Mac offers no comforting arm around her shoulder, no promises that the move is temporary. Rhea knows she deserves to be benched—she has a total of four points in her last four games. Still, she hoped. She walks away, looking for a place to hide. Her chin quivers. And then the tears roll. Standing close by, Sharon and Amy try not to watch.

Despite Central's 2-5 record, it's a team that worries Coach Mac. They've lost their last three games by a total of only five points. In the pregame huddle, she reminds the team of the importance of getting off to a fast start and taking the crowd out of it.

Her stomach churns. She hates Billings Central, the Notre Dame of the prairie, a team everyone loves to beat: it's Catholic school versus public, white versus Indian, city snob versus small-town hick. She hasn't forgotten the taunts and racist slurs Central's fans hurled at Sharon and Roberta Yarlott during last year's Divisionals. She can still see that miniature megaphone flying out of their rooting section and missing Roberta's head by inches.

"You gotta attack them," she directs.

Hardin responds, coming out on fire. Midway through the second quarter, they lead by 20. It has all the signs of a blowout. The end line bleachers, known as the dog pound, is silent.

"Don't let up!" instructs Coach Mac.

Tiffany is everywhere, a whirlwind of arms, legs, and nasal congestion. Despite problems getting a deep breath, she already has 15 points, mostly on layups after stolen passes. The Central guards can't cope with her and Anita's swarming pressure. The first unit stays in the game.

A timeout is called and Tiffany grabs her inhaler, trying to coax air into her lungs. She wants to ask out, but doesn't. At the end of the bench, Amy mentally readies herself to check in.

Just before the half, Central reels off eight straight points and narrows the margin to 13, bringing life to the dog pound. "Don't look now, squaw, but we're gaining."

Sharon turns away, remembering Coach Mac's advice— "Don't let them know you hear them." It's impossible to miss.

Don't look now, squaw, but we're gaining. The margin continues to shrink until finally, with three minutes left in the game, the margin is one. From a 20-point lead to one. Coach Mac is apoplectic.

Everyone is to blame . . . easy misses by Sharon, turnovers by Owena, passive play by Anita. DyAnna picks up her fourth foul, and Rhea replaces her, wasting no time in tossing up an air ball. Tiffany continues to be the only bright spot, but she struggles for air.

Sharon misses another wide-open 10-footer, and the dog pound chants, low and insidious. "Go back to the rez . . . go back to the rez . . . go back to the rez."

She tries to ignore it. It's not as if she's never met overt racism. As a child, she and her grandmother went to a restaurant in Billings and were refused service; another time, she and her aunt had to ask for a key to a basement rest room at the County Courthouse because Indians weren't allowed to use the one on the main floor. It's tough to ignore.

Following another turnover by Owena, Central works the ball around the perimeter. A basket will give them the lead. But Tiffany intercepts a pass and takes off, her nearest defender ten feet behind her. As she goes up for the layin, her long arms and legs flop out of control. She has played the whole game. Her shot clangs off the rim and Central takes it the other way for an easy score . . . and the lead.

The noise threatens to turn The Dungeon to splinters. But Tiffany scores, then scores again, putting Hardin back up by three. One minute left to play. Timeout.

Heading to the huddle, Tiffany stops and doubles over, grabbing her chest. "I can't breathe," she gasps.

She staggers to the bench and collapses, desperately trying to breathe, her face turning ashen.

"Quick, breathe into this," instructs Coach Mac, handing her a paper bag.

Tiffany breathes into the bag, and slowly the air returns to her lungs, the color to her face.

"You going to be all right?" asks Coach Mac.

Tiffany nods.

The horn sounds and the players return to the court. Tiffany continues to sit, then slowly rises and joins her teammates on the floor.

A Central free throw cuts it to two with 30 seconds left. "Don't shoot!" implores Coach Mac, a plea that went unheeded last game.

Rhea stops her dribble at the free throw line. Unable to spot an open teammate, she sees no alternative: she shoots. Never mind what Coach Mac just yelled. Never mind that she hasn't scored in four games. Never mind that Anita is wide open under the basket. Her shot misses badly and Central grabs the rebound. At the other end, they score, tying the game.

Total bedlam in the stands. "Time out!" screams Coach Mac, signaling DyAnna back into the game. Eight seconds left.

More tears roll down Rhea's cheeks.

With Central pressing full-court, the inbounds pass is deflected and the ball rolls loose toward midcourt, players scrambling from all angles. Sharon wins the race, scooping it up on the run, her path to the basket wide open. But her feet tangle and she stumbles, struggling to control her dribble. With only three seconds left, her only hope is an off-balance, half-court heave. There's no chance.

Then the prayers of a thousand sweat lodges are answered. Behind her, a Central player is somehow confused and thinks Hardin still leads. In desperation, she shoves Sharon intentionally, not a little paddycake push, but a two-handed slam job. Sharon bounces hard on the floor, then bangs hip-first into the wall bordering the court. It sounds like a 2x4 slamming against plywood. The final buzzer sounds.

Lying motionless, she stares up at the rafters, pain shooting through her body. Standing nearby, the ref blows his whistle—it's a flagrant foul. Two shots. Only one is needed to win. Slowly, Sharon struggles to her feet, Coach Mac next to her.

"I'm okay," Sharon asserts, heading for the free throw line.

In the bleachers behind the basket, everyone in the pound is on their feet, stomping and screaming. It's a party for the obnoxious.

"Choke it . . . choke it . . . choke it!" they chant.

Sharon waits for the ref to hand her the ball, the other players standing behind her. Directly under the basket, two Central students whip themselves into such a frenzy that they tumble out of the bleachers and fall to their knees, wildly pounding the floor. Another student hops over the end line and onto the court, howling like a coyote.

"Get them off the court!" screams Coach Mac.

The refs do nothing.

Sharon takes the ball and eyes the basket. She appears calm while all around her is pandemonium. On the season, she is an unimpressive 22 for 39 (56 percent) from the line, but in this game she is five of six.

She bends at the knees and releases her shot, the ball arching high. It hits the back rim and bounces away.

But she has another chance.

"Choke it . . . choke it . . . choke it!"

How many times has Sharon rehearsed this moment? At the court in Crow Agency. At practice. At Danetta's. A thousand times and more.

Standing alone, she repeats her routine, dribbling once, bending at the knees, and arching it high. All eyes in The Dungeon follow the ball. It is straight and true.

But it dips in and out.

"Choker . . . choker . . . choker!"

For the second night in a row, the Lady Bulldogs are going to overtime.

In the seven years I've known Marcie, I can't remember any sporting event she has attended as a spectator. She is a competitive rower, driven to be on the river every morning at dawn, but she is not a spectator unless you count the Westminster Dog Show. She considers the guys in the cheese hats and painted faces to be idiots. Her life is too full to waste time cheering for the home team. She'd rather garden, jog, or read a book. She's a mental health therapist, straightforward and no nonsense. But from the second quarter on, she has been Looney Tunes, screaming herself hoarse, covering her face with every Hardin miss, jumping for the rafters with every swish. All she's missing is a giant foam finger.

Sharon hits the first basket of overtime and Marcie pounds my shoulder. Anita and Tiffany both hit two free throws and it's a veritable Mardi Gras in our section.

With a minute left and Hardin up by four, the ball pops loose near midcourt. Tiffany dives after it, her head arriving at the same time and place with the knee of a Central girl. The ref whistles a foul on the Central girl.

Tiffany is face down, her nose pressed against the floor. Sharon kneels next to her. "Are you okay?" she asks.

"No."

Tiffany is helped off the court and placed prone on the bench. Her head feels like a punching bag. "Can you shoot the free throws?" asks Coach Mac.

"No," she whispers.

A player on the bench will have to shoot the free throws. Coach Mac looks at Rhea, then points toward sophomore Kassi Elk Shoulder, who has played less than five minutes with the varsity, but is champ of the free throw contests at practice.

Calmly, Kassi makes the first, then misses the second. Hardin's lead is now five with only 55 seconds to play.

"We're going to win!" shouts Marcie.

We? Two hours ago she was telling me that she felt the outsider, now she's being fitted for a Lady Bulldogs sweatshirt.

Central scores, then steals the ball right back. Now, a three-pointer will tie it. Forty-five seconds remain.

"Don't let them shoot the three!" begs Coach Mac. It is less than twenty-four hours since Colstrip's Darcy Jensen was left as open as the Arctic and drained a three.

So naturally, with ten seconds left, a Central guard gets the ball just outside the three-point line with no defender in the same zip code. The girl shoots. The ball swirls around the hoop, then rims out. It's a wild scramble under the basket. Central's Molly Roscoe muscles it loose and hurriedly shoots from five feet. As she releases the ball, Sharon hacks her hard across the arm—a foul Stevie Wonder could call—but the refs miss it. The ball eases through the net. The margin is one. Four seconds to go.

Sharon takes the ball from the net. Standing inches from

the screaming fans, she cradles the sphere calmly in her arms. Frantically, the other nine players run in circles, waiting for her to inbound it. She plants her feet, and the clock ticks down. Three . . . two . . . one. The horn sounds. The game is over. Hardin 72, Central 71. The Lady Bulldogs are 7-1, all alone atop the conference.

"Unbelievable!" concludes Marcie.

CHAPTER EIGHTEEN

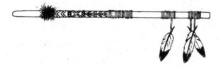

After saying a sad goodbye to Marcie at the Billings airport, I drive back to Hardin on I-90, not seeing a car for miles, not even a hay truck. Then I see the flashing red and blue lights. I'm doing ninety. Busted. Again.

I know the drill—this is my third speeding ticket in a month, although getting busted for speeding in Montana isn't all that bad. With no speed limits on rural roads, a speeding ticket is termed an "environmental infraction" and doesn't go on the violator's driving record; the fine is only $5, payable right on the spot to the State Trooper. I'm beginning to wonder if it's possible to just call ahead and announce that I plan to speed and that the check is in the mail.

Back in Hardin, I go to assistant coach Dave Oswald's house. He's my new best buddy on the prairie. The players also like him, especially Sharon, who says in private that sometimes she wishes he was the head coach.

A big Palooka of a guy, with black hair, sideburns, blue eyes, and teeth his parents couldn't afford to straighten, he is as unpretentious as the double-wide Detroiter mobile home he lives in with his wife and three kids. On this sunny Sunday, he's taking me to his family's farm. It's a late harvest, and there is still much to be done.

"We'll find out if you're cut out to be a farmer," he says.

"How about if I end the suspense right here and tell you I'm not."

We climb aboard his propane-fueled '69 Chevy pickup for the ride to the farm. I am a little disappointed to be going in the pickup because he promised we'd take his cherry '66 Pontiac LeMans. But he isn't finished rebuilding its engine because he got sidetracked replacing the trannie on his '78 Chevy van. Or maybe it's the other way around. Either way he's up to the task. At Hardin High, where he has never taken a sick day in fifteen years, he teaches auto and wood shop. A week earlier he paid a surprise visit to my duplex to deliver a lamp he'd designed and built in the shape of a water pump. He said he didn't want me to have to read under the bare bulb I was using.

Leaving town, we drive down Center Street, passing the Hardin Ford dealership. An Indian couple is on the lot, examining a deluxe new pickup. Dave taps the dashboard of his battered '69 pickup, then speaks, choosing his words carefully.

"I'm not prejudiced, but I have to admit it bugs me when I see these Indians around here driving their new pickups," he says. "How do they get the money to buy them?"

He answers his own question. "They get all the benefits," he says. "Welfare, subsidized housing, free medical care, food stamps, no taxes, tribal handouts. That's how they can afford new pickups.

"It's not fair," he continues. "I work my butt off as a teacher and my wife works in a bank. Yet it's all I can do to scrounge up the money to buy used engine parts to keep this heap running. But if I complain about the pitiful 2 percent pay raise the school board wants to give us, I'm treated like a thief. Sure, this country screwed the Indians.

But that was six generations ago. Why punish me? It's not my fault."

These are hard times for Coach Oswald. He's still steaming from getting passed over for the boys' coaching job, but that's not even on his radar screen compared to his concern for his wife, Susan. She has multiple sclerosis, and recently it has gotten worse. She is still able to work as a teller at First Interstate Bank, but last week her vision blurred again and she fell twice. Dave and their three teenage children are doing everything to ease her discomfort, but as he describes her weakening condition, his voice cracks.

He is also concerned about Sharon. Where once he held out hope that she might be the one to break free, he now doubts it. He has worked around Indians long enough to recognize the signs.

His relationship with Sharon goes back to her sophomore year when she starred on his junior varsity squad, a team that went undefeated. He remembers the nights she stayed after practice and worked on her inside moves. He helped her develop the little drop step she has and the spin move to her left. They grew close that year. In her junior year, she went to him in tears early in the season, upset at Coach Mac for yelling at her. She said she was going to quit and transfer to Lodge Grass. He convinced her to stay.

The warning signs he sees this year aren't anything huge, just the way her attention wanders in practice, or the way she sometimes goes into a funk during a game and makes careless mistakes. She didn't do that as a sophomore. Another thing he notices is her weight. She's never had much meat on her bones, but when he tapes her ankles before practice every day, her arms and legs seem skinnier. She claims she is eating like she always has, but he doubts it.

When he asks her what she's done regarding college applications, her answer is vague, evasive. He takes it to mean she hasn't done anything about it, just like every other Indian student he's had.

His voice changes from concern to anger when the topic turns to his not getting hired as the boys' coach. In his interview with the board, a tribal member asked what he'd do if a father complained that his child wasn't getting to play. The question irritated him—it seemed racially charged. He answered by telling the story of how a Crow mother accused him the year before of being prejudiced because he didn't start her son on his junior varsity team. "She didn't bother to check that the five starters were all Crows," he tersely told the board. "What was I supposed to do, start six kids?"

Clearly, he is still irked. "How can they say I'm prejudiced?" he says. "I don't see color. The kids in my classes and on my team are just kids. I don't think of them as Indian or white."

We are greeted at the farm by two of Dave's four brothers, his father, and his two teenage sons. They all worked until midnight the night before, toiling under the lights of the combines, then went back at it at sunrise. There is an urgency to the work. A big storm is forecast, and the possibility is real that any wheat not yet harvested will be ruined. It doesn't help that one of the combines is broken. Dave's first task is to get it running again.

Dressed in dirty bib overalls, Dave's father surveys me suspiciously. "Guess you won't be no help," he concludes.

The farm, first homesteaded by the Oswald family in 1908, is a dry land farm on unfriendly alkali ground, with barley and spring and winter wheat the cash crops. It is truly a family farm, with no hired hands. Most years it is a struggle just to break even, success always at the mercy of nature, always just a swarm of grasshoppers or sawflies or a bad hailstorm away from having thirty bushels an acre wiped out. According to Dave, the original farmhouse was spooked by ghosts, with exploding windows, slamming doors, burning rooms, and even a UFO sighting. The family abandoned the house and moved to Billings; they now stay in the trailer home when they come to work on the land.

While Dave works on the combine, I wander the farm, eventually accompanying the senior Oswald on what he calls "the money run," a trip to unload the wheat at the grain silo ten miles up the road. When we're done, it's time for lunch. On the menu this day is biscuits and gravy, and plenty of it. "You must have worked up a big appetite carrying that little notepad around," observes one of Dave's brothers.

The night before, the other brother poached an antelope, shooting it from the front porch with a scoped rifle. The meat is already in the freezer. "You can't tell nobody," instructs the brother.

"I won't," I promise.

After lunch, I make another money run with Mr. Oswald. He talks about how proud he is of Dave, and how hard it must be to coach the Indian kids. "But I'll tell you what," he concludes, "I'd rather watch those Indian kids play any day of the week than those niggers in the NBA."

Everyone I meet keeps telling me that the Big Horn River is the greatest trout fishing spot in America. According to the locals, all I have to do is cast my line and then start reeling in the big four-pound rainbows and German browns. Good thing, because I'm no fisherman. The last time I went was with my uncle Ralph when I was nine.

That's when I concluded that spending a day untangling a fishing line out of a tree limb wasn't my idea of fun.

Before I decide to invest in equipment and license, I go see Dick Imers, a PE teacher and ex-football coach. I'm told he's the ultimate guru on Big Horn River fishing. But before he shares his fishing secrets, he sets me straight about why the Crows are so good in basketball. He says it's because of the 10th Cavalry.

He explains that after the Battle of Little Big Horn the government sent the 10th Cavalry out west to Fort Custer to help settle the Indians on the reservation. The 10th Cavalry was a regiment of black men, part of the famed Buffalo Soldiers. "There weren't a lot of women around these parts in those days," he says. "So naturally, these black soldiers started foolin' around with some of the squaws. Now, a hundred years later, these Indians kids around here still have some of that black blood in them. That's how come they're so good at that racehorse style of basketball. It's true."

The sounds of Garth Brooks on KTCR "Cat Country" radio jar me awake. It is 5:20 A.M. and still dark on the prairie.

I roll off my futon and fumble through my closet for my high-top Nikes and sweats. In ten minutes I am supposed to be at the Hardin High gym. I've let Coach Oswald talk me into joining him and several of his buddies for some predawn basketball. It seemed like a bad idea when he asked me, but now that I'm struggling to get dressed, it seems idiotic. Still, I'm determined to try it for a few weeks.

These guys, all of them white and middle-aged, have been exercising their hoop jones for years, regularly playing full-court rat ball. I haven't played anything more strenuous than H-O-R-S-E since the last of my four broken ankles fifteen years earlier. Golf is my sport. But it is too late to back out now. Tiffany's dad will be there, as well as Ron Johnson, Holly's dad, and Don Gordineer, the girls' freshman coach, a nice guy whose day gig is minister of the Lutheran Church.

Arriving at the gym, I think about returning home and crawling back under the covers. I've been working out a bit—riding my bike, swimming at the Community Center, jogging on country roads—but I'm not in basketball shape. Not even close.

"Let's play some half-court," I suggest.

"That's not how we do it here in Montana. It's full-court."

Nine other players have showed up, which by my count, means that there'll be no substitutes. "Can we call time-outs?" I ask.

"I guess you didn't hear me . . . this is Montana."

At least these guys don't look like the second coming of Larry Bird. Or even tribal legend Larry Pretty Weasel. At 6'3", I am the second tallest, and as I watch them warm up, I can see that most of them are not shooting specialists. Nor do any of them look like they've been spending too much time in the weight room. I feel encouraged.

It doesn't last. On my third trip downcourt, I suddenly realize I'm going east and they're all going west. I gasp for air, the hemoglobin being sucked right out my eyeballs. Do they honestly expect me to get a rebound?

My redemption, I hope, will be my shooting. I have been on target the last couple days in my games of H-O-R-S-E against Anita, especially with a little turnaround jumper from the right side. So when I get the ball in my favorite position, I go for it. My defender, Coach Oswald, who weighs in at 235, is leaning on my back. As I start my move up, I realize there is no up. I lose the ball out of bounds. Huffing and puffing back downcourt, I'm sure that whatever credibility I have to write about basketball in Big Horn County is in danger. Maybe I can fake an injury.

I have read that when mountain climbers near the summit on Everest, the air is so thin that the body literally begins to eat itself and delirium sets in. That's how I feel. My only solace is that I know the man I am guarding, Gary Ostahowski, is a doctor at the Hardin Clinic. If I collapse with a thrombosis, he'll be right there. I also know from Aunt Marlene that he is the doctor who gave Sharon her Norplant.

Somehow, in one of the great minor miracles of bad basketball, I continue to stay upright. We've been playing about 45 minutes when the side door opens. In walks the Lady Bulldogs and Coach Mac. It is her policy to have the team practice before school on the day before a game, the theory being that it gives the girls an extra half-day of rest before the next game. They need all the rest they can get before going up against Billings Senior, a school with four times the enrollment of Hardin High.

Chugging downcourt, I glance to the sidelines where the girls are stretching, some of them stealing peeks at our game. Sharon and Tiffany spot me. They look surprised.

As luck would have it, I get the ball at the top of the key. With a quick fake to my left, a direction I have never driven, I stop and fire up an 18-footer. Bingo, bango, bongo. Nothing but net.

Coolly, I backpedal downcourt, acting as if I've been doing it all morning. It is, in fact, my first basket. I steal a quick peek to check Sharon's and Tiffany's reaction. Neither of them are watching.

On our final time downcourt, my teammate Ron Johnson, easily the best player on the court, misses a short jumper. With one last burst of energy, I go for the rebound, climbing up and over the back of Tiffany's dad to miraculously tip it in. This time, Sharon and Tiffany are watching. Heading off the court, I puff my chest.

"Don't you guys call fouls?" asks Sharon.

*   *   *

I stay to watch practice. It has a crispness and energy I haven't seen before. Sharon is particularly focused, encouraging her teammates, hustling in every drill. Somehow, I haven't thought of her as a morning person.

At the close of practice, the girls spread out to the side baskets to shoot their free throws. I ease to where Sharon is shooting, and start retrieving her shots. She hits several in a row, then stops, motioning me toward her, like she has a secret to tell.

"Remember when that girl shoved me against the wall at Central?" she asks.

"Yes."

"Want to see the bruise I got?"

"Sure."

She looks around the gym, making sure nobody is looking, then quickly pulls down the left side of her shorts, revealing a hematoma the size of Delaware on her upper hip. It isn't sexy. Then she trots off to the locker room.

For the first time, I sense a trust.

CHAPTER NINETEEN

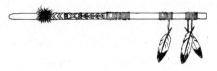

Marlene turns off I-90, heading for home. It has been a long day—eight hours at her new job as a teacher's aide at the day-care center at Little Big Horn College, and another two hours as a student in an early childhood development class. She still has to fix dinner, tend to the kids, and cope with a drunk husband. If he's home.

On a reservation filled with hopelessness, Marlene Fallsdown stays positive. She is employed, sober, and supporting a family. Her teenage daughters, JoJo and Christie, are staying out of trouble, and her niece is the star of the reservation, averaging 20 points a game. Plus, she was just named the first woman pipe carrier in the Crow-Sioux Sun Dance, a tribal honor equivalent to being elevated to Archbishop of Canterbury. Sharon is still ambivalent about taking part in the Sun Dance ceremony with her next summer, nervous about fasting for three days in the hot sun.

Driving her Chevy van, one of the five cars Danetta bought with the proceeds of her land sale to the tribe, Marlene nears Bair's Truck Stop and Cafe. She spots her sister, Karna's, black Mercury Sable in the parking lot and debates whether to stop. The last time they were together it ended in a wrestling match, Marlene ripping off Karna's shirt in front of the whole family. She turns into the parking lot anyway.

She parks next to the Sable, the car Karna was driving when she got her most recent DUI, this one for falling asleep at the wheel while waiting for a stop light at a busy intersection in Billings. Marlene steels her resolve as she approaches the entrance to the bar.

To her, Karna has always been the spoiled child, the older sister who got the fancy dresses, piano lessons, and new pony. It was Karna, not Marlene, who got to stay with Danetta and Blaine when they moved to Busby on the Northern Cheyenne reservation for two years while Danetta worked as a matron at a boarding school. Marlene got left behind with an aunt. And it was Karna who got the most expensive wedding in tribal history when she married Sharon's father. When Marlene married Evon, all she got was Karna's hand-me-down wedding gown. And when Karna was pregnant with Sharon, Danetta sewed Sharon a dozen elks tooth dresses; when Marlene was pregnant with Christie and didn't marry the father, Lee Plainfeather, Blaine disowned her for two years. Now the roles are reversed; Marlene is the star daughter. She and Danetta have become more than just mother and daughter; they are good friends, talking almost daily.

Despite this new favored status, Marlene still resents Karna. It's no longer about who got the prettiest dress, it's about Karna's alcoholism and irresponsibility as a parent. As much as Marlene loves Sharon, she resents that she is the one, not Karna, raising her. As far as she is concerned, Karna's only contribution as a mother has been childbirth.

She spots Karna at the end of the bar, slouched, drunk, pathetic. Her first impulse is to knock her off the stool.

"What the fuck you want?" growls Karna.

Marlene doesn't respond.

"Did you come to save me?" asks Karna. "Did mother send you?"

Marlene still doesn't respond.

"Well, fuck you!" declares Karna.

Impulsively, Marlene grabs her by the wrist and jerks her off the stool, the two sisters tumbling to the floor, four hundred pounds of flailing, kicking fury. Karna grabs a handful of hair.

The bartender, no stranger to Indians fighting, wastes no time in calling the sheriff. He collars them both and herds them out the door to the parking lot. Karna turns to go back in.

"I need my purse," she says. "It's got my keys."

"You're not driving nowhere," says Marlene, blocking her way.

Karna takes a step back, then kicks her in the ankle. Marlene, a shot-putter back in her days at Hardin High, bear-hugs her, wrestling her to the cement.

Two sheriff's cars pull into the lot. The officers, no strangers to Indians fighting either, shove Karna into the back seat of one car, Marlene into the back seat of the other. And off they go to jail, both charged with disturbing the peace.

Two hours later, they are both out of jail, Marlene heading home, Karna heading to the Wagon Wheel. The night is young, and she still has money in her pocket.

At the Wagon Wheel, she leans against the jukebox, studying the man at the end of the bar. If he is who she thinks he is, then she has some things to say to him. But in the smoky haze, it's tough to get a clear fix. The half-dozen shots of Seagram's 7 she had back at Bair's still cloud her vision. She can make out that he is an Indian, and judging from his tight jeans and big belt buckle, probably a rodeo guy, too. Slowly, she eases toward him, her bloated body listing to starboard.

"I hear you're dating my daughter," she says, her voice gravelly from the years of Marlboro Lights.

The man shoots her a suspicious glance, then takes a long pull on his beer. "Who's your daughter?" he asks.

"Sharon LaForge."

He nods, offering a small, crooked smile.

She steps closer, less than a foot between them, then shakes her fist in his face. "If you do anything bad to her," she proclaims, "you'll have to deal with this fist."

He smiles but doesn't respond.

"I mean it, too," she reiterates. Then she turns and retreats to the jukebox and her seventh shot of Seagram's 7.

Chapter Twenty

Life is good for the Lady Bulldogs. They are coming off a good week of practice; they are leading the conference; they are 7-1; they just won two clutch games in overtime against tough opponents; and for the first time in school history, the coaches' poll in the *Gazette* has them ranked number one, passing western Montana powerhouses Dillon and Ronan. *Number one.*

But it's no time to relax. Their next opponent, Billings Senior, is the biggest high school in the state, an athletic powerhouse, a tough place to play on the road.

Seconds before the end of the first half, Karen Weyler, the big, strong redheaded center for the Lady Broncs, pulls down a rebound and swings her elbows like a pair of wrecking balls, one of them nailing Sharon dead center in her upper chest. She staggers back, the air smacked from her lungs, her knees buckling. But she doesn't go down. No foul is called.

"Are you blind, ref!" screams Danetta.

The horn sounds, ending the half, Hardin leading 26–20. In the locker room, Sharon struggles to regain her breath. Her chest throbs from her sternum to her shoulders. "I'll be all right," she promises.

In the first two quarters, Sharon and Tiffany, coming off her career high 33 points against Central, have 20 of the team's 26 points. Against Weyler, one of the best players in the state, Sharon is holding her own, both players with 11. But Coach Mac's strategy confuses her. Why isn't she playing Christina Chavez or Stacie? Especially Stacie. This seems like the perfect game for her. Weyler is strong, nearly impossible to stop down low, but so is the 6'1", stronger-than-a-plowhorse Stacie. Sharon has guarded them both, and for her money, Stacie is the bigger load. So what if she is only a tenth grader and sometimes has a feather duster between her ears?

Near the end of the third quarter, a black Mercury Sable pulls into the parking lot. It's Karna. Originally, she planned on arriving for the start of the game, but a detour by the Melody Club in south Billings for a quick drink turned into three quick drinks, then five quick drinks.

She turns off the engine, then eases a flask of Seagram's from her purse and takes a long hard swig. She knows the reception by her family inside the gym will be chilly. She needs to get warmed up.

The Lady Broncs score at the end of the third quarter to tie the score 37–37. Their band, with its crazed drum corps, rattles the rafters.

From behind the Hardin bench, I can smell Sharon. She smells like a liniment factory, a heavy balm coating her bruised chest and hip. I can hear Anita coughing and wheezing. She caught Tiffany's bronchitis. This is not a healthy team.

At the scorer's table a few feet away, three more Billings Senior subs check into the game, the fourteenth time their

181

coach has gone to his bench. Coach Mac has subbed only once, Rhea replacing DyAnna, who started despite Rhea's dominating her in practice all week.

"This is where we find out if we deserve to be number one," shouts Coach Mac, straining to be heard.

Sharon grimaces, rubbing her chest. She feels like she has a torpedo lodged in her lungs.

"What's wrong?" asks Coach Mac.

"I can't get a deep breath," she answers.

"Do you need to come out?"

Sharon shakes her head.

In the lobby just outside the gym, Karna stops at the snack bar and orders a Coke. She hears the announcer inside call her daughter's name, and momentarily feels a surge of pride. Behind her, two Billings policemen casually chat. She walks around the corner, then furtively pulls out her flask and pours a shot of whiskey into her Coke. Entering the clamorous gym, she keeps her eyes straight ahead, her course deliberate, like balancing the line in a sobriety test. She walks in front of the bleachers, then turns up the aisle and squeezes in next to her father. Blaine, who superstitiously never sits with Danetta at a game, greets her with an icy silence. Three rows back, Danetta and Marlene stare in disbelief, shocked at the temerity of her showing up in the fourth quarter of one of the biggest games of her daughter's career. In front of Karna, the game is a blur.

"Come on, babycakes!" she yells.

Sharon doesn't see or hear her mom. With two minutes to play, she scores on a soft lefthanded hook, putting Hardin up by four. Then she steals a pass, and Coach Mac holds her palms down, the signal to run time off the clock. In practice earlier in the week, they worked on their half-court stall.

The stall lasts less than ten seconds, Owena casting off from 15 feet. The ball clangs off the rim into Weyler's hands.

"Shit!" yells Coach Mac.

It's hard to figure what she sees in Owena, who's an okay rebounder, but not much else. One theory is that Coach Mac is intimidated by Owena's family, including a very menacing uncle who sits near the bench and yells at her. Another theory is that she's afraid to move Stacie up to the varsity for fear of alienating Coach Oswald, who takes great pride in his winning junior varsity team and has lobbied against weakening it. His 6'1" daughter, Maria, a very likable young lady but very awkward athlete, plays twin post with Stacie on the JV, and to promote Stacie over her might prove delicate, even though Stacie is the much better athlete. Coach Mac admits to worrying about this. She can't afford to have Coach Oswald get upset and quit.

With 20 seconds to go, Senior scores, then gets the ball back and scores again. The game is tied.

"Run the clock down for the last shot!" yells Coach Mac.

It takes Owena four seconds to cast off again.

What is this girl thinking? In her last three games she is five of 22 from the field, an anemic 23 percent. The shot misses everything. "Air ball!" taunts the crowd.

Senior hurries the ball upcourt, everybody in the gym knowing it's going inside to Weyler. She gets it with five seconds left, Sharon all over her. She turns and shoots. The ball grazes the front rim, then falls off to the side.

For the third game in a row, the Lady Bulldogs are going to overtime.

In the huddle, Sharon struggles to get a deep breath. She has played the entire 32 minutes. So have Anita and Tiffany. Anita coughs, then takes a hit on her inhaler. She is playing tentatively, favoring her bad knee. Her torrid shooting touch has turned cold—11 of 34 since the injury.

In the stands, Karna grabs her drink and staggers down the aisle, heading straight toward the Hardin huddle. She stops ten feet away and waves her arms, trying to snag her daughter's attention. Sharon's back is turned. Karna stops flapping, then turns and heads for the rest room.

With 31 seconds left in overtime, and Hardin trailing by one, Anita is fouled, sending her to the line for a one-and-one. The noise is deafening. She sinks the first shot, tying the score. Then she misses the second, the ball caroming off the rim into Sharon's hands. She dribbles back out of the key, then shoots. It's a perfect swish—her 20th point of the night. Hardin now leads by two with 20 seconds left.

Senior inbounds the ball, but at midcourt Tiffany deflects a pass, the ball bouncing to Sharon. In desperation, Weyler fouls her from behind. Six seconds left.

Exhausted, Sharon walks to the free throw line for a one-and-one and a chance to ice the victory.

"Time out!" yells the Senior coach.

Coming to the huddle, Sharon is mobbed by teammates.

Hardin's fans are delirious. But not Karna. She feels the bad vibes—from her father, her mother, her sister. It's time to leave, she decides. It doesn't matter that her daughter is about to go to the line with six seconds left.

She stumbles down the stairs, stopping behind the Hardin bench again. "Sharon! Sharon!" she yells.

Standing at the far side of the circle of players, Sharon looks up and spots her mother for the first time. Her heart sinks.

Coach Mac also spots her. "Don't let her into the huddle!"

she barks, motioning players to form a blockade. Tiffany and Geri quickly lock arms, blocking the way.

"Goodbye, babycakes," slurs Karna, leaning on Tiffany. "I gotta go."

Sharon's jaw drops. She hasn't talked to her mom in months, and now here she is, making a fool of herself, trying to crash the huddle with six seconds left in overtime.

"Get her out of here!" orders Coach Mac.

Marlene and Danetta run down the stairs, grabbing Karna's arms, pulling her toward the exit.

"Let go of me!" yells Karna, shoving Marlene.

"Goddamn you, Karna!" Marlene yells.

"Fuck you!"

Stunned, Sharon's eyes fill with tears. She has never felt such humiliation.

The horn sounds, calling the teams back onto the court. Sharon turns and walks to the free throw line, tears streaming down her cheeks. Tiffany, who leads all scorers with 25, pulls next to her, easing an arm around her shoulder. "It's okay," she whispers.

Marlene and Danetta, joined by Carlene Old Elk, a member of the Hardin school board, push Karna out of the gym into the lobby.

"Stop shoving!" Karna bellows, her voice carrying back inside the gym.

She glares at Marlene. "Come on, tough girl!" she challenges. "I'm not as drunk as the other night. Let's go!"

"How can you do this to your daughter?" Marlene pleads.

"Go to hell," says Karna, fumbling for her car keys. "I'm leaving."

"Gimme the keys," Danetta orders, moving to block the exit.

"Get out of the way . . . I'm warning you."

Hearing the commotion, the two Billings policeman approach. "Everybody calm down," one advises.

Sliding away from the officers, Marlene eases toward the door to the gym, Danetta right behind her.

"Ladies, get back over here," commands the policeman.

"But that's our daughter out there," says Danetta.

Sharon has always been able to block out the outside distractions when she steps onto the basketball court . . . an argument with Randy, a racial taunt from an obnoxious fan, a midterm she's blown off. It is this concentration that makes her excel, that allows her to play with such intensity. But this is different. Her tough veneer melted the moment she saw her mother.

At the free throw line, she wipes the tears on the shoulder strap of her uniform, then eyes the basket. She can't hear the ruckus outside in the lobby. She doesn't need to—Karna's courtside barrage still echoes in her ears.

She misses the free throw.

Weyler grabs the rebound and fires an outlet pass, everyone racing to the other end, Sharon backpedaling, crying. Six . . . five . . . four. With three seconds left, Senior's Mary Holden gets the ball at the top of the key. A three-pointer will win it, two points to tie. With a foul to give, Anita wisely grabs her.

"Time out!" yells Coach Mac.

Danetta stands in the doorway, keeping one eye on the court, the other on Karna. Her voice is hoarse from four quarters of yelling for her granddaughter; her emotional tank is empty, too, drained from two decades of watching Karna destroy herself.

A cop takes Karna's keys. "How am I supposed to get home?" she asks, grabbing to get them back.

Blaine grabs her arm. "I'll give you a ride after the game," he says. "Where you staying?"

"Take me to the Melody Club."

Three seconds left . . .

Waiting for the ball to be put in play, Sharon and Weyler jockey for position under the basket, Sharon trying to catch the last reservoir of energy in her battered body, her forearms pressed against Weyler's sturdy backside.

"Watch the lob!" yells Coach Mac.

On the sideline, Holden arches a lob toward the key in front of the basket. Weyler and Sharon jump, but with a four-inch height advantage, Weyler comes down with the ball. She hurriedly turns and shoots, the ball leaving her fingertips as the buzzer sounds. It kisses the front rim and tantalizingly hangs suspended above the cylinder . . . then it bounces away.

It is pandemonium on the Hardin side. But the ref's whistle quickly interrupts the jubilation. It's a foul on Sharon for hitting Weyler's arm in the act of shooting. If Weyler sinks both free throws, the game is tied and it's on to another overtime.

Calmly, she toes the line. On the night she has 23 points, hitting her last five shots. Now, she stands alone, the other players positioned behind her, the Hardin fans trying to stomp the bleachers to smithereens.

Weyler releases the ball, and it is straight on target . . . but it hits the back rim and bounces away.

For the third game in a row, Hardin wins in overtime.

* * *

As Blaine escorts Karna outside, Danetta hurries across the court, dodging the fans pouring across the floor in celebration. At midcourt she finds Sharon, who stands alone, hands covering her face, sobbing.

"I'm proud of you," Danetta says, putting her arm around her.

"I hate her," cries Sharon. "I hate her, I hate her . . ."

Danetta walks her to the locker room. "The whole tribe is proud of you," she says. "You're the one they come to see."

Inside, the team celebrates, its lock on number one secure. But Sharon stands to the side, still crying.

Coach Oswald sees her despair. "You just have to shake it off," he counsels. "Don't let these things get to you."

She knows he means well, but how is she supposed to *shake it off*? How is she supposed to *not let these things get to her*? For two years she's tried not to think about her mother, but it hasn't worked. Every night she goes to bed worrying about her, wondering if Karna is in a safe place, wondering if she is even still alive. Sometimes she wonders what it would be like to just once wake up and feel what Tiffany and Anita do, to be loved, to have normal parents, to know that tomorrow will be just like today, safe and secure.

On the way back to Hardin, the team stops at a Billings's Burger King. Sharon is the last off the bus. Wearing a T-shirt with the inscription "Relentless Quest" printed over a drawing of a basketball player scaling a mountain, she holds an ice pack to her chest.

She sits at a table with Amy Hanson and picks at her Whopper and fries. Her face is ashen and her hand is pressed to her chest. "My heart feels like it's beating too fast," she says.

"Should I tell Coach Mac?" asks Amy.

Sharon shakes her head, but her breath is coming in short gasps. "I'm having trouble catching my breath," she utters.

"Coach Mac, Coach Mac!" yells Amy. "Sharon can't breathe!"

In the emergency room at Deaconess Hospital three blocks from the Burger King, the nurse pushes Sharon's wheelchair through the double doors leading to the rooms for her X-rays and EKG. Sharon turns and gamely waves goodbye to the quintet of people who have accompanied her into the hospital—Coach Mac, Coach Oswald, Tiffany, Anita, and myself. Everyone else is waiting on the bus in the parking lot, including Amy, whose feelings are hurt because Coach Mac picked Tiffany and Anita over her to accompany Sharon to the hospital.

"What do you think is wrong with her?" asks Tiffany.

The options are numerous: a collapsed lung, a bruised rib cage, a pulled cartilage in the sternum, stress.

It's 1:00 A.M. when the nurse finally reappears and tells us we can see her. In the darkness of a small room, Sharon sits on the edge of a bed, her face drawn, her eyes puffy. Her skinny arms hang out of her hospital gown like monofilament from a fly rod. But she is breathing normally.

The doctor enters and says that tests show no broken bones, no collapsed lung, no internal bleeding. "It's a severe contusion to the sternum," he says. "It'll take time, but she'll be all right."

"When will she be able to play again?" asks Coach Mac.

"Not for at least a week," he answers.

"You mean, I can't play tomorrow night?" asks Sharon.

"Absolutely not."

She cries.

CHAPTER TWENTY-ONE

Sharon agrees to try anything—a sweat with Aunt Marlene, prayers to the Great Spirit, a visit from the medicine man. "I'm okay to play tonight, really," she assures her grandmother.

"I'll call the coach and tell her," says Danetta.

After all, whose decision is this? The medicine man says it's okay to play, and so does the family, so why shouldn't Sharon be allowed to play? Why should a white doctor's opinion take precedence over the family and a tribal medicine man? Isn't this another case of infringement on tribal rights? Who controls Sharon's health anyway? Whose "medicine" counts in this situation?

Coach Mac listens to Danetta's case and agrees to think about it. "But no promises," she says.

Concerned about her friend's health, Amy Hanson pays a short visit to Sharon, then heads down the steps toward her car. She is accompanied by her boyfriend, Cody's, beautiful seven-year-old niece, Trina. Sharon walks them to the car.

"I told my aunt I'm spending the night with you," she says.

"Whatever," replies Amy, annoyed at being part of Sharon's little subterfuge.

Amy wants her friend to heal quickly, but there's also a part of her that hopes Sharon can't play tonight against Miles City. With Sharon out of the lineup, it might mean playing time for her. In the team's three straight overtime wins, she hasn't played.

Standing next to her car, a metallic gray '87 Pontiac Firebird, Amy bids Sharon goodbye. Although close, theirs is not a huggy relationship—that's not Sharon's way. Amy opens the door for Trina, then slides behind the wheel. Neither puts on a seat belt.

As she drives away from the house, Amy feels somehow awkward about the visit. Maybe she feels used. Or maybe she feels bad for hoping Sharon can't play tonight. Or maybe she didn't like hearing about the white man's medicine being no good. Whatever the reason, her mind is hatching weird schemes. Like maybe if she doesn't get to play tonight she'll have a talk with Coach Mac and subtly let slip that there are players on the team who are—how would she say it?—doing bad things off the court. Smoking dope and stuff like that. This wouldn't be snitching. It would just be letting Coach Mac know the straight skinny. It would be for the good of the team.

Despite feeling awkward about the visit, Amy is glad she and Sharon have put the fight at summer camp behind them, or at least swept it under the carpet. Except for her mom, sister, and Cody, she feels closer to Sharon than anyone. She is the only girl on the team to know about Randy, the only one to know about Sharon's implant. She would never betray her. And Sharon is the only friend she's confided in about her own troubled childhood, the only one who understands the hell she's been through. Still, maybe there are certain things Coach Mac should know.

But even if she does go to Coach Mac, it's not to get

Sharon in trouble. After all, wasn't it Sharon who stood by her when she was so depressed? Wasn't it Sharon who stood up for her when other kids called her "white trash"? Isn't it Sharon who always praises her for how hard she works in practice?

Amy has made little effort to hide her resentment of Tiffany. She doesn't like anything about her—her nice house, clothes, car, boyfriend, athletic skills. In practice, she resents the way Coach Mac doesn't yell at Tiffany but chews other players out for the same mistake. It bothers Amy that her mom has slaved away at the Crow School cafeteria for ten years for barely minimum wage, and Tiffany's parents "probably make ten times as much and don't work half as hard." The final straw was when Tiffany's dad, who is in charge of repossessions for First Interstate, hounded her mom when she fell behind on her car payments. He kept calling the house, demanding payment, threatening repossession. Finally, he took the car away, coming right onto their property to tow it. Since then, Amy has found it hard not to want to knock Tiffany on her butt in practice.

Driving south out of town toward St. Xavier, Amy steals a peek at Trina and smiles. Yesterday, they were coming out of the IGA together and a total stranger stopped them and asked to take Trina's picture—Amy figured the man was a tourist and wanted to show his friends back home a picture of the beautiful little Indian princess he'd met. That was fine by Amy. Lately, she's become something of a second mother to Trina, a role she enjoys. She loves the idea of motherhood, telling Cody she wants to be a mother by her twentieth birthday, which is in eleven months. He is lukewarm to the idea, but says he'll consider it. Meanwhile, she isn't using birth control.

The Firebird speeds south on the road leading through the heart of the county's flatland farms and ranches. Amy loves to drive fast. In St. Xavier she will drop off Trina with an aunt. As it always is when she comes to St. Xavier, her childhood home, it's hard not to think about the rough times.

"We're almost there," she promises Trina.

Amy Hanson wonders if her life would be different if her real dad wasn't murdered. A roughneck with an oil company, he was, by her mom's account, an excessive man, fond of booze, women, and brawling. It was a jealous lover, pregnant with his child, who shot him dead. This lover went ahead and had their child in prison, a half-brother or sister that Amy is now determined to track down and meet. "Maybe I can do one of those *Unsolved Mysteries* things," she says.

After the murder, Amy's mom remarried and Amy never took to her stepfather, a beer-vacuum she nicknamed "Slick." She can't count the times he staggered home at three in the morning, or all the holes in the wall where her mom threw kitchen utensils at him, or the restraining orders filed against him for domestic assault, or the times he promised to change but didn't. He financed a lot of his binges with Social Security money intended for Amy and her older sister's support. Many times he came home drunk and took the two girls out behind the barn and gave them the belt. The worst beating was in the sixth grade when he caught Amy switching an F to an A on her report card—he took a cribbage board to her that time.

When she reached high school, she hoped he would back off, but he didn't. Even though he is a quarter Cherokee himself, he hated her dating Indian boys, convinced they were using her for sex. He found footprints in the dirt outside her window—footprints left by an Indian boy who'd gotten drunk and sneaked into her bedroom in the middle of the night—so he boarded up the window and grounded her for two months.

As her depression grew, she found a sympathetic ear in an older hunting guide known around town as a shameless womanizer. He promised to take her to California, and she believed him. They'd leave as soon as school was out, he promised, so she packed her bags. But it was a lie. She felt duped, not to mention ugly, cheap, and worthless. She opened the medicine cabinet and swallowed four large handfuls of aspirin, then lay down to die. When she started throwing up bile, Slick heard the noise and rushed to investigate. She told him what she'd done, and he jerked her off the bed by her hair and began hitting her as hard as he could on the side of her head with his shoe, again and again and again. She screamed, trying to fend off the blows. "I'm beating some sense into you," he explained. After his arms grew weary, he threw her into the car and drove her to Crow School so that her mom could deal with it. Within a couple hours Amy was admitted under a suicide watch to Rivendell, the teen psychiatric center in Billings, where she stayed for a month. After her release, she didn't feel safe returning home, so she moved in with a friend of her mother's in Hardin. Slowly, she started the road back. Her attendance and grades improved; she joined the yearbook staff and played on the tennis team, working her way up to the number two spot; and she met Cody, a big and burly twenty-year-old, half Crow, half Kiowa. Of all the boys she'd dated, he was the first to treat her with respect, opening the car door for her, showing up on time, buying her gifts, not demanding sex. Over the summer, they moved in together in his recently deceased grandmother's two-story, faded yellow prefab house halfway between Hardin and Crow Agency.

She credits him with saving her life . . . with Sharon's help.

Nearing St. Xavier, Amy passes two recently erected small white crosses marking the spot of a fatal drunk-driving accident that took the lives of two young Crows. (In America, alcohol is involved in 73 percent of all fatal auto accidents involving Indians, compared to 44 percent for whites.) She also passes a small convoy of double trailer trucks hustling their sugar beet harvests toward market. She and Trina still aren't wearing seat belts.

With her Firebird on cruise control at sixty-five miles an hour, she reaches across the seat for a Tanya Tucker tape, then fumbles to insert it into the cassette player. She hears a loud bang. At first she thinks it's one of the trucks back-firing. But her car swerves hard to the right, the right front tire blown to shreds. She's going off the road.

"Get down," she shrieks, shoving Trina's head toward the floor.

The car hurtles off the highway, bouncing over a drainage ditch. Rocks bang against the underside. Without slowing, it plows forward through a barbed wire fence, the wire grinding across the hood, sparks flying. Finally, it slams into a tree.

Pinned against the steering wheel, Amy struggles to get loose. She glances to her right. Trina is on the floorboard, upside down, arms and legs splayed in every direction. Amy sees no blood. Not on herself, not on Trina. But she sees smoke leaping out from under the hood and hears ominous hissing sounds.

Frantically, she pries herself loose from the steering wheel and pulls on the door handle. It's jammed. But the window is open.

"Are you okay, Trina?"

Trina nods yes.

Amy reaches down and pulls her toward her. Then, with all her strength, she shoves her out the window. Trina tumbles to the ground. Amy crawls out right behind her.

Afraid the car is about to explode, Amy takes off running with Trina in her arms, not stopping until they reach a farmhouse a quarter mile down the road. She calls 911, then Cody.

He assures her everything will be fine. "My family has good medicine," he explains.

In the locker room, Tiffany walks past Amy's locker and wrinkles her nose. "What's that smell?" she asks.

"Perfume," answers Amy, who rode with Trina to the ER, where they were treated for minor cuts and abrasions, then released.

"You're wearing perfume?"

Amy nods.

"This is a basketball game, not the prom," says Tiffany.

"What difference does it make?" replies Amy. "I never get to play, so I might as well smell good."

In the hallway outside the locker room, Coach Mac paces, waiting for the principal, Jerry Slyker, to arrive at the gym. After thinking about it all day, she has decided Sharon can play, but she needs Slyker to sign off on it. She doubts he will. It's understandable. If Sharon plays and gets hurt, the school will be looking at a lawsuit; on the other hand, if Sharon isn't allowed to play, the school and Coach Mac will have to face some angry Indians. It will be yet another case of whites being insensitive to tribal religion and customs.

The battle line is predictable, the Indians knowing they've been getting a screw job for a hundred years, going back to the late 1800s when the federal government outlawed medicine men and most of the Crows' "medicines"—vision quests, self-mutilation, peyote, the Sun Dance. It was all part of the white man's effort to kill off the Indians' traditional religion and replace it with Christianity. At the end of the nineteenth century, Native American religions were seen as foci for organized armed rebellion. According to some of the militants on the rez, the feds could have cared less about religion per se, they just wanted docile, disorganized Indians. And if the Indians were half starved and drunk? Fine, cheaper to control. And if they were broke? Fine, easier to rob their land. Despite these government policies and restrictions, including the harassment and arrest by the sherriff of anyone participating in a peyote ceremony in the 1940s, many Crows clung to their old beliefs. Gradually, the government got a little wiser after the 1960s, and rituals like the Sun Dance and peyote meetings started reappearing, Crow religion evolving into a mixed bag of traditional Indian ceremonies and Christianity. In Sharon's case, she was baptized in the Baptist Church as a youngster, but now as a teenager, she rarely attends church, choosing instead to sweat out impurities in the sweat lodge. But she still calls herself a Baptist. There was even a time in junior high that she went to several Mormon services, although she is hard pressed to remember why.

Principal Slyker, blond and blue-eyed, arrives and huddles with Coach Mac. They quickly come up with a plan, one that should get the school and Coach Mac off the hook legally. They'll get Danetta to sign a release that it is okay for Sharon to play, then Sharon will be allowed to dress out with the team and participate in warmup drills. If she shows no adverse effects, then she can play on a limited basis.

"But you can't start," Coach Mac informs her.

*   *   *

It is Geri Stewart, not Amy, who starts in Sharon's place. With foam padding wrapped in an Ace bandage under her jersey to protect her contusion, Sharon looks as if she's had a breast implant.

The visiting Miles City Cowgirls take the opening tap and score. Then they score again . . . and again. Just like that they lead 6–0. Coach Mac turns to Sharon. "You're in," she instructs. A minute has gone by.

Geri hasn't even broken a sweat. She sits down next to Amy and glares at Coach Mac. "I hate that woman," she mutters.

On the court, Sharon feels a sense of urgency. Five seconds after entering the game, she dives for a loose ball, tying up her longtime rival Joleyn Wambolt.

Her teammates, however, are lethargic. The crowd is dead, too, sitting on its hands, still drained from rooting themselves nuts in the three straight overtime victories. Sharon is called for traveling and angrily bounces the ball hard off the floor. The ref glares, contemplating a technical, but lets it slide.

Coach Mac is mad, too. Despite the team's lofty ranking and gutsy overtime wins, it still lacks a champion's attitude, that chesty mix of confidence and arrogance that separates the really good teams and athletes, like the way the New York Yankees take the field with their tradition and pinstripes and a we're-coming-after-you-with-more-talent-than-you cockiness. It's an intimidation thing; it's a go-for-the-jugular thing; it's an if-you-were-any-good-you'd-be-one-of-us attitude. It's what Hardin doesn't have. What they have is no history of athletic excellence, no state championship banners hanging in the gym, no pride in wearing a letterman's jacket into an opposing town, no killer instinct, no executioner's glare. And most of all, they are inconsistent. The really good teams don't have quarter-long meltdowns.

Near the end of the first half, the Miles City Cowgirls reel off 10 straight points to take a five-point lead into the locker room. For her part, Sharon has 12 points and a couple of floor burns. Since entering the game, she hasn't been back out.

But she didn't start.

Midway through the third quarter, with Hardin still trailing by five, Coach Mac walks to the end of the bench after a turnover by Rhea. "Amy, check in," she says.

Jumping off the bench and ripping off her warmups, she stumbles. Her teammates cover their mouths and giggle.

Seconds after checking in, she pulls in a defensive rebound and makes a quick outlet pass to Tiffany to trigger a fast-break basket. On Miles City's possession, she blocks the lane, forcing a turnover, then hustles to the other end to set a large screen for Sharon, who drills a jumper. Hardin now trails by only one and the crowd is back into it.

Running back on defense, Amy glances toward the bench, not for approval but because she's worried she'll be taken out. Not watching the court, her feet tangle with Joleyn Wambolt's and they crash to the floor, Amy on top. The refs don't see it. Amy rolls off and for an instant she thinks about offering an apology and a hand up. Then she remembers Coach Mac's rule about never helping an opponent off the floor. She runs to her position.

"Box out!" yells Coach Mac.

She boxes out Wambolt, the rebound going to Anita, who takes it coast to coast for an easy layin, putting Hardin in the lead. The Miles City coach calls a timeout.

Normally during timeouts, Amy stands on the perimeter in her warmups, paying little attention to Coach Mac's instructions. But this is different. She listens intently, feeling a part of it for the first time all year. Those are real beads of sweat rolling down her face.

"Stay tight on Wambolt," says Coach Mac. "Keep a body on her."

Trotting back out onto the court next to Sharon after the timeout, she peeks toward the stands where Cody is sitting. He gives her the thumbs-up; she gives it back. Over the summer, he spent long hours with her at the hoop in his driveway working on her inside game, showing her how to box out on rebounds, just like she did against Wambolt. When the season started and she didn't get into games, he offered to go talk to Coach Mac and demand more playing time for her. She told him no.

On defense, she smothers Wambolt, leaning on her back, pushing her away from the basket. A shot from the outside misses and she snares the rebound. At the other end, Sharon scores on a nifty crossover dribble to her left. Cody bellows a loud war whoop.

The horn sounds ending the third quarter, Hardin leading by six. It is an 11-point run, all of it since Amy entered the game. She hasn't scored, but her two rebounds, full-court hustle, and defense on Wambolt are at the center of the comeback.

In the huddle, sandwiched between Sharon and Tiffany, she beams. All the long hours of practice, the yelling from Coach Mac, the games on the bench . . . it is suddenly worth it. She is at the center of the action.

"Rhea, check back in for Amy," orders Coach Mac.

Amy takes her seat, hoping it's temporary. Cody leaves his seat in the stands and walks behind the Hardin bench, slowing to pat her on the shoulder. He doesn't speak—it's just a hand on her shoulder.

She beams even more . . . such a thoughtful boyfriend. On their one-month anniversary he gave her two stuffed animals; for her birthday he gave her earrings and a necklace; on their two-month anniversary, he gave her an engagement promise ring. No boy had ever given her anything. He even invited her to one of his sacred all-night peyote rituals. Even Slick likes him.

The fourth quarter starts with eight unanswered points, only this time the streak belongs to the Cowgirls. Hardin trails by two.

Coach Mac is livid. How can this team be so *inconsistent*? Back when her teams won three games a year and her ulcer was devouring her stomach, she looked at coaches with winning programs and imagined how smooth life might be. Yet now, with her team leading the league and ranked number one, she feels like crap, doubling over at the waist, a pain shooting through her stomach.

With 2:12 to play, Tiffany sinks two free throws and Hardin is up by three. Then Miles City turns it over.

"Smart passes!" yells Coach Mac.

Anita passes it right to a defender.

"Don't foul!" yells Coach Mac.

Owena fouls.

The free throw is missed and Sharon rebounds.

"Don't shoot!" yells Coach Mac.

DyAnna casts off from 18 feet.

Coach Mac slams down her towel. This can't be happening. It's almost as if the team purposefully disregards everything she says.

With 26 seconds remaining, Wambolt misses a jumper and Sharon grabs the rebound and is fouled. She knows the numbers—math is her best subject—two free throws ice the game. She also knows that this is the third game in a row that she's been to the line in the final seconds with a chance to sew up a victory. The first two times she missed. This time she swishes both shots, clinching the victory 55–50.

Hardin now leads the conference by two games, and with conference play at the halfway point, they are 9-1, their grip on number one secure. For the night, Tiffany and Anita each score 15, Sharon a game-high 21. With the exception of the first minute, she played the entire game.

Amy never got back in the game.

PART IV

THE SEASON
(Second Half)

CHAPTER TWENTY-TWO

Hardin High English teacher Katy Lytle stops by to borrow a book. She is the most popular teacher in the school, and her husband, the former editor of the *Big Horn County News,* recently became an ordained Presbyterian minister and is on a year-long church assignment in Wisconsin. The morning after her visit I stop for gas at Jay's Auto Service. "I saw Katy Lytle's car parked in front of your place last night," says Jay. "What's going on between you two?"

Did I mention that gossip travels fast in Hardin?

After my morning swim at the Community Center, I stop to chat with the director, a woman whose husband has been defeated in a run for one of the three county commission seats, two of which are currently held by Indians. She wants to talk politics.

"The elections around here are rigged," she claims.

"How's that?"

"I don't know if you noticed, but there's Indians around here who can't read. I'm not saying they all can't, but there's quite a few."

"What's that have to do with the elections?"

"Plenty. On election day a pickup truck with loudspeakers drives all over Crow Agency urging people to get out and vote. That's not right."

"Why?"

"As I said, a lot of these Indians can't read. But they've been trained to recognize the letter D."

"Huh?"

"Yeah, D, as in *Democrat*. They mark their X on the ballot wherever they see a D. It's true."

I meet Ron Johnson for bad coffee at the Chat and Chew. He's lived in Hardin his whole life and knows the scene as well as anyone. He gets his gossip from a lot of sources, including his various positions as greenskeeper at the local nine-hole course, volunteer fire chief, and school bus owner/driver. Because he is the father of Sharon's best friend, Holly, I figure he knows some of the dirt on Danetta, such as how it is she has the money to drive around in a big Lincoln Continental and pay cash for new cars for seemingly everyone in her family, including Sharon. He explains that she sold off twenty choice acres of her family's land to the tribe, land that will be the site of the new Crow Hospital.

"Danetta likes to make everyone think she's rich," he says. "But mark my words, sooner or later, she'll hit you up for a loan. Hang on to your wallet."

Later, I ask Danetta why it is she bought a Lincoln instead of a Mercedes. "'Cause half these dummies here on the rez would look at that emblem on the front and think I'm driving a Plymouth."

"Why didn't you buy a Cadillac?" I ask.

"'Cause that's what all the niggers drive."

Like most days, I stop in at the school during fourth period to spend time with Amylynn Adams. A high-energy, pretty girl, she's a member of the Honor Society, active in the Lutheran Church, and one of the most popular kids in school. She dreams of being a writer, so we've made a deal:

I'll help her with her writing and she'll provide me the inside scoop on life at Hardin High. I have already learned that despite her bubbly personality, she's had a rocky childhood, living under the fear of an abusive stepfather who recently got tossed out of the house by her mom.

Amylynn shares a new piece of writing with me. She knows I'm following Sharon and the Lady Bulldogs, so she's written an essay about her experience as a teammate back in the eighth grade:

I didn't understand basketball much and never tried for a basket, afraid of missing and letting down the team. But Sharon wasn't afraid. Heck, I was positive she could do anything. She had no fears. I had a respect and reverence for her, an awe. Part of it was because of her amazing grace on the court. Sitting on the bench and watching her every move, I'd imagine I was her. When she shot three-pointers, I'd tense my body and clench my fists, hoping with all my strength and emotions that she'd make it. If she missed, I'd blame myself for not wishing hard enough. I felt for Tiffany, too, but it wasn't as extreme.

This was all during my "I wanna be everyone but me" stage. I never told Sharon, but I was her biggest fan. I always wanted to talk to her, to be her friend. She reminded me of leather—soft and kind on the outside, strong and resilient on the inside. Where I was weak, she was strong.

Maybe it wasn't that I wanted to be Sharon—I doubted I ever could be that special—it was more like I wanted her to be my big sister, to stick up for me. Everyone respected her and no one messed with her. She reminded me of an Indian girl who wanted to fight me in the sixth grade back in California before I moved to

Montana. I figured that if I could be her friend, then she wouldn't want to fight me.

To me, Sharon was able to control the petty emotions that I always fought wars with. She always seemed in control. I guess people thought that about me, but I was a wreck inside. I wanted to cry on her shoulder. I wanted her to tell me how to solve my problems, to be strong like her. I was convinced that "LaForge the Basketball Queen" was above tears. I figured she never cried.

I was devastated when I heard they found weed in her locker at the end of our eighth grade year. All I knew about weed was that it was a drug. I couldn't fathom why she would do something so revolting. Then she disappeared from my life for a couple years. I became friends with Tiffany during that time.

I remember the first time I met Tiff. I'd just moved here from California and she and another girl came to the door to ask if I wanted to go bike riding. My first thought when I saw Tiff was that she was the prettiest girl in the world. She had these incredible long tan legs and a cute hair style. I thought, "Wow, if all the girls in Montana look like this, I'm in big trouble."

In the tenth grade I was hanging out a little bit with Holly Johnson, who didn't get along with Tiffany. Holly told me that Sharon had a really rough home life and lived with her off and on to escape. I was confused. I'd never thought of Sharon as having a mom or dad or family. She was independent, and in my mind she didn't need parents. Besides, I thought I was the only one with secret family problems. Anyway, Holly started dating Solomon Little Owl, an important basketball star who was really cute and sweet. But after a month or so, Holly's love for him fizzled out. One day she told me that Solomon thought I was HOT. Pretty soon I started dating him. I guess because he was a big basketball hero, he made me feel special. He was nice and I liked to listen to him tell me stories about his grandpa. I liked him, but to tell the truth, half the reason I went out with him was because Sharon was usually at Holly's house when I was there and she encouraged the relationship. In fact, a lot of the times I'd go to Holly's just in hopes that Sharon would be there. She had no idea what a big influence she had on me.

"You're going to a Tribal Council meeting?" asks Danetta as we sit in her dining room awaiting Sharon's arrival for dinner. "You better wear a flak jacket."

Although it's not for a couple weeks, I am indeed going, and she's referring to the reputation of these quarterly tribal gatherings for turning into raucous free-for-alls. At the last meeting, a brawl broke out and women were knocked to the floor, elders were stampeded into corners, and heads were banged with chairs. It took the BIA police thirty minutes to restore order and a dozen victims had to be treated at Crow Hospital for cuts and contusions.

Danetta knows firsthand about the hugely partisan world of Crow politics. As a young girl, she served coffee for her grandfather at political gatherings. In the 1960s, when Crow women had zero political clout, she tried to get her moccasin in the political door by joining a small group that called itself the Women's Club. But every time one of these women tried to speak up at a council meeting, the men shouted them down, or grabbed away the microphone, or fired off a dirty joke at them.

Danetta didn't give up. Because she is well spoken and comes from a family that didn't sell off all its deeded land at the first sign of a whiskey bottle, she kept pushing. Her enemies thought her arrogant.

"Our family is like the Kennedys," she boasts.

For many years she served on a variety of tribal committees, including the Land Purchase Committee, a position that put her in the middle of battles between the tribe and white ranchers, and got her accused of everything from being a tribal con artist to a flunky for whites.

"They can say what they want, but I'm the one who raised the leases for everyone in the tribe," she huffs.

In the early 1980s she was elected tribal vice chairperson, making her the highest-ranking woman in tribal history. "You should've seen me back there in Washington, D.C.," she says. "I'd show up to meetings wearing my fancy furs and jewelry, and I'll tell you, those Montana senators liked to show me off."

But back on the rez, her role as vice chair was more about making copies and fetching coffee. "I can't tell you what went on in the decision-making meetings," she confessed. "They always locked the door on me and wouldn't let me in."

She dropped out for a while, spending much of her time raising Sharon. Then her political fortunes rose again with the election of her cousin Richard Real Bird as the new chairman. A sharp-dressing former rodeo rider who survived a broken neck, Real Bird was a political maverick who openly opposed the Evil Empire of the BIA and advocated full tribal sovereignty, believing that the government's welfare handouts "enslaved" his people, and white ranchers wouldn't be happy until they had total control over Crow lands and there was no more Crow Nation. He was the bad-boy militant of the Crows, a tribe not known for its sieges and shootouts with the feds. Although Danetta favored a more moderate course, she gladly rode the family coattails to increased power.

Despite Real Bird's fiery rhetoric, he was a lot like his political predecessors, a chauvinistic alcoholic, a leader who let men under him turn little vices into big ones. Their shenanigans, i.e., loan-sharking and fraud, caught the attention of bureaucrats at the BIA eager to bring him down, most notably Clara Nomee. She snitched about an illegal loan transaction on a land purchase, a deal in which an elderly white couple from Billings lost their life savings. Danetta took the minutes at a meeting in which some plans were hatched. Next thing she knew, six Big Horn County sheriff's cars were circling her house and a deputy sheriff was thrusting indictment papers under her chin. Sharon was standing right next to her at the time.

"Aside from the day my son was murdered, that was my low point," she says, holding her hands out to show how they handcuffed her when she turned herself in to be fingerprinted.

She pleaded not guilty to charges of co-conspiracy to commit bank fraud and falsifying a bank loan application. For eighteen months she fought the charges, hiring an expensive lawyer in Billings. "I had to sell a choice tract of land along the Big Horn River to pay the guy," she says. "It was land I was going to use to pay for my grandkids' college."

Of the twenty-four people charged in the conspiracy, twenty pled guilty, accepting a government plea bargain to testify against Real Bird and two aides in return for no jail time. Danetta was the only one to plead not guilty, the only one with the resources to fight the charges.

"Why would I plead guilty when I'm innocent?" she asks.

On the first day of her trial, Danetta brought Sharon to court. "I bought her a new dress for the occasion," she says. "Anything to help my case."

But just before opening arguments, the prosecution surprised the courtroom and dropped its charges against Danetta. "That was a great moment," she says. "But it cost me $34,000 in lawyer fees."

It also cost her reputation, her name forever linked to

Real Bird, who was convicted and sentenced to seven years in federal prison. To bury the knife a little deeper, Clara Nomee, the ex-friend who she deemed stabbed her in the back, was hailed a hero and after a brief stint as secretary of the Tribal Council was elected as the new tribal chairperson despite having no political experience.

"I'm the one who should've been elected," claims Danetta.

Now she is a politically disgraced woman. "My main mission in life is to restore my good name and the family's honor," she says. "And if Sharon's the one to do it for me, that's fine by me."

The whole time Danetta talks, Blaine sits stoically, saying nothing, occasionally nodding in agreement. Tired of waiting for Sharon, we start to eat. It's the same macaroni and beef dish as before, except the meat is even chewier, if that's possible.

The door opens and Sharon enters, surprised to see me.

"What'ya doing here?" she asks.

"I've come to help you with your homework."

"Very funny."

After dinner—she limits herself to candy and Fritos—I move to the couch and she sits down next to me, a move I'm not expecting.

"How's your back?" I ask.

"I want to tell you about this weird dream I had last night," she says, ignoring my conversation starter.

In her dream she was in her basketball uniform driving the team bus, the person in charge of getting her teammates to their destination. The bus came to a steep hill, and halfway up, she tried to shift, but the gears ground and the bus started to roll backward. The harder she tried to stop it, the faster it rolled, finally rolling all the way back down the hill. Determined to try again, she started back up, but the bus stalled again and rolled back to the bottom. She tried and failed again. When the dream ended, she was sitting behind the wheel, crying, upset that she couldn't get her teammates over the hill.

"Do you think this dream was some kind of vision or revelation?" I ask.

"No, it was just a regular nightmare."

CHAPTER TWENTY-THREE

Sharon exits the small IGA in Lodge Grass, stopping as she passes Sunny Old Elk, a handsome seventeen-year-old basketball player who recently moved to Billings. She's known him since first grade. He stops to greet her, but she barely breaks stride, avoiding eye contact. She mumbles a hello and continues toward her car where Randy waits. He stiffens in his seat and turns away, glaring out the window.

"What's wrong?" she asks.

He doesn't reply, continuing his gaze.

Instinctively, she knows. Any Crow woman knows. On the rez, male jealousy is the dominant emotion.

She starts the car, wondering if she should just ignore him. Or should she try and talk about it? She knows the chances of him sharing his feelings are zero. The chances of her sharing her feelings aren't much better.

Randy's sulk may have its cultural origins in the days when the men in the tribe led the war parties, conducted religion, guarded the camp, brought home the meat, *counted coup*. In other words, totally ruled. Other than doing the dirty work of digging roots and packing the travois, women were there to reproduce. A Crow warrior even got to have more than one wife, and if he suspected infidelity, real or not, he beat her. This was known as *Indian loving*.

"Take me to my pickup," Randy says curtly.

"Is something wrong?"

What's wrong, most likely, is that Crow men no longer totally rule. The emerging status of women on the rez, including star athletes like Sharon, is threatening. Men can't be traditional warriors anymore; they can't lead a war party or kill buffalo. But a lot of them are still stuck in that old warrior game plan. They still want to drag the woman into the teepee. But that's not cool, they're told. So what's left for these Crow men? Most of them can't bury themselves in their work—there is no work. And what few jobs that do exist on the rez—waiting tables, filing papers for the BIA, cleaning bedpans at the hospital—are beneath their dignity. As a result, the unemployment rate for men is significantly higher than for women. Not surprisingly, many of these men are full of anger and jealousy. Randy has just been informed by his boss at Crow Tribal Housing that his construction job will be terminated for the winter.

"Come on, let's go!" he orders.

Sharon doesn't respond. She needs to talk, to clear the air, not just about this little sulk job, but a whole lot of things, such as how come he seems to always have an excuse why he can't see her? It's always something—a rodeo out of town, his job, a chore he has to do for his mother. Or why is it that every time she invites him to meet her family, he can't come? Or how come he's never been to one of her games? He rarely even asks about them, yet she's been to three of his rodeos, and has listened to him go on and on about roping this lil' dogie or that one. And she can't remember the last time he called. She's always the one who initiates contact. She wonders if sex is the only reason he sees her, but no, that can't be true. If it is, then why did he tell her he doesn't want her to go away for college? Why did he tell her how much he'd miss her and how much better off she'd be not leaving the rez? Doesn't that mean he really cares? Then again, what about that whole Raylene Pretty Elk episode? Was that a mirage?

In silence, she pulls away from the store and turns the corner. A car approaches and Randy suddenly slides down in his seat, shielding his face with his hand.

"What are you doing?" she asks.

"Keep driving!"

Sharon glances at the passing car and recognizes the driver. It's Rona Hugs, a twenty-two-year-old with long black hair, a hot temper, and a killer body. She is Randy's ex-girlfriend, the one Holly claimed she'd seen him with recently.

"Why are you ducking?" Sharon demands, slowing down. Rona's car abruptly turns around.

"Go!" he orders.

"No."

"Come on! Take me to my pickup!"

Sharon relents and speeds up, swerving to avoid a huge pothole. Rona's car closes behind her.

"Shit!" he shouts. "Go faster!"

Sharon slams on the brakes. "This is stupid," she says. "Go talk to her. Find out what she wants."

"No, just take me to my pickup!"

Rona jumps out of her car and runs toward the passenger side of Sharon's car. "You asshole, Randy!" she screams, slamming her fist against his door.

"Go!" he yells.

Sharon hits the accelerator and the car roars away, leaving Rona standing in the dust, shaking her fist.

They ride in silence to Randy's pickup, then Sharon turns and glares. "You said you weren't seeing her no more," she fumes.

"I ain't," he says, getting out of the car.

She surveys him skeptically.

"What? Don't you believe me?" he asks. Then he gets in his pickup and drives away.

*   *   *

It's a few minutes before the start of the Lady Bulldogs' home game against Glendive, the team that handed them their only loss, and I'm waiting in line at the snack bar to buy a couple bags of Nibs. It's part of my pregame superstition—one bag of the little red licoricettes for me, one bag for Stacie's stepmom. The team hasn't lost a game since the first time I did this Nibs thing, so why jinx it? I'm working my voodoo.

Out of the corner of my eye, I spot him. Or at least I think it's him. Sharon's father. Michael LaForge. Danetta and Marlene had pointed him out to me at an earlier game, but it was from across the gym and I didn't get a close look. Now he's just a few feet away. At least I think it's him.

Danetta and Marlene had also given me the lowdown on the guy. He has always lived within a couple miles of Sharon, but he has never been in her life, made no contribution to her childhood, financially, emotionally, or otherwise. Not one dime, not one phone call, not one hug.

Danetta could recall only one face-to-face meeting between him and Sharon. It was at the Montana State Fair in Billings—Sharon was six—and they bumped into him. "Sharon wanted nothing to do with him," she recalled. "She had these two goldfish in a water-filled plastic bag that we'd won, and as we stood next to him, she clutched those goldfish to her chest like he was going to steal them or something. Or maybe she thought they'd protect her against him."

Waiting in line for my Nibs, I study him. Dressed in Wrangler jeans and a snap-button cowboy shirt, he's thin as a swizzle stick, timid-looking, with a wisp of a mustache. There's no mistaking he's Sharon's father. The physical resemblance is strong—slender frame and butt, small mouth, sharp bone structure. From the angle I'm seeing him, they look almost identical.

It was Marlene who told me some of his background, including the story about the chaotic scene at his wedding to Karna. "My mother was determined to make it the biggest wedding in tribal history," she said. "She hosted a reception the night before and four hundred invited guests packed the gym at the old tribal headquarters. Wedding gifts filled an entire room. But things got out of control when somebody spiked the punch with a couple gallons of vodka."

Michael, twenty-two at the time, got so wasted that he ended up in a Billings jail after a car chase and the police discovered a couple outstanding warrants. It didn't look like he would make it back in time for the wedding, but Danetta came to the rescue, paying his bail just in time for him to make it to the ceremony at the Baptist Church in Crow Agency. But the marriage didn't survive the first year. He was drunk most of the time. When Karna kicked him out, she was five months pregnant with Sharon.

When I finally get to the head of the snack line, there's a problem—they're out of Nibs. Evidently they don't understand that the team's number one ranking depends on me and my Nibs.

I turn around and Michael LaForge is no longer there. He's heading into the gym. Somehow, I get the impression that he's an elusive sort, here one minute, gone the next.

I follow him inside. There's much I want to ask him, such as why hasn't he had any contact with his daughter? I'm curious as to why a man, whether he's on the rez or in Scarsdale, can throw away such a relationship. Maybe Michael LaForge has an explanation.

He climbs the bleachers toward the top of the gym and I continue to follow. I feel like Mike Wallace stalking some chiseling weasel to ask him why he's such a loser. But that's not my idea here. I'm not out to challenge him about his parental irresponsibility. Not now, not in a packed gym anyway. I just want to introduce myself.

Actually, it's not just his relationship—or lack of one—with Sharon that interests me. For instance, I find it fascinating that he and Sharon are connected by birth to one of the watershed events in American history—the Custer massacre. The paternal side of Sharon's family traces back to Thomas LaForge, a handsome American of French descent who in 1868 set off to travel through the Big Horn Mountains in search of game and adventure. A spunky kind of guy, he made pals with a band of Crows who soon adopted him into one of their families, thus making him one of the first whites to have a clue about tribal ways. Eventually, he recorded his experiences in a book, *Memoirs of a White Crow Indian*. One of his buddies in the tribe was Mitch Bouyer, one of the six Crow scouts who rode with General Custer on his fateful journey to the Valley of the Little Big Horn. (It was Bouyer who said to Custer, "General, I don't think you should go down there.") The other five scouts said no thanks on going down there and turned back, but Bouyer rode into the valley with Custer, a choice that got him prematurely dead. A couple years after the battle, LaForge stepped in and married Bouyer's Crow widow and together they had three children, including a son, Sharon's great-great-great grandfather.

Michael LaForge takes a seat a couple rows from the top, surrounded by people. Several rows below him, I pause. Maybe now isn't the best time for introductions. With the game about to start, I decide to wait until later. Maybe I'll catch him at halftime.

On Hardin's first possession, Sharon forces an off-balance shot and misses everything. On the next possession, she clangs one off the front rim, then scowls all the way downcourt. She looks out of sync. Already I'm thinking I need to make a dash to the Town Pump for some Nibs.

Glendive is a hard team to figure. After blowing out the Lady Bulldogs in their first meeting, they've lost three games and are two full games behind Hardin. The scouting report is that they have trouble with teams that slow the tempo. Coach Mac will eat worms before she tries that.

Sharon misses her next shot.

It hasn't been her best week. Besides the Randy and Rona incident, she's been bothered all week by her various injuries. On Wednesday she ran out of the medication for her chest contusion and barely slept. On Thursday she got a failure notice in Mr. Nelson's Senior Comp class. It isn't that the class is too tough . . . it's that she hates Mr. Nelson, a guy with a "Rush Is Right" bumper sticker on his classroom wall. In her view, he has "prejudism."

Midway through the first quarter, playing without the ball, she rolls off a screen by Tiffany and breaks wide open under the basket. Anita has the ball at the free throw line and doesn't see her. Instead, she shoots and scores.

"Damnit!" snarls Sharon as they retreat on defense. "Pass me the ball when I'm open."

Anita glances at her, dumbfounded. "I didn't see you," she says. "Sorry."

For the next three minutes, the Hardin fans witness a clinic—hustling defense, crisp passes, aggressive rebounding, great shot selection—12 unanswered points. But it's Glendive putting on the clinic. At the end of the first quarter, Hardin trails 27–14. Sharon has no points and three fouls.

Across the gym, her father sits on his hands.

As in the team's first game against Glendive, the zone press is being shredded by quick passes upcourt before Rhea, Owena, and Sharon can move to stop the penetration. The few times they have been able to force Glendive into a half-court game, the Lady Red Devils' Michelle Frenzel is wide open and connects from outside. Just like she did in the first game.

Coach Mac is determined to stick to the game plan. The problem, she thinks, is in its execution not its design. She also opts to leave Sharon in, despite the three fouls.

To start the second quarter, Sharon tosses up another brick.

"Relax!" yells Coach Mac.

The second quarter rolls on and it's ugly. Sharon misses three more shots, then yells at Owena, "Stop standing around!" It's as if she's back in her dream, grinding the gears, struggling to get her teammates over the hill.

She hits a short jumper at the buzzer, her first points of the game, then slinks off the court, head down, Hardin trailing by 14.

I watch Michael LaForge descend the stairs and walk out the gym to the lobby. I set out to meet him.

Reaching the lobby, I watch him buy a Coke and then walk out the doors to the outside. It's cold and I don't want to follow. Maybe he's going for a smoke and will be right back. Or maybe he's going outside to pull a Karna and spike his drink.

From what I've been told, he and the curse of alcohol go back to the tenth grade. He was expelled from Hardin High because of missing too many classes, absences that were usually alcohol-related. He managed to make it through the army relatively sober, but he was hitting the sauce pretty hard by the time he married Karna. After the divorce, he shaped up for a while, first landing a job on the production line at the ill-fated Big Horn Carpet Mill, then as a welder at Sarpy Mine. But he fell to drink again and pretty soon he was too drunk to even call in sick. That was it for that job.

His second wife, who had another daughter by him, temporarily dumped him, too.

I continue to wait for Michael LaForge. According to Marlene, who sees him around Crow Agency from time to time, he's on the wagon again. The story has it that he found religion in the Mormon church, gave up the booze, got a job as a janitor at Crow Hospital, remarried his second wife, and now lives with her and their daughter just north of Crow Agency. Then again, Marlene hasn't talked to him in a few months, so all that could've changed.

I see him reenter the lobby and I move swiftly toward him before he has a chance to go back into the gym. He is alone. I stop him at the door and introduce myself. His handshake has all the pep and power of linguini. I tell him that I'm writing a book that will most likely focus on his daughter. He stares blankly. I don't smell alcohol.

He has no reaction to my introduction whatsoever. None. From his stare, I might as well have just told him I am a book. Or linguini. Usually, when two people meet for the first time, at least some degree of response occurs, even if it's just body language that says get out of my space. In this case, there's nothing, a total flat-liner.

"Hardin didn't play too well that half," I say. "Maybe they'll be able to get it together."

He responds with a nod, although if I hadn't been looking straight at him, I would have missed it. I don't know what to say next. Should I tell him I think his daughter is terrific? No. Any lame attempt at conversation at this point seems an intrusion, or too complex. I'm afraid that if I ask if I can come to his house for an interview, he either won't get what I'm saying or will report me to the BIA police. But maybe I'm all wrong, maybe he's just ultrashy.

"Well, it was nice meeting you," I say. "I'm sure we'll meet again."

With no goodbye, he turns and returns to his spot in the bleachers. It's clear I need a new strategy.

Maybe I'm missing something, and maybe I've never been a basketball coach, but it seems clear that Hardin needs a new strategy against Glendive. Neither Coach Mac's two-three zone press or her diamond and one zone is working. They didn't work in the first game, and they aren't in this game. Glendive is running around and through them like soup through a fork. Maybe a man-to-man will stop the bleeding.

"Let's stick with the press," exhorts Coach Mac as the team retakes the court.

The third quarter starts with a run of 14 unanswered points. Glendive points. The Lady Bulldogs are in total collapse, everyone moving without purpose.

"This is embarrassing!" Coach Mac yells following another Glendive layup.

For the quarter, Glendive outscores them 24–4. A public flogging. There are not enough Nibs in the universe to stop the onslaught. For the first time ever, Sharon wants out of a game.

It isn't until midway through the fourth quarter that Coach Mac pulls the first team. Sharon slumps on the bench, a towel covering her face. She has played the worst game of her varsity career, scoring only six points, a miserable three for 15 from the field. And Coach Mac has probably coached the worst game of her career, too stubborn to change a lousy game plan. The final score is 83–49. But as they say, it wasn't that close.

CHAPTER TWENTY-FOUR

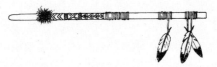

He's lying through his teeth," Tom Hopfauf whispers to Coach Oswald.

School superintendent Rod Svee doesn't hear the comment. He's too busy explaining to the rest of the audience at the school board meeting how the latest crunching of the district's numbers doesn't add up to give the teachers the pay raise they're demanding. Hopfauf is there to show his support for the teachers.

A motion is passed to table the debate until the union can present numbers of its own. The next item on the agenda is the announcement of the formation of a Crow parent advisory committee to study cultural issues facing the district, such as the lack of Native American personnel and curriculum.

Hopfauf whispers to Oswald again. "Funny, I don't remember hearing anything about a white parent advisory committee."

A handout sheet from American Indian Educational Commission is distributed to the audience. On it is a list comparing "traditional Indian values to European industrial values: *Indians are patient, whites aggressive; Indians honor cooperation, whites favor competition; Indians believe in harmony with nature, whites seek to conquer it.*

Hopfauf briefly examines the list, then flings it down on an empty chair next to him. "If Indians believe in nature so much," he mutters, "then why do all their houses look like junkyards."

He and Oswald leave the meeting.

There is a single light on in Bullis Mortuary. Inside, Kent Bullis and Tiffany sit in the office, just like they do on many school nights, Kent doing odd jobs, Tiffany hanging out and doing homework. On this night, she is studying for her SAT on Saturday morning in Billings.

For her, hanging out in the mortuary has become no big deal. She's even seen a couple corpses and toured the embalming room. But that's not why she comes. She comes to see Kent, and when you're in love, according to her, "it doesn't make any difference where you are."

Kent is boyishly cute—Holly calls him a pretty boy—but there are those among Tiffany's friends who are convinced it's just a matter of time until she realizes she's got more going and dumps him. She's in the Honor Society, he gets Cs; she's a senior, he's a junior; her basketball team is in first place, his football team is in last; she plans to go to college, he thinks maybe he'll go to trade school. That's not to say he doesn't have goals. He dreams of one day playing on the PGA tour, although so far he hasn't broken 85 at the local goat track known as Hardin Golf Course.

If his pro golf career doesn't pan out, he's always got the mortuary. For three generations, the funeral business has been good to the Bullis family. Kent's parents have a private plane and a cabin on Seeley Lake in western Montana, where Tiffany went with Kent and his parents on a family vacation over the summer. But Kent has seen the long hours his dad puts in, and so far, he's more interested in going his own way.

225

None of that matters to Tiffany. Ever since their first kiss at the barn dance in May, she's had the hots for him. They're not officially going steady, but she now considers him her best friend. She loves it that he's so polite and mannerly, opening doors for her, spreading his napkin on his lap, sending her roses. Her first boyfriend, Deano, was always late or standing her up altogether. Kent is always on time, and the one time when he was late, he called.

The phone rings. Kent hopes it's not a call that a new body is on its way. It isn't. It's Tiffany's mother. She's calling to tell her that Geri called.

"What's she want?" asks Tiffany.

"I don't know. She didn't say."

Tiffany promises to call.

"Why is your mom calling?" asks Kent.

"Just checking up," answers Tiffany.

The next day Geri and Tiffany exit the locker room on their way to practice. They make a striking pair, Tiffany long and lean, Geri with her sultry, sexy sneer. "Did your mom tell you I called last night?" asks Geri.

"No. What did you want?"

Geri looks at her askance. By her estimation they'd talked on the phone "a zillion" times since becoming best friends in the seventh grade and they never needed a reason to call. "I was just calling to talk," she answers.

"Guess my mom forgot."

As they reach the gym, Tiffany is flagged down by Laura Sundheim, her volleyball coach and counselor. Geri keeps walking.

"You got another letter from a college today," says Sundheim, handing her an envelope.

Tiffany opens it. It's from the volleyball coach at Carroll College a small private school in Helena. He's writing to say he has been following her career and hopes she'll consider Carroll College when she makes her decision where to continue her education. There might even be the possibility of some scholarship money.

Tiffany smiles. It's the third letter from a college she's received in ten days, joining Dickenson College in North Dakota and Rocky Mountain College in Billings, both of which expressed interest in her for volleyball *and* basketball. Sharon has received no such letters.

Tiffany rejoins Geri, and despite feeling good about the latest letter, doesn't mention it. Geri has seemed moody lately, unhappy, and it seems like bad timing to bring up her own good news. Although they don't talk about it, the fact that Tiffany will leave in a few months for college and leave Geri behind is creating a wall between them.

"Wanna do something after practice?" asks Geri.

"I've already got plans with Kent," Tiffany replies.

"What else is new?" sighs Geri.

To Geri, it's clear that their once tight friendship is losing its glue. Since meeting in the seventh grade, they've been best friends, spending countless nights together, talking on the phone, gossiping. It was Tiffany whom Geri confided in after being sexually abused when she was younger; it was Geri whom Tiffany confided in when she first became intimate with Deano.

Tiffany's house has always been a refuge for Geri, a place to escape her own unhappy home life where she lives with an alcoholic mother and a very strict grandfather. Last week her mom found out she was flunking algebra and said, "You're too stupid for that class. Why are you even bothering? You're never going to graduate anyway."

As important as her friendship with Tiffany has been, it has come at a price. Some of Geri's Indian friends have accused her of being an apple. They remind her that an Indian isn't supposed to have a white as a best friend. Until now, Geri has ignored them. Tiffany and her family have always been friendly and generous toward her, although she admits that there have been times when she's wondered if Tiffany's parents are racist, like the way they won't let Tiffany go to the reservation, or the way they were so happy when Tiffany split up with Deano.

Geri moves to a side basket where Sharon is lazily loosening up. "Let's go to the Corner Pocket after practice," she suggests.

"Okay," replies Sharon, spinning a hook shot off the backboard.

Lately, Sharon and Geri have started spending more time together. In the complicated world of teenage friendships, Geri has always felt caught in the middle of the tension between Sharon and Tiffany. She has always wanted to be friends with Sharon, too, but it seemed as if she couldn't be good friends with both girls, especially not when Holly was still around back-stabbing Tiffany. It bothered Geri that Sharon would go along with it, especially when they bitched about Tiffany being spoiled. Who was Sharon to talk? Nobody got more than she did: a new car, an expensive homecoming gown, gas money whenever she needed it.

But ever since Tiffany hooked up with Kent, Geri has felt like the third person out. All the times they used to hang out together—lunchtime, after school, weekends—those are now Kent times. Geri's not convinced, however, that he's the sweet, well-mannered guy Tiffany thinks he is.

"Guess what I heard," she says, motioning Sharon closer. "Kent took another girl out to lunch the other day and was acting all cozy."

"Does Tiffany know?"

"No, but maybe I should tell her."

*　　*　　*

Tom Hopfauf is a firm believer in hard work. It shows in our early morning basketball games. He's a player with limited skills—can't shoot, can't jump, can't dribble—but he's always scrapping and clawing for the ball, a persistent pain in the ass. He shoots the ball like he's shot-putting a garbage can, but somehow it goes in. I can see where Tiffany gets her competitive grit. Her dad is a bulldog.

On this night, I've invited him and his wife, Karen, to my duplex for dinner, a chicken cacciatore recipe I got off a soup can. Judging from the food left on their plates, they're not big cacciatore fans, at least not mine. Or maybe they're just tired. They've been moving all week, having sold their house, a comfortable two-story, three-bedroom on a cul-de-sac, the only home Tiffany has ever known, and downsized to a mobile home one hundred yards off the Interstate. For Tiffany, the move is a definite bummer, going from thirty cable channels to no cable hookup, going from a full basement bedroom of her own, where she could sometimes entertain Kent, to a cramped, thin-walled bedroom right next to her parents. And if it wasn't going to be crowded enough, one of her older sisters, Tammy, is pregnant and moving back home.

The move to the mobile home is a first step toward Tom's dream of saving enough money to buy some land and raise a few cattle. It's also to save money for Tiffany's education. Although Tom and Karen both work, they are part of the growing segment of middle-class America in which the combined income of the parents is too much to qualify for financial support, but not enough to afford the skyrocketing cost of a college education. With Tiffany being the youngest of three daughters, Tom and Karen have already drained the funds they socked away for their kids' college.

"It's pretty important that Tiffany gets a scholarship," says Tom.

"It's too bad she's not Indian," says Karen. "Then she'd have access to tribal and federal grants for college that white people can't get. To be honest, I don't think it's fair. I just think it should be equal."

The Hopfaufs have definitely worked for what they have. For the past ten years, Tom has had a moonlighting job with the bank repossessing cars. He's been spit at, cussed, and chased off property. It doesn't deter him. He's developed his own tricks of the trade, like waiting in the parking lot of the IGA, then hauling away the car while the delinquent owner is inside buying groceries. He likes to see their faces when they come out and find their car gone. Another method is to sneak out to the parking lot during halftime of Hardin High basketball games and snatch the cars. He can usually tow it away and be back for the start of the third quarter. Most of the repossessions are from Indians.

"It irritates me when I hear them complain about how us whites broke all the treaties we ever signed, yet these same Indians don't think anything about breaking a contract with a bank," he says. "Isn't a contract a treaty? They can't have it both ways."

I store the leftover cacciatore in the refrigerator, then we adjourn to the living room. Tom notices my copy of the list comparing Indian and white values sitting atop a bookcase.

"I don't get it," he bristles. "I learned that whenever there is a war, the loser has to abide by the winner's rules. That's the way it was for the Germans after World War II. Right? So why should the Indians be any different? Why don't they have to abide by the rules?"

Karen nods. She is in the repo business, too, sort of. She manages the credit department for Montana-Dakota Utilities and is the person in charge of turning off a customer's lights for failure to pay.

"Tiffany likes to joke that her dad takes away a family's

car and then I come along and turn off their lights," she says. "She calls us Mr. and Mrs. Repo."

Prior to the tip-off of the home game against the Lodge Grass Indians, I see Sharon's father again. I don't approach him. My strategy is to wait. Maybe I'll just pop in on him at home. Or maybe I'll catch him just as he gets off his janitor job at Crow Hospital. Or maybe I'll invite him to dinner at the Chat and Chew. Or maybe have him over for some leftover cacciatore.

By Coach Mac's calculations, her team should blow Lodge Grass out of the building. But at the end of the first quarter, the score is tied. Hardin looks lazy, uninspired.

"Ladies, you're forcing shots," she fumes.

Tiffany sighs. Why does Coach Mac insist on saying "you're" forcing shots when everyone knows it's Sharon who is forcing shots? Is Coach Mac afraid of her? Tiffany can't remember Sharon ever getting chewed out.

Sharon is playing in a funk. It started against Glendive and is happening again against Lodge Grass. Forced shots. Glaring at teammates. Even at practice she seemed irritable. Why doesn't Coach Mac do something about it, like sit her on the bench, or talk to her, or yell at her? Anything would be better than just letting her black cloud roll down the court.

Just before halftime, Coach Mac bends at the waist and clutches her side, using Coach Oswald to shield her from the crowd's view.

"Are you okay?" he asks.

"Hanging in there," she replies.

From my seat right behind the bench, it looks like she needs an ambulance. Or a sabbatical.

*   *   *

231

It isn't pretty but Hardin pulls away in the second half. Coach Mac finally subs for the first team with a minute left. For the game, Sharon has shot a miserable three for 13 from the field, which coupled with her equally miserable three for 15 against Glendive, makes her a candidate for the Tom Hopfauf School of Shooting. On the positive side, her 19 rebounds are a career high and the team is back on the winning track.

In the locker room, Rhea sits dejected in the corner. For the fifth game in a row, her father isn't in the stands. Just as well. She stunk it up.

Tiffany is the bright spot, scoring a game-high 17, her steady play holding the team together. But she's not exactly lighting up the locker room with her smile either. Across from her, Sharon and Geri sit in a corner and talk in Crow. To her, it seems divisive, secretive. They should speak English.

CHAPTER TWENTY-FIVE

Driving up the dirt road to Danetta's, Sharon spots her mother's black Mercury Sable parked next to the house. She hasn't seen her since the courtside incident at Billings Senior. And she doesn't want to see her now.

Her instinct is to turn around. But she keeps going and parks her car next to the Sable.

Slowly, she enters the house. Danetta and Blaine are sitting at the dining room table, but there's no sign of Karna.

"Where's Mom?" she asks.

"Who knows?" answers Danetta.

"What's her car doing here?"

Blaine explains that they were driving past the Wagon Wheel earlier and saw the Sable parked in front. Figuring Karna was inside getting drunk, he used a key he had and drove it home. "I was doing her a favor and keeping her from killing somebody out there on the highway," he says.

"She's gonna be mad when she finds her car gone," says Sharon.

"It's not her car. We paid for it."

The next morning Blaine sits at the dining room table, drinking his morning coffee and scouring the sports page of the *Billings Gazette,* searching for any clue in the minutiae of the Eastern Montana Conference standings and statistics that he might pass on to Sharon to give her an edge. He notices that tomorrow night's opponent, Shepherd High, is on a five-game winning streak. He also notices that Sharon has slipped to third in conference scoring, her 16.5 average trailing Tiffany's 17.6 and the 18.1 of Michelle Frenzel of Glendive.

He hears a car approach. Who could this be so early? He gets up and peeks out the window. A car stops next to the Sable and a woman exits the passenger side. It takes him a second to realize it's Karna. She quickly gets in the Sable and starts the engine.

Blaine runs outside. "What the hell you think you're doing?" he yells.

Karna throws it in reverse, and with Blaine running alongside the car and pounding against her window, she peels off down the dirt road.

"Damn you, Karna!"

He turns back and gets into the Lincoln, tearing out after her. In less than a minute they are southbound on I-90, their speedometers pushing ninety.

Blaine pounds the dashboard. For years he and Danetta have done everything they could for Karna: they bought her cars, furniture, a house; they sent her to college, paid for her wedding, bailed her out of jail, raised her daughter. And all they've got in return is resentment, hostility, and drunken behavior. For her to come onto their property and hijack the car right under his nose . . . he's so mad he shakes. She has no insurance, no license.

How many times has she gone off to treatment and relapsed? How many times have they built up hope? How many times has she let them down? Let Sharon down?

She continues to speed south, passing the Lodge Grass exit, then twenty . . . thirty . . . fifty miles more, Blaine still a quarter mile behind her, no cops in sight. They cross the state line into Wyoming.

Karna reaches into her purse, pulls out a flask and takes a swig.

At Ranchester, a small town sixty-five miles from Crow Agency, she exits the freeway and stops at a park in the center of town. She's tired of the chase. Blaine pulls up right next to her.

"Get out of the car!" he orders, approaching her window.

She refuses, staying behind the wheel.

He bangs on the window, but she doesn't budge. He bangs it again, harder, and the glass fractures and spreads like a spiderweb.

"Go ahead, smash in the window!" she yells. "As long as you're at it, hit me."

It has been several years since he hit her, but not long enough for her to have forgotten. The last time was when he walked in on her and found her cutting herself. He didn't actually hit her that time—he just body-slammed her to the floor.

She starts the engine again and pulls from the curb. He steps back, and as she slowly heads back into the street, he stations himself in front of the car. She inches forward and he retreats, then suddenly leaps onto the hood and spread-eagles.

She keeps rolling forward, swerving back and forth to throw him off. But he holds on, clinging to the wiper blades. She turns a corner. "Stop!" he yells.

She slams on the brakes, and he rolls off the hood, tumbling to the pavement. As a rodeo bronc rider, he was bucked and thrown to the ground hundreds of times. But this is different. This is a concrete street, and it isn't a horse that's thrown him. It is a 300-horsepower car driven by his daughter.

As he slowly picks himself up, she floors it . . . up a hill and around a bend. He assesses the damage. Everything hurts, his arms, legs, hips. His elbows are bleeding. He hobbles back to the Lincoln.

At the edge of town, she jumps the curb and heads down an incline into a cow pasture. There is no path or trail, just alfalfa and cows. Bumping and bouncing, she navigates to the back side of a small slope, out of sight from the road. Opening her purse again, she takes another shot of whiskey, this time chasing it with a warm beer. Then she gets out of the car and crouches behind the rear fender, waiting for Blaine to drive by and fade into the distance. Cattle surround her.

She spots the Lincoln again, but instead of fading into the distance, it is parked on the side of the road across the pasture. He is scanning the field. She can see him, but he can't see her.

"What are you doing on my property?" asks a voice, startling her from behind.

She turns, face-to-face with a rancher. "See that man up there in that car?" she says. "I'm trying to get away from him. He's nuts. Is there another way out of here?"

The rancher points to a gate behind them. "Just make sure you close it," he instructs.

Slowly, she backs her car through the field to the gate, easing her way through the cattle. Blaine doesn't see her. After closing the gate behind her, she backtracks through town, then back onto I-90, heading north to Hardin. She has friends to meet at the Wagon Wheel.

Livid, Sharon storms out of Coach Mac's office, through the locker room, and out into the gym. "What's wrong with her?" asks Tiffany.

"I'm not sure," says Amy. "I talked to her this morning

and she was really pissed about Parent Appreciation Night."

"Parent Appreciation Night?"

"Her grandmother's making her take her father," explains Amy.

"I didn't know she had a father," says Tiffany.

"She hates him. I don't think she's ever talked to him."

"So why is her grandma making her take him?"

"I don't know."

Sharon grabs a ball off the rack and heads to a side basket to loosen up. She looks mad enough to kill.

Amy approaches. "What's wrong?" she asks.

Sharon glares across the gym to where Tiffany and Anita are talking. She purses her lips. "Coach Mac just told me that someone came to her and narced that somebody on the team is smoking dope," she says.

Amy contemplates her response. "Did Coach Mac accuse you of smoking dope?" she asks.

"No," answers Sharon.

"Then why'd she talk to you?"

"I don't know."

"So who do you think narced?"

Sharon looks in Tiffany's direction. "Who do you think?"

"Why would she do that?"

"'Cause she's an asshole," answers Sharon.

"I can't believe she'd do that," consoles Amy.

I'm already on *Bulldog I* when Sharon climbs aboard for the trip to Shepherd, a farming community fifteen miles northeast of Billings. I notice a big bulge in her back.

"What's that?" I ask.

She lifts the back of her shirt, revealing an electronic stimulator taped to her back. It's to relieve the spasms.

They've gotten worse. Last night she ran out of her medication, again, barely sleeping.

As the bus pulls away from the school, I lean forward and ask Coach Mac her game plan for Shepherd, a team as dangerous as Glendive. She says that she's studied the tape of their first game, the one where Hardin scored 86 and looked unbeatable, and she noticed how Shepherd liked to work the ball to the left side to Mauri Newman, their best outside shot. "We worked all week on rotating quickly in our half-court zone to force their offense to the right," she explains. "Of course doing it in practice is one thing. Let's see if we can do it in the game."

Shepherd wins the opening tap and zips the ball to the left and Mauri Newman. She hits a wide-open shot.

Hands on hips, Coach Mac takes a deep breath.

On Shepherd's second possession, they again work the ball to the left as easy as humming, and Newman hits another wide-open shot.

"Come on!" shouts Coach Mac.

Next time downcourt, Shepherd works it—you guessed it—to the left, and once more Newman hits. Coach Mac calls a timeout.

"Why do we even bother to practice?" she asks. "The game starts and you go brain dead." She substitutes DyAnna for Rhea.

On offense, Hardin struggles. Sharon misses her first four shots and looks ready to scream.

The Lady Bulldogs' dispirited play isn't the only thing stinking up the gym. Somebody has left a side door to the outside open, and the smell of cow manure from the giant feed lot next to the school floats through the gym. The door is closed, but the smell lingers.

Sharon misses her next four shots, making her zero for

eight. She finally connects on her ninth attempt, then misses three more. All are forced. Over the last ten quarters, she is shooting seven for 40 from the field, a woeful 17.5 percent.

The horn sounds ending the first half. Not only have the Lady Bulldogs been outplayed, they have been outhustled. It is a minor miracle that they only trail by one.

Head down, Sharon walks to the locker room side by side with Rhea. It's a picture of despair.

During halftime I talk with Tiffany's and Anita's parents in the lobby. "What's wrong with Sharon?" asks Karen Hopfauf.

They all look at me as if my growing connection with Sharon's family somehow gives me insight into Sharon's slump. I'm not at a loss for theories:

- Nutrition. She eats like a bird, and what she does eat is crap. Coach Oswald is sure she's losing weight.
- Bad shooting mechanics. She's releasing the ball too soon, taking her eye off the basket, not following through. It's partially the coaches' fault. Neither of them can shoot a lick. They don't know how to teach shooting technique.
- Karna. Sharon hasn't been the same since that incident at the end of the Senior game. How's this kid supposed to concentrate when she has a mom who's off-the-charts whacky and just led her grandfather on an absurd hundred-mile-an-hour chase into Wyoming?
- Lifestyle. She has no discipline off the court. No curfew, rules, or parental control. Her family loves her— that's not the issue—it's that she's basically on her own. How can she perform when she's staying out late, smoking cigarettes, blowing pot? She needs structure in her life.

- Randy. This guy has her all messed up. He's jealous, he likes to drink, and she's madly in love with him.
- Tribal pressure. Basketball is life around here. She's got everybody's hopes on her shoulders. Everywhere she goes, people are telling her how great she is and how they know she'll lead them to State. She's seventeen years old. She believes it's all up to her.
- Father. What father?
- Injuries. My God, if I had as many injuries as she does, I'd be in a cartoon graveyard. Let's see . . . she's got muscle spasms in her back, a contusion on her sternum, hematomas on her hip and thigh, a swollen ankle. Now she's walking around with a voltage regulator taped to her back. And don't forget her bum knee. She'll probably have surgery on it after the season.
- Chemistry. This team is a time bomb. Whites against Indians. Indians against whites. Sharon against Tiffany. Tiffany against Sharon. It's a wonder they can all ride on the same bus together.
- Playing time. She never comes out of the game. It's ridiculous.
- No half-court offense. Our ragtag, predawn games have better passing than the Lady Bulldogs. When her teammates do finally get her the ball, she's usually surrounded by half the conference. So she gets frustrated and forces shots.
- Family pressure. Special sweats, feasts, and clan gatherings, all to honor her. Not to mention Danetta expecting her to salvage her good name.
- Racial oppression. It surrounds her every day.
- Narc. Somebody is snitching on her behind her back.
- Holly. She was Sharon's best friend and now she's two hundred miles away. It can't be easy to lose your sidekick and soul-mate going into your senior year.

- Scholarship. It's coming at her from every angle: people telling her she needs to sign up for her SAT; she's flunking Senior Composition; her classes bore her; Tiffany has colleges writing her letters; no college coach has contacted her; Randy tells her she doesn't need college; Danetta tells her she should go to Montana State.
- State. Anything less than a trip to the state finals at Whitefish and the season is a bust.
- Herself. She's never satisfied with how she plays. She's her own worst critic. It keeps her up nights.

What could be wrong?

In the third quarter, Sharon hits her first shot, a jumper from 15 feet. Her next shot goes in, too, as does the next one. All swishes. Suddenly, she's back in the zone.

With one minute left in the third quarter and the game tied 42–42, she scores from underneath and is fouled, hitting the free throw, too. The Hardin fans, outnumbering the hometown Shepherd rooters, act like it's carnival time, leaping and dancing and war-whooping. The three massive guys in their satin tournament jackets move down to the first row and pull out their imaginary bows and fire their imaginary arrows at the Shepherd guard trying to bring the ball up against the Hardin press. They're almost close enough to tomahawk her. I have never seen eyes get that wide. She dribbles it off her Nike and out of bounds.

Coach Mac sends Rhea into the game, and Sharon hits her with a behind-the-back pass. Rhea scores on a short jumper, her first points of the night. Then she steals the ball and scores on a layin.

Thirty seconds later, just as the horn sounds, Rhea swishes a 15-footer from the key. Six points in 40 seconds. That's more points than she's scored in all but one game.

Smiling as she comes to the huddle, she is pummeled by her teammates. Even Coach Mac gives her a hug. The fans cheer. All that's missing is her father.

Hardin wins the game 71–61, holding on to their conference lead and upping their record to 11-2. The black cloud and the stench from the cow manure that followed them into the locker room at halftime are gone.

At the postgame meal, Stacie is in particularly fine form, placing a Burger King crown on Rhea's head.

"I present to you the lovely Princess Di," she announces. "Get it? Princess Di . . . DiaRhea."

Rhea laughs, something no one has seen in a while. On the night, her 13 points is only three less than her previous nine games. She can't wait to tell her dad.

Amy asks Stacie if she can borrow fifty cents. Stacie thrusts out her chest. "Can't you see I'm flat busted," she replies.

Even Sharon laughs, her first sign of a smile in days. She has played a great second half, scoring 16 of her game-high 18 points. Stacie eyes her half-eaten burger and fries. "Aren't you going to finish your Whopper?" she inquires.

"I'm too tired to eat," replies Sharon.

"Praise the Lord for this bounty I am about to receive," proclaims Stacie, swooping down on the Whopper and fries like a giant hawk.

CHAPTER TWENTY-SIX

No games are scheduled this week because it is Montana's annual statewide teacher convention. The Lady Bulldogs are happy for the chance to rest their various aches and wounds. Coach Mac gives them a day off from practice. They need more.

I walk down center hall and glance through the window of the counselors' offices. Sharon is sitting at a computer, staring into space. I enter.

She frowns, explaining that her counselor, Ms. Sundheim, has her writing a letter to colleges requesting admission and scholarship forms. So far, all she's got is her name and address.

My first impulse, as it was with my own daughters' schoolwork, is to offer a helping hand. I resist. I suppose my inclination to help Sharon comes from my growing personal experience that when it comes to Indians and college, there's no track record of success. Part of the reason is the application process. It's intimidating. Indians have experience filling out applications, but it's for welfare or food stamps, not to get ahead; they know there are deadlines, like for signing up to take the SAT, but they miss them; they hear about the importance of getting good grades and taking honors classes, but nobody pushes them.

A few nights earlier, Little Big Horn College sponsored a college financial aid workshop for Native American students at Hardin High. Nobody showed up.

It's not just the application process. There's no family support system for education. Families, including Sharon's, can somehow make plans and save money for powwows and Crow Fair and a pickup, but not for a college education. They seem incapable of the it's-going-to-cost-me-$20,000-to-send-my-kid-to-Montana-State kind of planning. With a $3,100 average yearly income, why bother?

"Have you signed up for the SAT?" I ask, offering a little nudge.

She looks at me as if I've just told her to go double dribble.

"What about Little Big Horn College?" I ask. "Have you thought about going there?"

She shakes her head. "There's no basketball program," she says. "Besides, my grandma wants me to go to a four-year college."

I back off. It's disheartening to realize how confining her choices are. She has received scant instruction in career opportunities and has encountered people only in a few professions—health care providers, teachers, welfare workers, service providers. She has no exposure to the worlds of business, engineering, science. Math is her best subject, but nobody has explained potential careers in that field. She has a vague notion about accounting, but no real clue what is required.

I say goodbye. When I pass by the room a couple minutes later, she's gone and the computer is turned off.

I've come to visit Little Big Horn College, a two-year accredited community college in Crow Agency and the biggest success story on the rez. It's a school that started in an abandoned trailer and now has an enrollment of three hundred. I'm anxious to meet the college's president, Janine Pease Windy Boy. She's infamous in Big Horn County, her supporters claiming she's the Joan of Arc of the rez, a savior, her critics sure she's the devil. Everyone agrees, however, that she is very good-looking.

I don't have an appointment. I've learned that making appointments with Crows is like scheduling a tumbleweed. They may show up or they may not. My plan is to just pop in on Ms. Windy Boy.

The campus, such as it is, is a hodgepodge of rusty trailers and run-down buildings that once housed Crow Tribal Housing. The exterior is painted a powder blue that clashes with the dead brown grass surrounding the place. Frankly, the place is an aesthetic pinkeye.

Entering the main building, visitors are greeted by a huge sign on the wall: "With education we are the white man's equal; without it we are his victim."

Windy Boy is not there. "When will she be back?" I ask a woman in an office next to hers.

"Oh, let's see, um, maybe . . . you know, hmmm, I'm not sure."

"Is it okay if I just wander around?"

"Suit yourself."

I mosey down a hall and peek in a classroom. It's a converted shower room. Several students are sitting at computers, diligently working. I move to the cafeteria/commons, which was once a gymnasium. I assume it's the cafeteria because of the vending machines lining the wall. A handful of students study at picnic-size tables, unfazed by a four-year-old darting in and out of the tables, screeching as he goes.

I'm noticing a pattern. Kids on the rez seem to run wild. At Lady Bulldogs games, Sharon's four-year-old cousin charges up and down the bleacher stairs as if he's running wind sprints. Nobody seems to care; nobody tries to mellow him out. Maybe it's just too much candy.

I sit down and try to soak up the academic ambiance. My table is littered with empty pop cans and candy wrappers. At the next table, a young woman is rattling her box of Mike & Ikes, trying to shake loose the candy at the bottom of the box. The noise is distracting, but evidently, only to me. Everyone else seems to be focused, earnestly reading and writing.

The woman shakes loose the last of her Mike & Ikes and goes to the vending machine to buy a box of Good & Plenty. I continue to explore.

I've come to the college a little desperate, hoping to secure, or at least check out, some good future for Sharon, a future that, among other things, does not include her turning into her mother, Karna.

For I can see a bad end to this. I'll finish my book about a season on the brink with the Lady Bulldogs, go back to Portland, and then what will become of this girl?

I've spent a chunk of my life around athletics, having whiled away many an hour with professional athletes, including members of the NBA, and when I first met Sharon I thought: this girl is fabulous, she can make it in college. Yeah, she is a little short to be playing the post, but Spud Webb wasn't exactly a tree-topper.

Now, three months after arriving, I have fewer illusions. Now I am afraid no matter how far she takes her team, Sharon is doomed. In any suburb, a young woman with her talent, nice looks, and intelligence is destined for college and yuppiehood. At the very least she'll end up married to some Generation X lawyer and wind up a Suburban-driving soccer mom.

Now I figure, at the very least, Sharon might wind up

with a steady job at Burger King. That is if they open up a franchise in Hardin. In any other American town, she would have already had scholarship offers. But not in this one. Plain and simple, the cowboys who run Montana colleges don't like Indians. And it doesn't help that Sharon is a so-so student and hasn't even signed up for her SATs.

So what to do? It's hard not to feel responsible. Not only because I care for her, but because I, the lone city slicker in her world, know there is a better life out there for her if she can just go after it, not a life that rejects her own culture, but one that works in concert with it.

It has occurred to me that perhaps I can look out for her after she graduates. Maybe she can go to Portland State. On the West Coast, Sharon would not face even remotely the prejudice she faces here. She would be just another slender, dark, pretty face. But she would also be a fish out of water, likely to become part of the staggering 98 percent of Indians who don't get by the first two months in college. Or she'll fall in with whatever proverbial "wrong crowd" she runs into first. And I am in no position to be her father—even if she wanted me to be, which she doesn't. So here I am.

I head back to Windy Boy's office. She's still not there. I browse a brochure. Maybe Little Big Horn College, despite its not having a basketball program or a pretty campus, is Sharon's best hope for the future. It has some positive things for Sharon to hook up with, such as a learning environment created to prevent the culture shock experienced by Indians when they try to leave the reservation for college. It's a school run by Indians for Indians.

And it has some positive numbers going for it. Since its inception in the early 1980s, 25 percent of its two hundred graduates have gone on to continue their education, with twelve having already earned a four-year degree and twenty more working toward one. Modest numbers, perhaps, but on a reservation with an obscene unemployment rate, 85 percent of its members on welfare, and a per capita income less than what Grant Hill gets paid per dribble, it is a dramatic improvement.

Despite the school's pluses, I still share Danetta's dream of Sharon going to a four-year college, even if Little Big Horn College is a more realistic choice.

In the college library, I say hello to Carson Walks Over Ice, the assistant librarian. He's a regular at the Lady Bulldogs' games and we've talked on several occasions. A Vietnam vet wounded twice in combat with the Purple Hearts to prove it, he is one of the few Crows in the twentieth century to have *counted coup,* actually touching an enemy in battle. He took out nearly a whole enemy platoon with a machine gun. As a souvenir, he has two braided Vietcong scalps hanging from a coup stick in his living room.

He's an amiable, jovial man, but on this day, he's subdued, worried. A crisis confronts the college. A resolution to remove Windy Boy as the school's president has been filed by Frederick Lefthand, an economics teacher she recently fired. In two days the resolution will be voted on by the Tribal Council, which is to say all registered members of the tribe. Lefthand has the support of tribal chairman Clara Nomee.

"That means he's got the votes," says Walks Over Ice.

Lefthand's crusade to oust Windy Boy will not only strip her of her job, it will close down the school. Federal guidelines prohibit getting rid of a college president by a political vote, the penalty being the loss of accreditation. Windy Boy and her supporters maintain Lefthand's firing was justifiable, with documentation to prove her case. His retaliation, they say, is born out of jealousy and resentment, a Crow man angry at being a subordinate to a woman. Despite the potential consequences to the school, he and Nomee are insisting on taking the case to the tribe. If they win, the college not only will cease to exist, but with it will go the best chance most of the kids on the reservation have of ever continuing their education, including Sharon.

Talking to Walks Over Ice, I feel a tap on my shoulder. I turn around and my jaw surely drops. It's Janine Windy Boy and she is even more beautiful than I'd been led to believe, a willowy six feet, with long dark hair braided in two pigtails that hang almost to her waist. She is dressed in an ankle-length navy blue skirt, white blouse, multicolored shawl, and lots of silver and turquoise jewelry. Her teeth are straight and white, her dimples huge. She offers a firm handshake and friendly greeting, her voice soft and smooth.

"I only have a few minutes," she apologizes. "As you might have heard, we've got a little crisis on our hands."

We go to her cramped boxcar of an office. Her desk is a mess. She sits down, then stands up, then sits down again. "I'm sorry," she says. "I've got a lot on my mind right now. Everything I've worked for with this school is on the line."

Behind her, a picture of her and Desmond Tutu adorns the wall. On another wall hangs an architect's rendering of the modern campus and facilities that Clara Nomee and the tribal government voted down. She keeps it on the wall as a reminder of what could be.

She quickly tells about the school, a speech she's obviously made hundreds of times. When she initially created the concept for the school, she wanted it to be a place that not only empowered Indians and prepared them for the workplace, but a school that actively attempted to achieve cultural preservation and protection with courses in Crow culture, history, and language.

In 1980, armed only with the belief that Crows have the ability to be successful, she forged a team of volunteers and together they turned an abandoned, dilapidated gymnasium into a learning center. They scrounged the dump for secondhand furniture and brought rocks from the Little Big Horn River to weight down a roof that threatened to lift off its moorings and fly away.

In the first year, fifty-nine students came, most of them women, most of them battered and abused and trying to get by on welfare. In the winter when the pipes burst and the building flooded, they put the files up on stilts and studied in the middle of the flood. When the tribe refused to give the school money, she wrote grants and squeaked by on donations. She and her staff worked for peanuts. When the feds cut back on funding, she took a part-time job working for a Hardin attorney and bought the school's toilet paper herself. But the college survived, eventually growing to three hundred students, becoming the first truly independent institution on the reservation. Her ability to succeed beyond the control of the tribal government gained the school outside recognition and more support. But it came with a price—Crow jealousy. Many in the tribe, including Madam Chairman, as Nomee prefers to be called, were threatened by her power and notoriety. They resented that she didn't grow up on the reservation, that she was educated, that she was a half-breed. Nationally, however, she was honored and respected: Indian Educator of the Year; four honorary doctorates; an offer to move to Washington, D.C., and join the Clinton administration. Once, Senator Claiborne Pell of Rhode Island walked across a crowded room just to tell her she had an "aura." Her efforts were compared to those of blacks who created culturally sensitive learning centers like Tuskegee and

Howard, institutions that were crucial in creating the black educated middle class.

She has little patience for the whites in Hardin, most who detest her. "The white people around here are outdated and outmoded, a bunch of cranky, unfriendly, immigrant bigots," she says. "They're in a defensive stand, crowded against a hill, doing the Custer thing. It pisses them off just to see Crows. We're a constant reminder that they don't have all the land.

"Our values aren't on common ground. We have never shared a common plane, and we never will. They are morally, legally, and ethically wrong. They treat Indians like shit, constantly making us walk the gauntlet. There's nothing subtle about it. It's overt, and it's unacceptable."

After my visit to the college, Danetta calls and invites me for a dinner and a sweat. I wonder if this will be, as Ron Johnson warned, when she hits me up for cash.

I survive the sweat. In fact, I improve my performance, entering the lodge clockwise like I'm supposed to and keeping my head off of other people's butts. I even manage to sit up longer than one of the Indians. When Blaine opens the flap after the last round, I crawl out, feeling proud, refreshed.

It's dusk and as I head for the house, I see Sharon lazily flipping up shots at the netless rim next to the abandoned house trailer. Since my last visit, a chunk of the plywood backboard has broken off, making bank shots from the right side a thing of the past. I ease over and join her.

We trade shots, nothing fancy, just little flips and hooks. Behind us the sun disappears over the horizon and an easy darkness moves in, but it's still light enough for lazy shooting. She spins in a lefthanded flip and I match it. There's a calm between us that says let's don't play H-O-R-S-E, let's just keep it nice and quiet.

As we continue to shoot, I am reminded of the countless days that my father and I stood on our front lawn, tossing a ball between us, saying nothing, just connecting on some deeper level. Handing her the ball for another shot, there's a feeling of—how can I put this without sounding cheesy?—something ethereal happening. The dusk, the crickets, the calm.

Maybe it's that I just came out of a sweat with her beloved grandpa, or maybe it's that I've been around long enough now that she feels comfortable with me. Whatever it is, the gap between us is closing—the ice cream sundae, the peek at her hip bruise, the family feasts, our sit-down interviews—I'm no longer the stranger.

Finally, I break the silence. "So how's it going, Sharon?"

"Same ol', same ol'," she answers softly.

"No, I mean, how's it *really* going?"

She holds on to the ball and studies her response, then in a voice barely audible, replies, "Hanging in there."

She shoots and makes it, and I feed her the ball again. She connects again, then a third and fourth time in a row. I feed her once more, but this time I walk behind her, and as she shoots again, I reach over her shoulder and block it.

She turns and I grin like Dennis Rodman.

"You're like a teasing cousin," she says.

Yes! Of all the wonderful experiences I've had since arriving in Big Horn County—the sweats, the overtime victories, Crow Fair—this is the tops. I've been honored. In Crow culture, a teasing cousin holds a special place of esteem. It is the role of the teasing cousin to use jokes and subtle put-downs to remind the other person of the need for humility. The teasing cousin is always treated with kindness and respect.

My instinct is to reach out and give her a giant hug that

tells her I truly care. But of course I don't. We just keep flipping up shots, wearing out the rim.

After dinner, Sharon and her grandfather sit on the couch, talking basketball while Danetta and I sit at the dining room table discussing Clara Nomee. Their conversation is low and quiet, ours is not.

There is an easy comfort between Sharon and Blaine. He is the calm in her life, his laconic manner a sedative to the howling chaos surrounding her. With others, she often listens with one ear; with Blaine, she is tuned in, relaxed. It isn't a spill-your-guts relationship—Blaine doesn't even know Randy exists, let alone that she has an implant.

"We gotta figure out a way to get that Tiffany girl to pass the ball more often," he says.

She nods, then excuses herself to go to the bathroom, moving stiffly, limping. She is a wreck. Contusions. Hematomas. Spasms. Sprains. Twenty years down the line, will she be able to get out of bed without grimacing? Will the gains of Title IX be measured for her in crutches and painkillers? It doesn't take four years of med school to know she needs a rest.

Danetta pours me a cup of Instant Folgers. "Clara Nomee is a liar and a cheat," she says.

"Then how'd she get elected?"

"Her support comes from the uneducated and unscrupulous, people with no moral fiber," claims Danetta. "When you go interview her, ask her about the stuffed ballot box in the last election. Ask her what happened to the $5 million that has disappeared from tribal funds."

"I take it you're not a big fan."

"Let's put it this way. When I saw a photo of her ugly face standing next to Bill Clinton when he came campaigning in Billings against George Bush, I switched my vote to Bush."

Prior to attending the Tribal Council meeting that will determine the fate of Little Big Horn College and Janine Windy Boy, I inquire around Hardin about her character. "She's a militant," says Hardin mayor Joe Koebbe. "A real troublemaker, one of them half-breeds that's never happy less'n she's stirring things up."

Windy Boy started stirring things up back in the 1980s and it seems the local whites have never forgiven her. At the time she was struggling to get Little Big Horn College off the ground, as well as serving as the chair of the Big Horn County Democratic Central Committee. She began examining some assembled facts about the county: no Indian had ever been elected to any office despite being 48 percent of the population; only one of the 250 county jobs was held by a Crow; Indian unemployment was twelve times higher than that of whites. It was clear, at least to her, that the county government was diluting the Indian vote by maintaining an illegal pattern of harassment and intimidation of Indian voters. With the help of the ACLU, she filed a landmark suit in U.S. District Court in Billings (*Windy Boy v. Big Horn County*). She charged the county commissioners and the school board with violating the 1965 Voting Rights Act, the first time a case under that law had been brought on behalf of American Indians.

"She was determined to make a mountain out of a molehill," says Mayor Koebbe.

To win the case, she had to prove a consistent pattern of racism in the county. It took two years to bring the case to trial, but when it finally opened, she and two other plaintiffs had two hundred people ready to testify. It was a litany of abuse: segregated rest rooms in the County Courthouse;

a teacher at the high school who'd never given an Indian student higher than a C in thirty years; ambulance drivers picking up a white accident victim but leaving an Indian to bleed on the side of the road.

"Those were isolated cases," says the mayor.

She received death threats and was investigated by the FBI. The editor of the *Big Horn County News* called her a "sugarcoated devil." When the case finally went to trial in the spring of 1985, it was assigned to Los Angeles District Judge Edward Rafeedie, a Reagan appointee. Windy Boy took one look at him and figured she didn't have a chance. She was wrong. After hearing the testimony of witness after witness, he found Big Horn County guilty of "official acts of discrimination that have interfered with the rights of Indian citizens to register to vote." He ordered the county to pay ACLU's legal expenses of over $500,000, and directed the county to be divided into three large voting districts, which would give Indians a fair chance at representation on the school board and the county commission, as well as hiring, jobs, and services. And most importantly, a voice in the all-important issue of land control.

"Windy Boy's mother is white and well educated and her father was a teacher," says Jean Koebbe, the mayor's wife. "That's what makes her so dangerous. She can use the white side of her brain."

It's the eve of the Tribal Council showdown on the resolution to terminate Windy Boy. At stake is nothing less than the educational hopes of the tribe's young people. Not to mention Windy Boy's future. On a reservation with so few female role models, to lose someone of her prominence would seem a certain setback.

I have an appointment to see Clara Nomee. As I wait in her outer office, forty-five minutes past our scheduled time,

I simmer. Finally, I am ushered into her office. It is big and cavernous. On the wall hangs the photo of her and President Clinton. Nomee is short and plump, with jowly cheeks, tightly permed hair, narrow eyes, and thick glasses. She lights a cigarette and starts by telling me of the recent miracle healing she experienced.

"I had a growth the size of a fist on my esophagus," she explains. "But then every morning I went out behind my house up by Lodge Grass Creek and prayed to our Heavenly Father. He blessed me and the growth disappeared."

"How come you're still smoking?" I ask.

"Now I pray to Him for the help to kick the habit."

She also used to have a problem with booze, and was one of the biggest drunks in Hardin, with frequent trips to jail. Despite working for the BIA, she was constantly in debt. Everything she owned was repossessed at one time or another, her heat and lights regularly turned off, her friends always having to bail her out.

"Then I found Jesus and all glory goes to Him," she exudes.

She denies the accusation that she was elected by voter fraud, pointing out that all efforts to prove it failed. "God knows I didn't cheat," she says, "and He knows the love I have for my people, and that I give all praise to Him."

But what about the missing funds? Not only were there accusations of vote tampering, but she's been accused of having large sums of tribal money disappear under her watch. The tribe's reserve balance has dropped by $6.5 million during her first term.

"That money has gone to pay off the debts of the corrupt administration that preceded me and to create jobs," she says. "The accusations against me come from people who are jealous of my power. But I don't answer to them. I answer to Him."

There's also the question of how it is that her administration has spent millions awarded the tribe in a coal severance tax case and has little to show for it in terms of economic development or long-range investment beyond plans to build a casino.

"Since I took office we have seven hundred new jobs for tribal members," she asserts.

Seven hundred? Strange, but I don't see a lot of people getting up and going to work every morning. And here at tribal headquarters there are lots of people milling around, smoking cigarettes, doing very little. But I might be wrong.

"I am the education chairman," she proclaims.

If that's true, then how come her submitted tribal budget of $7.5 million allocates only $200,000 for education, none of it to Little Big Horn College? What good does it do for her to give $100 to every Crow that gets his/her high school diploma? Wouldn't that money be better spent giving full scholarships to a handful of deserving students with high potential. Like Sharon LaForge?

"Young people like Sharon are the reason I serve my people . . . to insure an honest tribal government for the future."

What about the charge that she's a snitch for the BIA, the agency that has historically set Indians up to fail if not openly rip them off?

"I am proud to call myself a 'government informant,'" she says.

At the main entrance to Hoops Memorial Hall in Crow Agency, the site of the council meeting, I join a congregation of angry reporters from eastern Montana newspapers and Billings's TV stations. In front of the doors, three menacing BIA policemen stand with arms folded across their big chests, blocking our entry. Stationed between them, like George Wallace at the college entrance, Madam Chairman shakes her finger at a reporter, telling him again that the meeting is closed to the press. It's the first time the media has ever been barred.

"What have you got to hide?" asks the reporter.

"We're discussing private tribal business," Nomee explains.

As the reporter reminds her of the freedom of the press and that these tribal forums are constitutionally mandated to be open, I feel a tug on my arm. It's Carson Walks Over Ice. He motions me to follow him.

I slip away from the pack of reporters. Out of view, he hands me a big black cowboy hat and instructs me to pull it low over my eyes to hide my face. "I'll sneak you in a side door," he whispers. "You can sit with me in the back. Nobody will know you're here."

I don't question him, I just pull the hat low and turn up my jacket collar, then follow him inside. It's a dimly lit, wooden, octagonal hall, with horseshoe-shaped bleachers and a thick, choking cloud of cigarette smoke.

Through a crack in the door I see the media guys get in their vans and drive away. So now it's just me and six hundred Indians. I stay tight to the side of Walks Over Ice.

Traditionally, supporters of the administration sit in the bleachers on the south side, while the opposition sits on the north. On this day, the south side bleachers are filled, most of the people employees of the tribe hired by the Nomee administration; the north side is sparse.

"Doesn't look good," forecasts Walks Over Ice.

We take our seats high up in the bleachers of the north side. I've got my eye on those three BIA behemoths. I hunch forward, pulling the cowboy hat even lower over my face.

Standing at the podium, Nomee waits for the late arrivals to get settled. Behind her, Marla Fritzler, a north sider, angrily brushes past her and commandeers the microphone. "This is a dictatorship!" she shouts. "Nomee must go!"

Below me, Danetta shouts her approval.

The BIA policemen swoop in and forcefully escort Fritzler away from the podium. Nomee grabs back the microphone, chastising her opponents for questioning her honesty.

"Thief!" someone yells.

The meeting hasn't even been gaveled to order and I smell a brawl brewing.

Somehow, order is maintained and Nomee leads the council into the agenda items. The first three items drag by. It's hard for me to concentrate, those three big guys patrolling the vicinity.

In the front row, Windy Boy sits tall and straight, her hands folded calmly in her lap, her fate about to go on trial. She gets up briefly to confer with a supporter, then sits back down. Her boyfriend, John Pretty On Top, stands twenty feet away, scanning the crowd like a Secret Service agent. He and Windy Boy have agreed that he will watch her backside. Yesterday, two large women confronted her at a children's play, bumping her, threatening her. For safety's sake, she sent her two children to stay with her parents in Billings.

I'm having trouble keeping my eyes off of Pretty On Top. He's a legend on the rez . . . an infamous legend. A tattooed ex-marine and a veteran barroom fighter with the knife scars to prove it, he's been married seven times, and by his own admission, less than a gentleman to several of those wives. The rumor is that he regularly flies into jealous rages every time Windy Boy even glances at another man. This contradicts his role as a spiritual leader of the tribe, a medicine man, and a Sun Dance leader.

I don't get it. Here is a woman, Windy Boy, who wins battles against all odds, a woman who is beautiful, educated, compassionate, endlessly capable, a woman who wins a $250,000 MacArthur "Genius" Grant (that goes unreported in the local papers), a woman who, by any logical definition, should be termed a "great American," and a woman who has a jealous lout for a boyfriend.

This is hard to believe. I try again to get it straight in my mind. Windy Boy builds a college out of nothing, is gorgeous, gets complimented on her aura by a powerful senator, and is in love with a possessive bully, a guy who's a seven-time loser at the altar. Like I said, I don't get it.

"You have to understand Crow politics," says Walks Over Ice. "Those people over there on that side are a bunch of sheep. They do whatever Nomee tells them. The vote won't even be close."

It's time for the resolution. Nomee reads the list of complaints against Windy Boy: no audit reports, increased tuition fees, no election for new trustees, failure to adhere to provisions of the faculty handbook.

"Before we hear from the involved parties," says Nomee, "I need to announce that yesterday President Windy Boy rejected a compromise offer to reinstate Mr. Lefthand to her staff. If she would have accepted, Mr. Lefthand would have withdrawn the resolution."

Wearing Wrangler jeans, black leather coat, and matching hat, Lefthand addresses the audience, his voice echoing through the round hall. A slender man with a thin mustache and delicate features, he doesn't look at Windy Boy. Unaccustomed to speaking in front of such a large group, he seems nervous, but he speaks forcefully. There is no applause, just rapt attention.

It's Windy Boy's turn at the podium. She has spoken

publicly hundreds of times, but never with so much at stake. She is relaxed, voice smooth, hands gesturing gently.

"This isn't about me," she says. "I have other options. This is about the students, the ones that are going here now, and the ones that will go here in the future. If I am fired, the school will lose its accreditation. That means that not only will the school have to close, but all of the credits that students have worked so hard to earn will be useless, nontransferable to any other college."

She concludes her speech and there is an unexpected burst of applause. Then she returns to her seat, Pretty On Top standing nearby.

Lefthand returns to the podium, and where he was strong before, now his voice is weak, defensive. He repeats yesterday's compromise offer. Windy Boy signals Nomee that she's not interested and is ready for the vote. At this point, it seems inconceivable that the dirty little world of Crow politics could be so misguided that it would kill the best thing on the rez, but Walks Over Ice is still predicting defeat.

It is an oral vote. First comes the call for those in favor of firing Windy Boy. The hall falls eerily silent. Nothing. Walks Over Ice looks baffled.

"All those opposed to the resolution," instructs Nomee.

The hall erupts—north side, south side—a crescendo of nays rattling the boards.

"The resolution to terminate Windy Boy has failed," announces Nomee.

Walks Over Ice is in disbelief. So is Windy Boy. Once again I don't get it. Why is this such a shock? It seems a simple triumph of reason. Then again, Crow politics aren't about reason.

In any case, for Sharon and other young Crows, an option for the future survives.

CHAPTER TWENTY-SEVEN

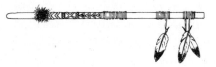

With less than a minute to play at home against Laurel, the worst team in the league, reserve guard Christina Chavez head-fakes her defender into Idaho, then shovels a pass to Stacie for an easy score. On the bench, Sharon laughs. She is sandwiched between Tiffany and Anita, also laughing.

There's reason for mirth. The Lady Bulldogs are cruising to their easiest win of the season, 71–37, a victory so lopsided that Coach Mac has seen fit to rest her three stars the entire fourth quarter, a first in their varsity careers. For the game, Sharon has 19 points and 11 rebounds. Tiffany has 18 points, Anita 11. Their conference lead over Glendive and Colstrip is back up to two games.

Watching sophomores Christina and Stacie dominate play, I wonder again why they don't start. Is Coach Mac blind? Can't she see that these two athletes are clearly more talented than Owena and Rhea? After the game, I ask her to explain.

"Stacie and Christina aren't emotionally mature enough yet," she says. "They still need more experience on the junior varsity."

Emotional maturity? If that were a prerequisite for playing time, there wouldn't be an NBA. And how is it that

Owena, a girl who keeps a teddy bear under the bench during games, is somehow "emotionally mature" enough? If she's a better athlete than Christina or Stacie, I'm Nolan Ryan.

And if Coach Mac is concerned about the seniors revolting if she promotes the sophomores, I say let 'em go. Stacie can outrebound all three of them with lead weights on her ankles.

Coach Mac settles in for a relaxing day at home. No washing uniforms. No watching game tapes. No correcting tests from Health class. Just her and her mutt, Spice, home alone, kicking back. She hopes a day of doing nothing will loosen the knot that is her stomach. The easy win over Laurel helps.

She hears a knock at the door. With Spice yapping, she opens it, surprised to find a short, plump Crow woman standing on her porch. At first, she doesn't recognize her, then realizes it's Lois Chavez, Christina's mom. Mrs. Chavez, a cook at Pretty Eagle School, is smashed, the smell of alcohol blasting Coach Mac.

Her first thought is to tell this woman to go home and sober up. She notices the black eye and deep bruise on her neck.

Before she can speak, Mrs. Chavez brushes past her into the living room, obviously agitated. "How come Christina doesn't play more?" she demands.

Coach Mac takes a deep breath. Where in her coaching manual does it provide instructions for dealing with a drunk parent invading her house and questioning her decisions? Patiently, she tries to explain.

"I'm bringing Christina along slowly," she says. "I want to give her a lot of playing time on the junior varsity so she'll be ready to step up for the playoffs. Remember, she's just a sophomore."

"Owena's just a sophomore," says Mrs. Chavez. "How come she gets to play?"

Coach Mac explains that Owena and Christina play different positions, and Christina has Tiffany and Anita in front of her.

"You're afraid of Owena's family, aren't you?" Mrs. Chavez asserts.

"No."

Coach Mac knows that there's bad blood between the Chavez and Spotted Horse families. It's a feud dating back to when Owena and Christina were teammates on the sixth grade basketball team at Pretty Eagle School in St. Xavier and Owena's aunt coached the team and gave favored treatment to her niece. Coach Mac also knows that Christina's life is troubled . . . she just doesn't know the details.

In June, Christina's drinking got so out of control that she was sent to Thunderchild in Sheridan, the same alcohol recovery program Karna attended. It didn't help. In August, she got picked up for minor in possession at Crow Fair and spent seventeen hours in the Crow jail, missing the opening day of practice. In school, she and her twin sister, Marilyn, have a reputation as two of the school's biggest party girls. She's flunking Algebra, barely passing three other classes, and is close to being ineligible. Then there's her family. Both parents are severe alcoholics, fighting and hitting a way of life in the Chavez household.

"You don't like my daughter, do you?" accuses Mrs. Chavez.

"Not true," replies Coach Mac.

"Then why don't you play her? Is it because we're poor?"

Coach Mac stares, dumbstruck. In all her years in education, this is the most preposterous statement she's ever heard. If she didn't play kids because they were poor, she'd never have a team.

She starts to speak, but stops, knowing that there's no hope for reasonable dialogue. She wants this woman out of her house. But what if Mrs. Chavez doesn't want to leave? What if she wants to fight?

Cautiously, she herds her toward the door. "I appreciate you stopping by and sharing your thoughts," she says.

Mrs. Chavez stops and waggles a finger in Coach Mac's face.

Coach Mac takes a step back, ready for anything.

"If you know what's good for that team of yours," slurs Mrs. Chavez, "then you better start playing Christina."

Then she turns and stumbles down the steps to her car.

"I'm not going out there with him," Sharon insists.

"Yes you are!" counters Aunt Marlene. "It'll be fine."

They are standing in the lobby outside the gym a few minutes before the start of the pregame ceremony for Parent Appreciation Night . . . and Sharon isn't happy. This is the maddest I've seen her.

Who could blame her. She's been told—by Danetta—that it will be Aunt Marlene and her father who escort her to center court. Her father? How can that be? The guy's never been there for her, never, and now he gets to walk with her on Parent Appreciation Night?

"I hope he don't show," she mutters.

"He'll be here," says Marlene. "I talked to him this afternoon and he said he would."

Sharon paces, jaw clenched. She is wearing tight-fitting fuchsia jeans and a matching western shirt. She even has on lipstick. Still, this makes absolutely no sense to her. Other than his last name, he has contributed nothing to her childhood. Not even remotely. It makes no difference to her that the father-daughter relationship in Crow culture has historically been remote. Theirs has been nonexistent. And now he's supposed to be the person on her arm on Parent Appreciation Night. They've never even spoken. She is not impressed that he now comes to all her games.

"Why did Grandma do this?" she mumbles.

Danetta insisted on it because, in her words, "People need to know Sharon has a father." It was Marlene who called to invite him.

The other players are also waiting for the ceremony to begin. For Sharon, seeing Tiffany and Anita huddle with their moms and dads makes it all the harder. Even Rhea is smiling with her parents.

From down the hallway, Michael LaForge appears. Marlene, who has spoken to him only a couple times in the last decade, offers a kindly greeting.

"How'ya doing, Michael?" she asks.

"Nervous," he replies, his voice barely audible.

Nervous? He should be downright embarrassed, required to walk out alone in front of the packed gym and get down on his knees and offer a huge apology. What nerve for him to think this is acceptable. Can Crow men possibly be this removed from reality?

Sharon edges away from him, her eyes on the floor.

Why has Marlene allowed this to happen? She is the most grounded of the adults in the family, the most sensitive, and yet she has encouraged it. Earlier, I asked her why, and she said that she had talked to Michael, and in his own limited way, he was trying to do the right thing. "Somewhere in the back of his mind he hopes this will be a first step toward reconciliation," she said. "He wants a relationship with Sharon. He just doesn't know how to build one. But I think he deserves a chance."

To his credit, he has managed to stay sober for two years. He has a job and a home, and tells Marlene that he dreams of buying some cattle, maybe starting with forty head, and building a house on his inherited land on the eastern edge of the rez. He even says he wants Sharon to someday come and live on that land with his family. But the chances of any bank in Montana loaning money to him for this dream are about as remote as Sharon wanting to come live with him.

Marlene introduces us and we shake hands, his hand-shake even limper than when I introduced myself a couple weeks earlier. If he remembers me, he doesn't show it. Or maybe he's just preoccupied with walking out into the middle of a jam-packed gym with a daughter he's never met.

It's hard to understand Danetta's purpose in making Sharon do this. Is her view of family so askew that she thinks this will magically start father and daughter down the road to reconciliation? If so, then why didn't she invite Karna and go for the trifecta? Sharon's wishes don't seem to count in this.

Sharon moves closer to Tiffany, almost as if to say . . . can I be in your family tonight? She peeks in her father's direction. She has no intention of breaking the ice. And it's unlikely he knows how.

The PA announcer beckons the assembled players and parents to enter the gym. "Take his arm," whispers Marlene.

Sharon looks as if she'd just been instructed to dance with a viper. They are in the middle of the pack of parents and players and they are swept along, the door opening before them. With Marlene on one side holding her arm, they slowly walk into the gym, assembling with teammates under the basket. Sharon still hasn't taken his arm. They don't speak.

One by one, the players and their parents are introduced and move to center court, the parents presented with corsages and boutonnieres by Mrs. Demars, the cheerleader adviser and French teacher. The seniors are saved for last.

Sharon and her father continue not to touch, not to talk.

Finally, the two of them and Marlene are the only ones left. "Ladies and gentlemen," intones Tom Worth, the PA announcer and IGA pharmacist, "the last player is senior co-captain Sharon LaForge. She is escorted tonight by her mother, Marlene Fallsdown, and her father, Michael LaForge."

"Take his arm," Marlene whispers again.

As they slowly move forward, Sharon awkwardly hooks arms with her father, her eyes dead ahead. At center court they stop in front of Mrs. Demars, Marlene and Michael accepting their gifts. Then all three turn and retreat quickly toward the lobby, unlocking arms as they near the doors.

In the lobby, Sharon turns to the left toward the locker room. She doesn't stop to say goodbye, or thanks, or anything else. She and her father still haven't uttered a word. She disappears around the corner. The game against Billings Central starts in half an hour.

Coach Mac flings down her clipboard in disgust. "Move!" she yells. "You're just standing around."

It's the start of the fourth quarter, and unbelievably, the score is tied. Unbelievable because Hardin should be blowing Billings Central, 3-9, off the floor. Three of the Rams' starters are back in Billings, suspended for drinking, their places taken by players from the junior varsity.

Coach Mac looks toward the end of the bench. "Christina, check in," she orders, a substitution that has nothing to do with Mrs. Chavez's visit earlier, and everything to do with energy.

"You guys are dead out there," she hollers.

Christina, who hasn't been in the game yet, checks in for

Owena on the next break, and five seconds later, nearly hacks the arm off the ball-handler. The free throws are good and Central takes the lead.

Coach Mac takes a deep breath.

On Hardin's turn downcourt, Christina dribbles right up the chute, penetrating the middle, then dishes off to Sharon, who banks it in from close range. It's a simple play that hasn't happened often for the Lady Bulldogs. For all their skills at guard, neither Tiffany nor Anita are penetrators—whereas Christina plays like a bowling ball . . . she steps on the court and things start to scatter and fly.

Central inbounds the ball and Christina about hacks off the ball-handler's other arm.

Scatter and fly.

Another deep breath.

But there's now a different energy in the game, a higher pitch. Christina's presence has turned up the volume—the crowd, the Lady Bulldogs, the Central players. She scores on a layin, commits another foul, turns it over, dishes off another assist, and the crowd goes wild. But Central refuses to die. Coach Mac calls a timeout. Standing next to Sharon in the huddle, Christina is all smiles.

For her, like a lot of her teammates, basketball is the most enjoyable thing in her life, the big escape. But unlike the other girls, she didn't start playing the game because that's what her friends do—her friends are the stoners and the party people. Nor does she get much support for the sport at home, at least not from her father. He works as a coal miner at Sarpy Mine and thinks school and basketball are wastes of time. On some days, Christina saw him start his drinking before he even left for work, downing a couple beers for breakfast. Lately, the fighting between him and Christina's mom has worsened. He didn't come to Parent Appreciation Night. In fact, he never comes to the games.

With 51 seconds left, Hardin leads by only two and Central has the ball. "Watch for the three," warns Coach Mac.

Central's Mary Early drains a wide-open three, giving the Rams the lead.

For the second time in the quarter, the clipboard slams against the floor. For the sixth time in the season, Sharon, Tiffany, and Anita have played the whole game. Christina is still in there, too. So is Rhea, although for her, the euphoria of the Shepherd game is long gone. In the last two games, she has hit only three of 12 and consistently failed to rotate to the weak side on defense. In the stands, her father looks ready to disown her.

"Be patient," instructs Coach Mac. "Don't force a shot."

Usually, the Lady Bulldogs have the patience of jackrabbits, but they work the ball around the perimeter, looking as if they're strolling the promenade. The clock ticks down. Then, with 20 seconds left, Christina spots Rhea all alone under the basket and whips her the ball.

Rhea gets it just to the right of the basket—the good side of her home court—and turns to shoot. With every cowboy and Indian in the building holding their breath, the ball glides up and over the rim and down through the net. Hardin is back up by one.

Central takes the ball out of bounds, and in a moment of high anxiety fostered by deafening war whoops, the guard tosses it to Tiffany standing right in front of her. This is not a steal. It is a gift-wrapped present. Tiffany calmly takes it in for a score. Hardin leads by three.

Christina, with four fouls already, is all over the dribbler, practically inside her jersey. Flustered, the girl passes the ball across court, then turns and plows into Sharon, knocking her to the floor.

Sharon sinks the free throws and seals the victory, upping the Lady Bulldogs' record to 13-2, one win away from the conference title.

As Sharon leaves the floor, her father watches her every step, applauding, smiling. A few rows back, Mrs. Chavez also watches her daughter, and she, too, applauds and smiles.

It's been a good Parent Appreciation Night.

CHAPTER TWENTY-EIGHT

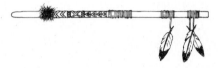

The student body files into the gym for the annual Hardin High Indian Club assembly. "What are they gonna do this year?" wonders a skeptical young cowboy. "Sit in a circle and drink Lysol?"

He is referring to a group of young Indians called the Lysol Gang, whose new trick for getting high is to soak slices of white bread in Lysol and eat them.

The students in the Indian Club gather in a far corner. They are dressed in Halloween-like costumes. Standing at the rear of the gathering is the 350-pound Miss Fry Bread. I know she's Miss Fry Bread because the beauty contestant's ribbon across her mammoth bosom tells me so. She says something to me but it's hard to understand. Her rubberized old lady mask muffles her voice.

Miss Fry Bread turns, asking a friend to adjust the pillows stuffed into her hind side. "So what are we supposed to do when we go out there?" she asks.

"Just dance and be funny," replies the friend, who looks as if he can't decide whether he's Herman Munster or Farmer John.

"This is gonna be stupid," predicts Miss Fry Bread.

She could be right. They haven't rehearsed. For that matter, there's no script or plan other than to "just dance and be funny." This lack of preparation is no surprise. Around school, the joke is that Indian Club meetings "never start on time, have no agenda, and always leave a mess." On this day, they're counting on loud music.

To many whites, the Indian Club is yet another example of the double-standard treatment for Indians, right along with All-Indian rodeos, All-Indian basketball tournaments, and All-Indian beauty pageants. Resentment toward the Indian Club, however, is minimal because the club is small, only twenty-five members, and maintains a benign presence in the school, limiting itself primarily to bake sales and raffles. Recently, members voted down a suggestion to perform a tribal dance, afraid the cowboy redneck students might try to disrupt the celebration like they did the previous year when 80 percent of the white kids refused to come to school on Native American Day. After that boycott, racial tension was heightened when somebody left racist flyers on doorsteps all over town in the middle of the night, flyers that smacked of the Ku Klux Klan. Indian students countered the white boycott by holding an all-day study-in in the gym.

I look around for Sharon. Her name is on the Indian Club roster, but she has always been ambivalent about it, rarely attending meetings. She joined not out of any cultural imperative but because her teammates DyAnna and Geri, the club president, talked her into it. For this gathering, she's nowhere in sight.

Somebody starts the music—a Bobby Brown rap—and the costumed Indian Club members sprint out from under the bleachers into the middle of the gym. Norbert Hill, the captain of the boys' team, grabs the mike and starts to twist and shout. If anybody can pull this thing off, it's him—he's the class clown, a regular Shecky Green. He instructs everybody in the gym, teachers, too, to get on their feet and start dancing.

273

For some mysterious reason—maybe it's the rap—everybody obliges. The joint is suddenly jumping. Good, clean, unrehearsed fun. Everybody, including Coach Mac, is dancing. Everybody except me. I haven't danced since my ex-wife informed me in a very serious way that I was the worst dancer she'd ever seen. I stand off to the side of the bleachers.

I am surprised to see the teachers dancing—most of them arrived at school testy from another failed negotiation session with the school board. Another song goes on and Miss Fry Bread climbs into the bleachers and pulls Tiffany and Kent out to center court. The trio dances rump to rump to rump.

"This is the way it's supposed to be," observes teacher Katy Lytle.

Pretty soon Miss Fry Bread drifts in my direction. I look the other way. She doesn't go for the fake. She grabs my hand and pulls me out onto the court, out in front of God and the student body. I am smiling, but I am wishing I'd gone to Billings to get a latte.

She starts to shake her booty, and there's a lot of booty to shake. I shake a little myself. Then she dips and twirls and does the shimmy, shimmy ko-ko-bop. I do something in return. Is that the student body I hear laughing?

I didn't know a rap song could last this long.

"Now isn't this more fun than taking a sweat?" asks Miss Fry Bread.

Whoa, wait a second. Now I get it. Miss Fry Bread is Sharon. Amazing. I've been watching her for twenty minutes and didn't have a clue. Interesting. The real Sharon, a diffident, self-conscious, walk-with-her-shoulders-hunched kind of girl, would no more get up and gyrate in front of the student body than she'd shoot free throws backward in overtime. But hidden inside a costume and a rubber mask, she's a wild woman.

I curtsy when the song mercifully ends. Then I head to Billings for a double espresso.

Sharon peeks out the curtains. Still no sign of Randy. He is late. No surprise there. What is a surprise, however, is that he is coming to her house to meet Marlene. Or so he has promised.

It has been five months since Sharon started seeing Randy, and Marlene has finally put her foot down, demanding Sharon bring him to the house. Sharon sits down, then gets up to peek out the curtains again.

This little confab isn't her idea, of course. She's already apologized to Randy for making him do it. But she owes it to Marlene. After all, it's Marlene who's providing a roof over her head and food on the table, not to mention spiritual guidance. Sharon knows she can count on her aunt—for prayers in the sweat lodge, for secrecy about the implant, for a shoulder to lean on—so letting her meet Randy is a reasonable request.

"He probably had to help his mom or something," she says.

Marlene nods. It's not that she doesn't want Sharon to have a relationship with Randy . . . it's that she knows how things work on the rez when it comes to men's attitudes about women. Abuse isn't just a *part* of life on the rez, it is a *way* of life. She's been down the road a hundred times with her husband, Evon—wait for him to show up, smell the alcohol, get knocked around. It's the pattern, and every female member of the family has been through it: Blaine hit Danetta, Evon hit her, Karna's husbands hit her. Now, Marlene worries Sharon will become part of the cycle.

Sharon's fidgeting is making her uncomfortable. "Relax, he'll get here," she says.

She feels bad for putting Sharon and Randy through this.

Parental discipline isn't the way in Crow culture, the belief being that adulthood is so hard that childhood should be protected and prolonged, and Marlene is no exception, not with her own children, not with Sharon. She's tried not to butt into Sharon's personal life. For instance, there have been times when she's wondered if Sharon is dabbling with pot, but she hasn't asked. Let Sharon find her own way . . . that's her motto.

Marlene's only real complaint with Sharon is that she plays both ends against the middle when she doesn't get her way, like last week when she wanted to go to Billings. Marlene told her no, so Sharon pleaded her case to Danetta, and Marlene was overruled.

The phone rings. "Maybe that's him," says Marlene, moving to answer it.

Sharon shakes her head. She knows that Custer will rise from the dead before Randy calls to say he's running late.

It's Danetta calling to chat. Marlene doesn't let on that's Randy's supposedly on his way. She's pledged to secrecy; Sharon will get around to telling her grandmother about Randy when the time is right. Marlene keeps the chat short, no easy feat with her mother.

Another of Marlene's concerns is that Sharon will get pregnant and drop out of school. It happened to Karna, it happened to her, and it happened to dozens of women she knows. The teen pregnancy rate on the reservation is nine times the national average.

It's worrisome to her that Sharon already talks of having her implant removed. "Randy says it's okay because he can't have children," is how Sharon explained it. But if that's true, Marlene asked, then how come he already has a child by another woman? "That woman is lying," Sharon said. "Randy told me the child isn't his." To Marlene, it all sounds fishy.

* * *

An hour late, Randy's pickup rolls to a stop in front of the house. He's been there before, but never when Marlene was around. Sharon opens the door and ushers him inside, introducing him to her aunt. She feels silly, like this is *so high school* to a guy used to dating girls he meets in bars.

To Marlene, he seems stiff, awkward, his eyes wandering the room, down at the Navajo blanket covering the couch, up to the framed portrait of John Wayne on the wall. (The Duke is the unlikely hero of Marlene's four-year-old wildcat of a son, Evon Junior, an adoration developed watching old westerns on TNT.) Sharon and Randy sit on the couch.

Marlene wastes no time. "You gotta treat Sharon with respect," she says. "Treat her in a good way. Understand?"

"Yes," he answers, his voice barely above a whisper.

"We want Sharon to finish high school and go to college," she says. "Understand?"

"Yes."

Evon Junior temporarily interrupts the conversation, zooming through the room like a hellhound, squealing and chirping. He climbs under the coffee table and up into Sharon's lap, sitting still long enough for a hug, then races into the kitchen on his next mission.

"Sharon's got a good future," Marlene continues.

"Uh, yeah," Randy answers.

There's a few more questions, mainly about Randy's mother, whom Marlene has met several times, then the inquisition, such as it is, is over.

Sharon and Randy stand to leave. "Nice meeting you," offers Marlene.

"Same here," he mumbles.

They move toward the door. "Oh, I almost forgot," Sharon says. "I'm spending the night with Amy. Cody is at an all-night peyote meeting and she wants company." She follows Randy down the steps.

Sharon is pretty sure Randy didn't pass inspection. But so what? How can Marlene or anyone else possibly understand? They just look at the bad side, his drinking, his carousing, his age, his divorce. It doesn't matter to these people that he is hardworking, good to his mother, and really only fierce on the outside.

They don't know the sweet side, the part of him she fell in love with, the gentle way he touches her hair and talks to her when they're alone. That's the part of him she loves. Of course she likes the other side, too, the outlaw, the wild rush of being chased through Lodge Grass by his ex-girlfriend, the unpredictability of not knowing if or when he'll call again, the feeling that every girl at the rodeo wants to jump his bones. He is status. He is danger. She can imagine having babies with him. He is true love.

Chapter Twenty-nine

Waiting to board the bus for the trip to Colstrip and a chance to sew up the conference title, Sharon approaches Coach Mac.

"Can I ride home with my grandparents after the game?" she asks.

Coach Mac ponders the question. Because of liability and insurance concerns, the school requires that players ride the bus to and from games unless they submit a written note from home twenty-four hours in advance. Sharon has submitted no such note.

"I suppose," answers Coach Mac.

Geri and Amy hear the exchange and scowl. They both know that Sharon's cousin is bringing her Cougar to Colstrip so she can hurry off to meet Randy at a party in Lodge Grass after the game . . . Sharon is afraid it will take too long to get home on the bus and Randy will be long gone. Geri and Amy also know that Coach Mac wouldn't give them permission.

It's clear there's a double standard on this team and has been since the first day when Sharon got away with missing practice. As the bus leaves Hardin, Geri and Amy continue to scowl.

* * *

Bulldog I rolls east over State Highway 212 on the way to Colstrip, crossing the boundary of the Northern Cheyenne Reservation, one of the poorest reservations in America. We pass the dirt road where Sharon's uncle was murdered, then on through Busby and Lame Deer, grim towns of crushing poverty and unemployment rates near 90 percent. The houses look right out of Appalachia, with yards of baked dirt. Correct that . . . the houses in Appalachia look better.

"How'd you like to be a gardener in this town?" observes Stacie.

In Lame Deer, Don Gordineer, the Lutheran minister and girls' freshman coach, tells a story of when he was refereeing a football game between Lodge Grass High and Lame Deer. It was right after the end of the Gulf War, and because the conflict didn't last as long as expected, the army decided to unload its surplus supply of powdered milk on the reservations. But the tribes couldn't give it away, so they came up with the good idea of using it to line football fields. Or at least it seemed like a good idea until they used it to line the field for the Lodge Grass vs. Lame Deer game.

"In the third quarter, it started to rain really hard," recalls Gordineer. "I looked to the other end of the field and noticed a pack of dogs had wandered onto the field. The rain had turned the chalk lines into milk, and the dogs were lapping it up. Before we could stop them, they drank the end zone."

Traveling across the Northern Cheyenne Reservation with a busful of Crows gives an uneasy sense of being deep in hostile territory. Crows and the Northern Cheyenne have always battled over land. In the beginning it was the Northern Cheyenne, along with the Sioux, that coveted the Crows' rich hunting land. That is why Crow scouts rode with Custer as he chased after the bands of Sioux and Northern Cheyenne. It was a case of the enemy of my enemy is my friend. And it is still land that they fight over, disputing the boundary the government fixed between them, the 107th Meridian. Beneath that disputed land lies enormously rich mineral deposits, mainly coal. The two tribes are suing for the rights.

Approaching Colstrip, which lies just beyond the Northern Cheyenne boundary, the countryside is bleak and straggly, remote and inhospitable.

"I'd shoot myself if I had to live out here," says Stacie. "Either that or I'd study a lot."

The bus rounds a little bend in the road, and out of nowhere appear two monstrous smokestacks. These things are huge, ten stories high, rising to the sky like giant concrete phallic symbols, each belching out plumes of ominous, ugly smoke. They are connected to a monolithic coal-fired generating plant, a dreary gray structure plopped down in the middle of some of the most desolate country in America.

"Surreal," observes Anita.

"Who's Sir Real?" asks Stacie.

We enter Colstrip, a company town built by Montana Power in the 1960s after the discovery of a large coal deposit. It has rows of company-built houses and mobile homes, with a company-built community center and even a company-built golf course.

"No, really, I mean it," presses Stacie. "Who's Sir Real?"

When the town was first built, it thrived, the population reaching seven thousand in 1980. But then the market for coal shrank and the town hit the skids. It looks it. Except for one thing: Colstrip High School.

"This is the nicest building I've ever seen," Stacie exclaims as she enters the school. "Look at this gym! I might have my wedding here."

The gym was also built by Montana Power, and is the pride of the community, a three-thousand-seat state-of-the-art facility with carpeted locker rooms, radio broadcast booth, and an overhead scoreboard with a clock that shows tenths of a second.

"I could put a DJ up there in the broadcast booth," Stacie says.

It's still twenty minutes before the start of the freshman game and the gym is already half full. "Where else do these zoids have to go?" asks Stacie.

Although it's not a do-or-die game, a victory to clinch the team's first conference championship is crucial to the team's momentum. Their four-game winning streak after the blowout loss to Glendive has pushed them back up to number three in the state, trailing only Dillon and Ronan, teams on the other side of the Continental Divide. In the pregame huddle Coach Mac reminds them of their mission.

"This is when we find out what we're all about," she says. "I want intensity."

That's not what she gets. In the first half, the Lady Bull-dogs play poorly—no patience in their half-court offense, bad shot selection, sloppy passing. After two quarters, they trail 21–16, their lowest halftime output of the season. Sharon has as many turnovers as points, four, playing as if she's thinking more about the party in Lodge Grass than the game. Tiffany isn't much better, apparently exhausted.

After chewing out the team in the locker room, an ashen Coach Mac exits a side door to the outside, hoping that a shot of fresh air will settle her down. Her breathing and heart rate are scaring her. In all her years of coaching, and all the gastric attacks, this is the worst.

As she walks out the door, I am standing close by and notice her distress. It's hard to miss. She looks as if some-body drained her blood.

I stand by the door for a moment, then follow. Outside,

I can see her across the darkened parking lot, a shadowy figure leaning against a chain link fence, slightly bent at the waist, hands on hips, trying to catch a mouthful of the cold Montana air. I want to approach and offer my help. But she sees me and waves me off, so I stay back.

In the three months I've been around her, I've come to respect her tireless energy and the concern she has for her players, even though she usually keeps that part hidden. Her strength isn't in warm and fuzzy player-coach relationships, and I suspect the barrier that she keeps between herself and her players has something to do with where she comes from, physically and emotionally. She is a woman shaped by an austere background—no father, no nurturing role model, no close friends, no soul-mate, no hobbies or recreational escapes unless she counts *Home Improvement* reruns. Earlier, on an off day, I drove two hundred miles to check out Judith Gap, her hometown, a place so small and nondescript that after I drove through it and decided I wanted another look I didn't even bother to turn around . . . I just backed up and started the trip over. On the second time through, I realized I'd seen everything the first time.

Her commitment to the job is also her downside, the side that makes her so intense that she's now gasping for air at a time when she should be back in the locker room pumping up her kids for the most important half of the season. Watching her struggle next to that chain link fence, I wish she had somebody to put an arm around her shoulder and tell her that her efforts are appreciated. I'd volunteer but she's already waved me off.

At times I have wondered if she is a coach rescued from defects by her stars. But I'm not willing to conclude that. I'm convinced she teaches the game well in practice and does a good job of matching an up-tempo, pressing, fast-break style of play with the talents of her players. But for the life of me I still can't figure out her continued refusal to substitute when her players are ready to drop, or her insistence that Christina and Stacie aren't ready for varsity competition, or her reluctance to switch to a man-to-man when the press and the zone aren't working, or her failure to encourage her players to shoot three-pointers. In the team's last 11 games, they have not attempted a single three-pointer. None. Whenever I've questioned her about any of these things, she has responded defensively, so I back off in order to maintain a good relationship and access to her team. After all, I'm covering the Hardin Lady Bulldogs, not the New York Knicks.

After another minute of watching her struggle for air, I can't stay back any longer. I approach. "Linda, you okay?" I inquire.

She shakes her head.

"What's wrong?"

She points to her heart and chest. "Everything's going too fast," she answers. "It feels like I'm having a heart attack."

She looks up. I can see tears moistening her eyes. She explains that the pain in her stomach is so sharp that she can't catch her breath.

"Let's get you to a doctor."

"After the game," she says weakly. "I'll go tomorrow."

"No, you gotta see one right now."

She straightens, trying to catch her breath, and not doing a very good job of it.

"I'm going to find a doctor," I say, turning toward the door.

She grabs my arm. "I'll be all right," she pleads. "Honest. I've had these attacks before."

"Linda, this is not something to screw around with."

"I know it," she says. "But I'll see a doctor tomorrow, I promise."

"No, we're going right now."

She looks at me hard, her eyes telling me to back off. Although we're standing two feet apart, she looks so alone.

I feel suddenly awkward. We're standing in the darkness outside the fanciest gym in the ugliest town in America, and I don't know what to say or do next. It's just her and me. What if I let her go back inside and she collapses on the sideline?

I know the right thing to do. But her eyes and words are telling me no.

I let her go back inside.

Returning to the court, her path falls in step behind Sharon. She reaches ahead and tugs her co-captain's jersey, pulling Sharon back toward her. Sharon turns, surprised to see her coach reaching out to hug her. Hugs have never been part of their relationship. Awkwardly, they embrace.

"Lead the way, Sharon," she whispers.

The team huddles before taking the floor again. "It's time to suck it up," she advises.

If sucking it up can be taught, then she's certainly teaching it. Or she would be if the players knew her condition. They don't.

As the third quarter unfolds, I keep one eye on her, one on the game.

Hardin continues to struggle, falling behind by eight. She puts Christina in for Owena, hoping for a spark. It's only her second substitution.

Christina is a mosquito, instantly bothering the opposition. She steals a pass and hits Tiffany for a layin; she drives the lane and dishes off to Sharon for a score; she steals another pass and pushes the ball upcourt to Anita for a bucket.

At the end of the quarter, Hardin trails by only two . . . and Coach Mac is still hanging in there.

The fourth quarter starts with Christina back on the bench. Christina played three quarters in the JV game so she's done for the night; Stacie played four quarters with the JV so she's in her street clothes. Sharon, Tiffany, Anita, and Rhea have played the whole game.

In the fourth quarter, the lead flip-flops, but with 2:02 to play, Hardin is up by four and has the ball. "Don't shoot!" yells Coach Mac. "Make them foul!"

How many times has she offered this plea during the year and then watched it go unheeded? It seems like every game.

Trapped with the ball in the key, Sharon lobs an ill-advised pass to Tiffany. It is intercepted, her seventh turnover of the night, a season high. Colstrip scores, cutting the margin to two.

"Time out!" orders Coach Mac.

In the huddle, she strains to be heard. The noise is deafening. "I can't hear, I can't hear," she shouts, motioning the players toward center court. The Colstrip crowd takes the cue and stomps and yells even louder.

As the team moves back to the sideline, Tiffany looks to be on empty. In the last 10 minutes, she has taken only one shot. She leans against Sharon and tries to catch her breath.

"Only layups," Coach Mac instructs.

While the players return to the court, I catch Coach Mac's eye from my seat behind the bench. "You okay?" I mouth.

She nods yes. I don't believe her, but at least she looks better than she did at halftime, which is to say, she hasn't died.

"Remember, only layups," she repeats.

It takes 20 seconds for Sharon to launch an off-balance

12-footer. It misses and Colstrip takes it the other way and scores. Game tied. Fifty-eight seconds left.

Is this the seventh or eighth game that's come down to the last minute? I can't remember. I feel drained. It's been hard enough watching these Cardiac Kids all season, but to now feel as if I'm a heart surgeon keeping an eye on my transplant patient is way more than I bargained for when I started this project.

Sharon is fouled and hits a free throw, then Rhea takes a charge and is also fouled. Despite the noise, she hits both free throws, giving her 10 points for the night and Hardin a three-point lead with 40 seconds left.

"Don't let them shoot the three!" shouts Coach Mac.

And how many times has she shouted this warning in the waning seconds? By my count, it's the fourth time, and on all of the previous occasions, the other team's best shooter somehow gets wide open and drills the shot. No wonder her stomach, heart, and respiratory tract all feel like Vesuvius. No doubt Colstrip will somehow get the ball to Darcy Jensen, their best shooter, and she'll be wide open and connect.

Colstrip works it around the perimeter, and sure enough, they get it in Jensen's hands. With enough time to do her homework, Jensen takes aim and swishes it. For the fourth time, the Lady Bulldogs are going to overtime.

Midway through the overtime and with the score still tied, Sharon is wide open without the ball under the basket. Owena has it at the top of the key, but doesn't see her. Instead, she moves five steps to her left, which isn't necessarily a bad direction to go, except that she neglects to dribble. Walter Payton would have been proud of such a carry. The ref blows his whistle.

"How can you call that?" screams Owena's uncle.

I am waiting for the concomitant charges of favoritism or racism, which seem to accompany every call made against a Hardin player. But if there is racism involved in the officiating, it certainly isn't reflected in the statistics. On the season, Hardin has been to the free throw line 217 times, their opponents 122.

With 59 seconds left in overtime and the score still tied, Owena is fouled, sending her to the line for Hardin's 32nd free throw attempt of the evening compared to eight for Colstrip. On the season Owena is shooting a lousy 51 percent, and although she has played in every quarter of all 16 games, she has not attempted a free throw in seven of those games. Her form resembles a hood ornament for a '52 DeSoto. Nobody has worked on her technique.

As she steps to the line, she is greeted by mass hysteria. She lets it fly, and if she'd been shooting a gun, she couldn't have had a more bulletlike trajectory, the ball going up as it hits the front rim. It hits so hard that it rockets right back to her before the other players have time to react. She catches the ball, and with the defenders still frozen, drives right up the wide-open lane and shoots from three feet. It misses everything, an air ball from point-blank range.

In the seconds remaining, the teams trade turnovers, nobody getting off a shot. It's on to a second overtime.

With the exception of Owena, the starting five has played the entire game, 35 minutes of full-court-pressing basketball. By comparison, the Colstrip coach had substituted twenty-six times. It's hard to figure out who looks closer to death, Tiffany or Coach Mac.

With 34 seconds left in the second overtime, Colstrip leads by one. But Hardin has the ball.

In a rare display of patience, they work it around the perimeter until Sharon spots Rhea breaking wide open under the basket. She threads a perfect pass between two defenders and Rhea banks it in for an easy score, putting Hardin in the lead.

With every Colstrip starter except Jensen fouled out, they work the ball around the outside, waiting for her to get open. A nervous sophomore sub gets the ball at the free throw line, nobody within five feet of her, the crowd screaming for her to shoot. She panics, looking left and right for Jensen, and with only five seconds left, frantically lobs a crosscourt pass toward her. The ball floats over outstretched arms, right on target. But with one last gasp from her wasted body, Tiffany reaches out and deflects it. As the ball rolls toward midcourt, the final buzzer sounds.

For the first time in Hardin High history, the Lady Bulldogs, now 14-2, are champions of Montana's Class A Eastern Conference. In the middle of the oncourt jubilation and confetti, I congratulate a jubilant Coach Mac.

"I'll see a doctor tomorrow," she says. "I promise."

CHAPTER THIRTY

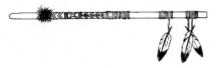

This sounds like it could be interesting. A friend, Tim Boyle, the CEO of Columbia Sportswear back in Portland, is on the phone telling me he's coming to Hardin in a few days with a bunch of guys to fish and hunt, and would I like to meet him at his lodge for dinner? The trip is a reward for his best clients and sales reps, and he's flying in a couple paid minglers to schmooz with them, legendary hothead Bobby Knight and NBA Hall of Famer John Havlicek.

"You can go fishing with us if you want," he says.

I see the headline: *Coach Knight Loses Lip in Fly-Casting Accident.* I tell Boyle I'll think about the fishing part, but definitely count me in for dinner. And wouldn't it be great, I think, if I can somehow persuade Knight and Havlicek to come to a Lady Bulldogs practice? I remember Coach Mac telling me that her favorite all-time coach is Bobby Knight and her favorite all-time player is John Havlicek. How would that be for a shock if I can stroll into practice with those two dudes?

I hang up from Boyle and the phone rings again. It's Danetta and there's an urgency to her voice I haven't heard before. She quickly explains that her brother, Bill Medicine Tail, is in the VA Hospital in Sheridan with cancer and has taken a turn for the worse.

"I need to get down there," she says.

I'm not sure why she's calling to tell me this, but I soon find out. "I hate to ask," she says, "but can I borrow $250?"

She explains that she'll have to stay in Sheridan a night or two, and needs money for gas, food, and lodging. "I've got a beautiful 30-06 I can give you for collateral," she adds.

"That's not necessary," I say.

She needs the money right away and she needs it in cash, so twenty minutes later I meet her in the parking lot behind the bank. We talk next to her car and the conversation is chatty, not like I'd expect of somebody off to see her dying brother. Yes, the weather is chilly, and yes, it's great that Windy Boy didn't get canned.

I'm never quite sure what to make of Danetta, but I've come to believe there are three of her . . . the good, the bad, and the godawful but kinda fun. One day I'll think she's Eleanor Roosevelt, generous with her time and money, a champion of tribal rights, a woman with courage, a pioneer among Indian women. The next day she strikes me as Imelda Marcos, power-hungry, dishonest, out to get whatever she can for herself and her family. Then I'll see her a couple days later and she's Zsa Zsa Gabor, garish, excessive, harmless, full of herself, the only woman on the reservation with two mink coats, a silver cigarette holder, and the audacity to have once hired a white cleaning lady.

I know she has a checkered financial history, one littered with repossessions, garnisheed accounts, unpaid debts, lawyer fees, and spending sprees. I'd heard all about the way she took her first check for the land she sold to the tribe for the hospital site and promptly shelled out $125,000 in cash for new cars, including Sharon's Cougar. Several people I've met have had a financial hassle with her at one time or another. Gary Stevenson, the owner of the IGA, fronted her $400 worth of groceries for a big feast and never got repaid. She also borrowed $1,000 from the Johnsons, and when she didn't pay them back on time, they figured the money was adios. Then one day she ran into Hjordis and peeled off ten crisp Ben Franklins.

It seems somehow sad and ironic that she's come to me for a loan: sad because it is yet another case, even if a small one, of the Indian coming to the white man with outstretched hand; and ironic because in this case it is the Indian coming to a white man whose idea of investment planning is *two* pizza discount coupons on the refrigerator door.

In the past the banks were willing to work with her because of her land holdings and a favorable work history. Never one to live off the tribal dole, she worked for twenty years as a clerk for the tribe and BIA, and another seventeen years as a sales clerk and administrative assistant for the National Park Service at Custer Battlefield until she retired in the late 1980s.

She opens her car's rear door and points to a blanket spread across the back seat. "Take a look under that," she says.

I'm not sure if I'm about to see a corpse or a case of powdered sugar donuts. I slowly peel back the blanket. It's the 30-06. "Sure you don't want to keep this for collateral?" she asks.

"No, it's a beauty, but I trust you," I say.

I hand her the money and she promises to pay me back out of the final payment from the sale of the land. She is supposed to have already gotten it, but there's been a mix-up with her lawyer. Or so she says.

I'm aware that Ron Johnson is probably right and I shouldn't believe anything she says about money. Watching her put the money in her purse I remember him telling me I'd be a fool if I gave her money because she'd figure me for a soft touch and just keep coming back for more.

"This'll be the last time," she promises.

As she gets in her car and drives away, I remember a story she told me during our first meeting. As she told it, she was at the track in Billings several years ago and saw a beautiful gray racehorse that she just had to have. A woman from Billings owned it. Danetta offered her $5,000, but the woman was suspicious of Indians writing checks and would only take cash. "So I reached in my purse and pulled out a thick wad of hundred-dollar bills and paid her right there on the spot," she said. "It was worth it just to see that white lady's mouth fall to the floor."

The Eagle's Nest Lodge, located on the west bank of the Big Horn River three miles south of Hardin, is a secluded retreat on private property, out of the price range for most residents of the county. I've come for a gourmet pheasant dinner and a little elbow rubbing with Bobby Knight and John Havlicek. My friend Boyle has advised me that they are there to recreate, not to do clinics and public appearances. Still, it's worth a shot.

I know that Knight is serious about his hunting and fishing trips to Montana, even going so far as to keep a big Suburban stored around here somewhere, a rig outfitted with cabinets and drawers for all his gear. One story has it that on a previous trip to the Big Horn area, he was doing some fly fishing way back up Lodge Grass Creek when he happened upon Bill Yellowtail, the state senator from the area who also works summers as a fishing guide. They got to talking and pretty soon they were having a sandwich together at Yellowtail's remote cabin. Not being a basketball fan, Yellowtail had no clue he was entertaining the shortest fuse in the NCAA. It wasn't until a friend stopped by and recognized Knight that the senator learned of his guest's notoriety. "He was a nice guy," Yellowtail recalled later, "but he didn't have the patience to be a good fisherman. It was cast and move on, cast and move on."

During the cocktail hour, I am introduced to the two paid minglers, and listen as Knight enthralls the sales folk with tales of his day in the woods and how his guide knew where every chukar, quail, and woman in the county was hiding. "That guy has to be the biggest Casanova in the county," he says. As I listen to Knight go on and on about this guy, I realize that this is the same dirtbag who sweet-talked Amy Hanson into thinking he was taking her to California so he could sleep with her. I don't tell Knight this.

At dinner I sit between him and Havlicek, who seems every bit as dignified and classy as he did in all his years in a Celtics uniform. Knight continues to hold court, explaining how the word "fuck" can be used as all eight parts of speech. Then the conversation turns serious. He's of the opinion that over the years a lot of college coaches, including the legendary Wizard of Westwood, John Wooden, have turned a blind eye on seedy boosters who shower their athletes with gifts and money. I don't tell him that Coach Wooden recruited me in high school and certainly never showered me with gifts and money. In fact, he wouldn't even promise me a scholarship.

After dinner and dessert, we all retreat to the lodge's rustic living room and a crackling fire. As Knight and Havlicek continue to mingle, I wait for the pesky sales reps to stop guffawing and let me have an opening. But there's no opening and the evening wears on. I'm having a nice time, but I'm afraid I'm about to strike out on my mission. Finally, Knight and Havlicek bid their admirers good night and start for their cabins. They will rise before dawn to fish.

It's now or never. I slice through the reps and cut them

off at the door. I feel like I'm back in high school . . . about to ask out the prom queen, scared to death I'll be shot down. Because the team will be practicing at 6:00 A.M., and Knight and Havlicek are leaving for home the next afternoon, the only window is first thing in the morning, before they go fishing. I state my case.

They glance quickly at each other, then Knight replies. "We'd be happy to," he says.

I take back all the nasty thoughts I've ever had about him.

Dawn is taking its sweet time arriving on the prairie as I return to pick up my two new heroes. I can't wait to see the look on Coach Mac's face when I walk in the gym with these two guys. Surely for such a deed I will be King of the Prairie.

Now to knock on Knight's door. What if he's still asleep and I piss him off and he goes sideline and throws a chair at me? I don't have to worry. He and Havlicek are already up, dressed for fishing, ready to go. Their only covenants for this favor are no fanfare, no autographs.

Arriving at the gym, we enter through a side door. Coach Mac and her players are all the way across the floor, working on their half-court offense. Slowly, we make our way toward them. Coach Mac briefly turns in our direction, but returns her concentration to her drill. Then she looks again, and as we move closer, she does a double take and then another, her eyes starting to bug right out of her head.

"My God!" she exclaims. "No, it can't be!"

I can almost hear her thinking: how the hell can Bobby Knight and John Havlicek be walking into my practice in tiny ol' Hardin, Montana, at 6:15 in the morning? Surely this is a mirage. Or at the very least, a sign that I should visit that doctor that I didn't go see.

Without saying a word to her players, she heads in our direction, walking right through the middle of the drill. She stops right next to Knight and stares up at him, then at Havlicek. She's too dumbfounded to speak, her mouth agape. Finally, she reaches out and touches Havlicek's arm.

"It's you," she stammers.

Then she turns to Knight and touches his arm. "And you."

Knight smiles, then notices the players beginning to creep in our direction, murmuring, pointing. "Hey!" he barks in his best impersonation of himself. "Who said you could stop practicing?"

The girls aren't sure whether to crap in their drawers or keep practicing. Slowly, they inch forward, buzzing, gawking. Most don't recognize Havlicek, too young to have seen him play, but they all know Knight. Anita draws close and offers a two thumbs-up salute. "Awesome!" she exudes.

I look to see Sharon's reaction, but she isn't there. Coach Mac has given her the morning off to rest her back.

Coach Mac tries to make conversation. "What are you doing here?" she asks.

Knight points at me. "He asked us," he says.

Coach Mac looks at me, not as if I'm King of the Prairie, but God.

Havlicek suggests she gather the team. "We can't stay long, but we heard they just won the conference title, so . . ."

"They're going to talk to us!" exclaims Coach Mac, motioning the players to take a seat on the floor.

For the next ten minutes, the men speak to the girls. It isn't technical stuff about backdoor picks or zone traps . . . it is straight talk about working hard, setting goals, focusing, avoiding distractions, enjoying one another. "You should really cherish these next few weeks," says Havlicek.

"You've accomplished something special. But you can't stop now."

Knight recalls how he and Havlicek were teammates on Ohio State's NCAA championship team in 1960, and the memories of that time are still fresh. "One of the things I remember most," he says, "is how hard we worked. I think we wanted it more than the other teams."

"That's what I've been telling them," injects Coach Mac.

"You have to listen to your coach," says Knight, putting a hand on her shoulder, "even if she's yelling at you. If she didn't care, she wouldn't be here."

"How come you seem different on TV?" asks Stacie.

"What'ya mean?" asks Knight.

"Meaner," she replies.

"Oh, that's just a little act I do," he answers. "Doesn't your coach holler at you once in a while?"

Heads nod. Coach Mac's smile is trying to rip a gorge in her cheeks. Her rantings have just been anointed.

Knight and Havlicek say goodbye, then with the girls still seated on the floor, head for the parking lot. It is still an hour before school, but somehow a dozen Indian boys have caught wind of the stars in their midst.

"Will you autograph my shoe?" one asks.

"How many As did you get on your last report card?" asks Knight.

The boy ponders the question. "Um . . . three," he answers.

Knight signs the shoes, and then he is gone fishing, casting and moving on, casting and moving on.

Anita and her youthful-looking parents greet me at the door of their spacious wood-framed house three miles south of Hardin. They've invited me to dinner, and I'm especially looking forward to dessert. Donna Dewald is a stay-at-home mom who brings in a little extra cash as a professional cake-maker, reputed to be the best in the county. Bob Dewald retired last month after twenty-five years as the Hardin postmaster and is now putting all his energy into raising cattle and growing wheat on the family's 240 acres. He plans to make his fortune, however, raising ostrich. Supposedly, the eggs are gold.

Anita gives me a tour of the house. In the entryway is a large framed photo of her in her basketball uniform that hangs next to an even larger painting of Jesus hovering over the United Nations Building. She shows me the Wurlitzer organ, hot tub, sunken family room, beamed ceilings, and the downstairs playroom that has more board games than a toy store. In her bedroom, a Michael Jordan poster hangs from the wall next to her neatly made bed. Her schoolbooks are neatly stacked on her desk. She takes only honors classes.

Dinner is served and for dessert it's a German chocolate cherry cake decorated with a basketball court on top. Anita's mom offers to box up an extra piece for me to take home. I'm disappointed. I want the whole cake.

Everything is so perfect, so wholesome. After dinner we adjourn to the music room and Anita plays a Mozart concerto on the family's black Hammond. Is there no end to this kid's talents? Her playing is so beautiful my eyes fill with tears.

We move to the sunken family room. The conversation drifts to the big controversy in town—the coming performance of four out-of-town exotic dancers at the History of the West Saloon. The Dewalds are outraged and plan to be downtown the night of the show to picket the saloon along with fellow members of their church, the Church of the Open Bible.

"This kind of show has no place in this community," says Bob. "It's morally wrong."

The conversation then turns, as it inevitably does, to Indians, alcohol, and public assistance. "I'm not saying they're all bad," says Donna. "I've met some really nice ones. But I guess when you come right down to it, I'm prejudiced against Indians. I admit it."

There is no malice or anger in her voice . . . she's quite matter-of-fact. It's the first time I've heard anybody in Hardin actually admit to being prejudiced. I suppose this qualifies her as one of the "cranky, unfriendly, immigrant bigots" mentioned by Windy Boy.

The manager of the History of the West Saloon on Center Street stands in the doorway, defiantly pointing to the message on his T-shirt. In big, black, bold letters it reads: "Just Blow Me."

On the sidewalk, the protesters, including Anita's parents and Pastor Don Morrisette from the Church of the Open Bible, continue to march, trying to ignore the message. It's impossible to miss.

It's dark and it's cold, but the protesters aren't about to abandon their cause. Inside the saloon, the exotic dancers, Mariah, Mercedes, Crystal, and Crimson, are about to go on stage. They've been brought in from out of state—Texas, according to the ads—to entertain the locals. The Christians in town, however, aren't happy about it: during the week, forty-seven people showed up at a City Council meeting to express opposition; 318 people signed a petition demanding a ban to such shows; and Pastor Morrisette wrote a letter to the editor of the *Big Horn County News* decrying the decline of morality and the damage the show will do to the town's "wholesome image."

"Get a life!" yells a passing motorist.

"We already have one," a protester retorts. "It's called eternal life."

Two weeks earlier, four out-of-state male Chippendale wannabe dancers strutted their stuff for a sold-out, ladies-only crowd, a show that didn't bring out the protesters but did have the town buzzing for days. This week it's the exotic dancers. Even the Lady Bulldogs were talking it up. "My dad will be there for sure," said Stacie.

Sure enough, he's one of the first to arrive. He ignores a man with a picket that reads, "Do you want your daughter doing this?"

Several of the protesters have brought their children, and the kids keep trying to peek in the door, their view blocked by the guy in the "Just Blow Me" T-shirt. He flashes a phony smile at their parents. I'm surprised at their restraint. I half expect them to pull him out on the sidewalk and show him some muscular Christianity.

The protesters finally leave and the show begins. The dancers aren't topless or bottomless—they're wearing string bikinis, the same kind worn on beaches all over America. The all-male audience laps it up, including two Big Horn County sheriff's deputies in street clothes who sit through both shows, drinking beers in the back row.

After the show, Mariah, Mercedes, Crystal, and Crimson put on their clothes and exit their dressing room, but as they head for the door, the two deputies step forward and slap handcuffs on them. "What the hell is this about?" demands Mercedes. Or is it Crimson?

A city ordinance prohibits the exposure of too much rear end flesh, so the arrest citation reads, "displaying too much buttocks."

As the officers lead the dancers outside to their patrol cars, forty of the dancers' devoted fans rally to their cause, marching en masse the four blocks to the sheriff's office to demand justice for Mariah, Mercedes, Crimson, and Crystal. Their demands are ignored. The dancers spend an hour in the hoosegow before posting $100 bond.

On her way out of town the next morning, Mariah drops off a letter to the editor at the *Big Horn County News*:

Dear Jesus. Wow! What a lord! You grant me the 36-24-36 figure that I so deeply cherish, but this town, filled with such pure and Christian people, elected a sheriff to come into a bar and drink and watch me dance. These poor brainwashed picketers, how much sicker are we when they bring their children to protest such "filth"? I know I am saved. Can this town really say the same? Love, Mariah.

CHAPTER THIRTY-ONE

W hat's up?" I ask.

"You know, same ol', same ol'," Sharon replies.

"Is your grandmother still down in Sheridan visiting her brother?"

"What are you talking about?" she responds. "He's been staying with us for a couple weeks."

Later, I drive to Billings for my espresso fix, and on my way out of town I pass Big B's, a bingo palace regularly frequented by Crows. Like most of the proprietors of the bingo and video poker parlors in the area, the management of Big B's is opposed to bringing legalized gambling to the reservation, fearful that it will draw away many of their best customers. I spot Danetta's Mark IV in the parking lot.

Danetta had told me that Big B's is her favorite bingo hangout. Sometimes she plays at the Cozy Corner in Hardin, but the jackpots are bigger at Big B's. Usually, she makes the 120-mile round-trip by herself, often returning home after midnight. It's not a new addiction. Her gambling habit dates back to the 1970s when she and Blaine made frequent trips to Las Vegas; she'd sit on a stool in front of a slot machine for hours, plunking in coins from her paper cup. Now it's just bingo—three cards at a time, sometimes six. But no more slot machines—that was gambling—bingo is just for "relaxation."

I turn into the parking lot and enter Big B's. It is a warehouselike building, with row after row of cafeteria tables, all of them packed with players, most of them Indians, most of them elderly, most of them smoking. A dense cloud of smoke hangs low.

"N-36," announces the caller, pulling a number out of the hopper.

None of the players look up, all eyes focused on their cards, three hundred bingo fanatics in muted frenzy, the only sound the hacking of cigarette coughs.

I wander the perimeter, scanning the tables for Danetta. It is like trying to see across Mexico City on a Stage 4 smog alert. Every tenth table is designated a no-smoking table, which is like declaring every tenth block in Chernobyl a radiation-free zone. Finally I spot her. She is all business, three cards spread in front of her, her bingo daubers held upside down, poised to mark. The game is blackout and all she needs on her middle card is B-7, then the jackpot is hers.

"I-14."

I squeeze into the seat next to her and she glances over, nodding a perfunctory greeting, barely breaking her concentration, in sharp contrast to all the other times she's greeted me, a geyser of enthusiasm.

"G-51."

She marks her two outside cards, then lights another Benson & Hedges menthol. Expressionless, like an accountant crunching numbers, she remains composed, absorbed. No groans. No signs of emotion. No mental lapses. The skill of big-time bingo is to not fall asleep at the switch and miss a number, especially not with a $500 jackpot just a number away.

"Sure would be nice to win that," I encourage.

"B-5."

"Bingo!" someone shouts from across the room.

Danetta peers over her black-rimmed glasses. No pout, no complaint. She takes another puff of her cigarette, then purchases three more cards . . . just for relaxation.

The first snow falls overnight, blanketing the Big Horn Valley in white. Despite the cold, Stacie Greenwalt charges out the door for school without a coat. Sound judgment isn't her specialty.

The last two games of the season will be especially crucial to Stacie. In her last three JV games, she has averaged 24 points a game, totally dominating, offensively and defensively. After the last game, Coach Mac pulled her aside and told her she could expect to see increased action with the varsity against Billings Senior and Miles City. It'll be good experience for the playoffs starting in two weeks.

Bounding down the steps, she waves to her father, who is getting ready to deliver hay to his cattle. The Greenwalts' property, twenty-three miles south of Hardin, is located in an area where the plateaus and bluffs bordering the Big Horn Valley begin to narrow, where the winds carrying the frigid air down from the Big Horn Mountains arrive more intensely, where the snow piles higher and the roads get more treacherous, and where ranchers like Doug Greenwalt must guard against frozen livestock.

Stacie scrapes the snow off the windshield of her dad's 4x4 pickup, then pulls out onto the highway for the twenty-three-mile drive to school. The road is newly plowed. No traffic. As always, she isn't wearing her seat belt.

Like she does every morning, she keeps the speedometer steady at sixty miles per hour. Never mind the snow swirling across the road. Approaching the Two Leggings bridge seven miles south of town, she passes a warning sign: "Beware of Ice on Bridge." She doesn't slow down.

As soon as the wheels hit the bridge, the pickup starts to slide, spinning sideways out of control. No cars are approaching. It spins all the way across the bridge, then plunges down a twenty-foot embankment.

As the truck careens down the hill, Stacie's shoulder bangs against the driver's-side window, shattering the glass. Then she flies through the opening, her book bag right behind her.

The vehicle bounces once, twice, then slams into a cottonwood, coming to rest directly on top of the book bag. Ten feet away, Stacie lies in the snow, blood flowing from a gash in her forehead.

She struggles to her feet. No use trying to get the truck going—it is totaled. Slowly, she climbs back up the embankment. Not seeing any cars approaching, she limps along the side of the road, shivering, crying, pain shooting down her back. She's only a couple miles from where her teammate Amy went off the road with Trina.

In the distance she sees a farmhouse and heads toward it, the pain in her back getting worse. No lights are on. She knocks on the door, but nobody answers, so she picks up a rock and slams it through a door window, cutting her hand. She lets herself inside and hurries from room to room, searching for a phone, blood dripping. Finally, she finds one and calls home.

By the time her father arrives, she is in shock. He quickly puts her in the car and drives to the emergency room. X-rays reveal no broken bones or internal injuries. That's the good news. Her back, however, is badly wrenched. "How long will it take before she can play again?" asks her father.

"At least a month," replies the doctor.

Hearing the news, I can't help but think that the Lady

Bulldogs' best shot at a state championship might have just slid off that icy bridge.

"I hate that woman," hisses Amy, plopping down on the bench with Geri and DyAnna.

It's just two minutes into the last home game, and Coach Mac, who had kept a promise to start her five seniors, has already yanked the three scrubs as soon as Billings Senior jumps out to a 5–0 lead.

"What an insult!" grumbles Geri. "Why'd she even bother?"

On the court, Sharon takes it right at Karen Weyler, putting up a lefthanded hook. Weyler blocks it.

"Be patient!" yells Coach Mac.

On Hardin's next possession, Sharon takes it right at Weyler again. This time, Weyler doesn't block it, but she spooks Sharon into an air ball.

Sharon forces up another bad shot, then another. Four possessions, four forced shots. Retreating on defense, she glares at Tiffany. "What are you doing!" Sharon snarls.

Sharon misses again, and for the first time in her career, she is pulled out of a game in the first quarter.

"Is something bothering you?" asks Coach Mac.

"They're not getting me the ball quick enough," she says, staring at her teammates.

Coach Mac sits her on the bench for 40 seconds, then puts her back in. But as in the team's two losses to Glendive, the Billings Senior guards use quick passes to shred the press, blowing by Tiffany and Anita, then dishing off to the wings, leaving Sharon overwhelmed in the middle. It's like she's home alone and burglars are breaking through every window in the house, Owena and Rhea sleeping through it all.

Senior stretches their lead to 15 midway through the second quarter. Coach Mac mulls her options. She can call off the press and go with a straight zone, or switch to a man-to-man, or throw in the towel and let the second-stringers gain experience.

Change has never come easy for her. She elects to stay the course, leaving the first unit out on the floor. Christina, who sparked the comeback against Colstrip, remains anchored to the bench.

Sharon continues her funk, forcing up more shots. "Take her out!" yells Tom Hopfauf.

Coach Mac leaves her in. It doesn't help the Lady Bulldogs' chances that Tiffany is also having her worst game of the season, with five turnovers, three fouls, and only two points midway through the third quarter. She glances toward Coach Mac, hoping she'll pull Sharon out of the game.

Dating back to junior high, Tiffany and Sharon have played over a hundred games together and been through a thousand practices, and in all those times, Tiffany has never seen Sharon lose her poise like this. Despite their differences, she has always admired Sharon's composure under pressure. In Coach Mac's preseason questionnaire, she listed Sharon as the player she'd most like to shoot the final shot with the game on the line. But on this night, Sharon is scary.

There will be no miracle comeback. Hardin loses 61–38, their worst performance of the season, even worse than the disasters against Glendive. Between them, Sharon, Tiffany, and Anita hit only 10 of 42.

I stand outside the locker room as the players head for home, sulking and pouting. Coach Mac finally exits. I feel compelled to ask: "Why didn't you switch to a man-to-man when it was obvious the press wasn't working?"

"'Cause I know best what works with these girls," she brusquely replies, brushing past me.

The next morning I make a run to the store for cereal and milk. A mean wind howls out of the north, blowing dirty snow down Center Street, making it look even bleaker than normal. In the doorway of the Little Big Horn Bank, a drunk Indian is curled up in a ball, no blanket to cover him. At the store, I hear someone call my name. It's Tiffany's mom and she looks like she's been up all night. "We had a tough time at our house last night," she explains. "Tiff barely slept. She did a lot of crying."

"Why?"

"You saw the game last night," she says. "It's as if the devil got ahold of Sharon the way she was yelling at the other players. Doesn't she understand what that does to somebody? It's tearing the team apart. That's what Tiff was crying about."

I see her point.

"Coach Mac needs to call a meeting before tonight's game," she says. "She needs to stop letting Sharon get away with this stuff. Maybe you should talk to Coach Mac and tell her what's going on. I'm serious."

"I don't think I should get involved that way," I explain.

"Well, if somebody doesn't say something to her, this team will self-destruct. I know it."

She heads for the exit and I go to the cereal section. Turning down the aisle, I hear my name called again. It's Danetta. Tossing a box of Cocoa Puffs into her cart, she looks upset.

"She makes me so angry," she states.

"Who?"

"That woman, you know, the coach."

"What's the problem?"

"She needs to call a meeting before tonight's game."

"Why?"

"For one thing, she needs to tell those other girls to pass the ball. Especially that Tiffany girl. She hogs it."

I've heard this before from Sharon's family, about fifty times. The facts don't support it. Tiffany leads the team in assists and most of her shots come off of steals and fast breaks, not forced shots; she almost never shoots from the outside. A ball hog she's not.

"Somebody has to tell Coach Mac that whenever she stands up and calls out a play it doesn't work," Danetta continues. "The girls watch her and forget what they're doing. She needs to sit down, shut up, and let them play. Maybe you should talk to her and tell her what she should do."

"I don't think I should get involved that way," I repeat.

CHAPTER THIRTY-TWO

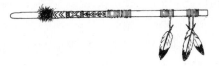

Waiting on a bench on Last Stand Hill for the start of the dedication ceremony to rename Custer Battlefield, I see a small group of Indians approach in the distance. They're on foot and carrying a red flag.

"Those are the guys from the American Indian Movement," says my buddy Carson Walks Over Ice. "Maybe they're here to start another Wounded Knee."

I check the crowd, wondering if those cowboys in the Stetsons next to us are FBI agents. I suggest to Walks Over Ice that we move our viewing spot for the ceremony . . . just in case. He reminds me that AIM isn't the radical Indian group it was back in the 1970s.

"They're harmless," he says.

I remind him that his last prediction was that Windy Boy would get fired.

Actually, I'm more worried about freezing my butt off than getting caught in a crossfire hail of bullets. A fierce wind is blowing off the prairie, and snow is starting to fall again. I wish they'd hurry up and start the ceremony.

Organized by the National Park Service, the ceremony is to commemorate the renaming of Custer Battlefield to the more politically correct Little Big Horn Battlefield. Back in 1881 a monument was erected at Last Stand Hill for the 7th

Cavalry soldiers who fell at the battle, but nothing had ever been done to recognize the members of the Sioux and Cheyenne nations who lost their lives. It took over a hundred years for Congress to pass legislation to change the name and create a monument formally acknowledging the Indians . . . and this is the day.

Seems fair enough. But the guys from AIM, led by Mr. Red Power himself, Russell Means, are mad. They claim it was pressure from AIM that won the battle to get the battlefield renamed to Little Big Horn Battlefield, and now they're getting stiffed, no recognition for their efforts.

The temperature plummets, and for a guy raised under the sun's rays in L.A., it's too cold. "I'm leaving," I declare.

Heading for the parking lot, I stop briefly to listen to the opening prayer delivered by Northern Cheyenne religious leader and tribal elder Austin Two Moons. His name sounds familiar.

On the way back to Hardin, I detour by Danetta's. "How come I didn't see you up at the ceremony?" I ask.

She scowls. "They shouldn't have changed the name," she says. "It's been Custer Battlefield for a hundred years and it shouldn't be up to the Sioux and Cheyenne to change it. This is Crow land."

Her face is flush, her eyes full of the hostility that still exists between the Crows and their neighboring tribes after two centuries of conflict over the land. But for her, renaming the battlefield isn't the biggest issue.

"How could they include Austin Two Moons in the ceremony?" she says. "How could they?"

It was Two Moons's son and nephew who brutally beat her son to death with a baseball bat. She can still see Two Moons's face at the sentencing hearing. "He stood up and argued for those boys' release," she says. "I can never forgive him for that. Never. It was a slap in the face then, and it's a slap in the face now. How can he be allowed to take

311

part in a ceremony on Crow land, my land? It shows total disrespect to the memory of my son."

When I climb aboard *Bulldog I,* Coach Mac is already in her seat. She looks as if she's been sucking on lemons all morning. "I barely slept last night," she says. "Just laid there worrying."

"About what?"

"Nothing much . . . just the offense, the defense, the chemistry."

"Are you going to have a team meeting?"

She shakes her head.

I don't tell her that renowned coaches Danetta Fallsdown and Karen Hopfauf think she should.

Sharon boards the bus. I expect her to look like she's been sucking on lemons, too, but she's smiling and whistling. I've never seen her so cheery and chipper.

Behind her, Tiffany shakes her head in wonder. Is this the same Sharon who yelled at her last night? Is this the same girl who had her so upset she barely slept? What's with the whistling and finger snapping? Did the medicine man slip her some Prozac?

"Let's get this show on the road!" Sharon encourages.

Tiffany smiles. She'd come prepared for a long, tense ride with dark moods, and now Sharon is acting like Miss Congeniality. It's so out of character. But Tiffany isn't about to question it. It's better than 150 miles of gloom. She's ready to flow with it. So forget the team meeting. What problems?

In Miles City, I head off for my usual walking tour, picking up brochures at the Chamber of Commerce. I read all about Colonel Nelson Miles and how he was dispatched west after Custer's misadventure, his assignment to force bands of wandering Indians onto reservations so that cattlemen could take advantage of the area's abundant grassland. Judging from the fact that there are no Indians living in Miles City, Colonel Miles must have done his job well.

During the JV game, I sit in the bleachers behind Sharon. She's still giddy. She'd gone to bed distraught, but woke up resolved to push aside all the negativity from yesterday, including the word that Karna is back in town. Why waste energy on what's past or what she can't control?

As she braids Amy's hair, she listens on her headset to "Humpin' Around" by Bobby Brown. Everyone knows it's "Humpin' Around" because the sound is vibrating at full volume through her earphones.

"Don't you listen to white people's music anymore?" asks Amy.

"I got to live in your world," replies Sharon. "Isn't that enough?"

In the pregame huddle, Coach Oswald, looking serious as a judge, addresses the team: "After last night's disaster, I think this is our biggest game of the year," he says. "We're going to learn what you're really made of tonight."

The Cowgirls, 9-8 on the season, are a hard team to figure. They took Hardin to the last minute in their first two games, but against weaker teams, they've been blown out. Lining up for the tip-off, Sharon looks calm.

Anita misses the first shot, but Sharon pats her on the back. On the next possession, Anita scores, taking it to the hole more aggressively than she has since injuring her knee earlier in the season.

Despite Sharon's calm and the team's sense of purpose, the Cowgirls don't fold, the first quarter ending in a 14–14 tie. But in the second quarter, there is even more harmony to Hardin's effort: Rhea scores on a backdoor pass from Sharon; Anita and Tiffany force the opposing guards into three straight turnovers; Owena grabs her own rebound and puts it back in. It's five girls playing in perfect concert.

"Way to go!" encourages Sharon after Anita scores on a fast break.

A few seconds later Sharon is trapped with the ball in front of the basket, but instead of forcing it up like she did last night, she whips a pass to Rhea, who scores. But the Cowgirls continue to play well. Led by Sharon's old nemesis, Joleyn Wambolt, they trail by only seven at the half.

"We've already won the conference," grouses Geri, heading to the locker room. "What's it gonna hurt to put us in?"

The usual cast of malcontents is upset—Amy, Geri, DyAnna. All seniors . . . but now a new frown has been added. Christina. After her excellent performance two games ago against Colstrip, she figured she'd get plenty of minutes in the team's final two games. Wasn't that Coach Mac's plan all along—to groom her for the playoffs? So why did she play only two minutes against Senior? Why hasn't she played tonight?

Early in the fourth quarter, Miles City scores to cut the deficit to three. The Hardin legs look tired. Coach Mac walks to the end of the bench and waves Christina into the game. A derisive cheer rises from the Hardin fans, who've been subdued most of the half. It's only the third substitution of the game.

Christina immediately steals a pass and scores, then creates another turnover and basket. Suddenly the crowd is back into it and the legs look fresher. Hardin's lead jumps to 14 and the victory is secure.

There is no wild jubilation or victory dance, just a quiet sense of accomplishment, not just for the game, but for the

15-3 season. By winning the league crown, they have earned a first round bye in Divisionals. For the game, Anita is high scorer with 20; Sharon is next with 16, adding seven rebounds, eight assists, four steals, and her most complete game of the year. In her four minutes of play, Christina contributed four steals and the vital spark.

On the bus, Coach Oswald addresses the team again. "Girls, you showed me what you're really made of tonight," he says. "This is a good win to take us into Divisionals."

I think they still need a meeting.

PART V

DIVISIONALS

CHAPTER THIRTY-THREE

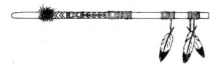

The bell rings, ending fifth period. In Mr. Scott's Marriage and the Family class, Amylynn Adams waits for the other students to gather their books and head for the door. She has spent most of the period with her head resting on a table, her vision blurred. When all the students finally exit, noisily parading off to their sixth period classes, she struggles to move her wheelchair to the door.

Without saying a word, Sharon slides in behind her and starts to slowly push her out into the crowded hallway. She stops, waiting for the crowd to thin, saying nothing, just holding on to the handles.

The school, as well as the whole town, is still in a state of denial about what has happened to popular Amylynn, the girl who wants to be a writer, the girl who used to pretend she was Sharon on the court. A month ago she was bounding down the hall, spirited, vivacious, then she was diagnosed with a fast-moving and particularly insidious form of multiple sclerosis, confined to a wheelchair, unable to walk, her body swelled from the cortisone treatment. On Thursday, the day her former teammates are scheduled to leave for Divisionals in Sidney, she is checking into Deaconess Hospital in Billings for a series of painful tests.

Spotting an opening, Sharon pushes the wheelchair into the center of the hall. To Amylynn, it feels almost as if they are going in slow motion. In the two weeks she's been confined to the wheelchair, she's been pushed by many students, but this is different, special. Until now, it has only been white kids pushing her, with lots of small talk and smiling. But this is Sharon LaForge, the basketball queen. There is no small talk, or happy face, or sappy promise to win the tournament for her. It is just the gentle vibration of the wheels rolling down the waxed floor.

Of all the days since being diagnosed, this day is the worst for Amylynn: she fell twice in the shower before school; she didn't have the strength to lift her arm to brush her hair; she stumbled down the porch steps and had to be carried to the car; and while sitting in her wheelchair during third period, she lost control of her bladder and wet her pants. On the bright side, she had finally tracked down her biological father, a man she's never met, a graphic designer living in Cincinnati, married, father of two. They talked on the phone, and to her, he sounded like the greatest guy ever. He said he couldn't wait to meet her. He agreed to a blood test, more to learn if there is any genetic predisposition to MS on his side of the family than to verify patrimony. According to Amylynn's mom, it was a brief college fling.

Continuing down the hall, they pass Amylynn's favorite teacher, Mrs. Lytle, in her doorway. Amy is too weak to even say hello. She just wiggles her fingers. Choking back tears, Mrs. Lytle retreats to her room.

The tardy bell rings, and with the hall now empty, they continue toward Amylynn's class. She doesn't want the trip to end. It feels soothing. There is a languid, graceful calm in the slow movement.

When they finally reach the classroom door, Sharon

pushes it open, then wheels her smoothly into the room. Heads turn to watch. Then she turns and walks back out of the room, gently closing the door behind her, not a word spoken.

Everything is on the line.

At practice, Coach Mac slams down her clipboard, frustrated at the team's poor execution in its half-court offense. "Guess I shouldn't be surprised," she fumes. "You haven't got it right all season."

Behind her, Stacie restlessly paces, bored at not being allowed to practice. Her injuries from the car crash are healing quicker than anticipated, but the doctor still says no to her playing in Divisionals.

"Stacie, could you sit down?" requests Coach Mac.

Stacie sits down, but quickly rises again, meandering over to the ball rack. With her back to the court, she pulls out two balls and stuffs them under her T-shirt, giving herself an instant Dolly Parton. Then she turns around and struts toward the court. Sharon is the first to spot her. She tries not to laugh, but can't. Soon everyone is laughing. Except Coach Mac.

"Damnit, Stacie!" she barks. "These other girls want to win a championship and you're not helping."

Stifling a smile, Stacie removes the balls and the team resumes working on its half-court offense. A few minutes later, a side door opens and two senior boys enter, one of them Brian Oswald, Coach Oswald's son, a faithful admirer of Anita. He and his friend sit down on a bench on the far side of the gym, silently watching the practice. They've been doing it on a semiregular basis all season.

"Get the hell out of here!" shouts Coach Mac.

* * *

Sharon hurries out of the gym to her car after practice, her hair still wet, her jacket at home on the floor. The temperature is eighteen, the wind chill factor at minus two. She is on her way to Danetta's for a ceremonial gathering in her honor, a pre-tourney feast, with sweat lodge, healing prayers, words of wisdom. Then, if she gets lucky, she'll meet up with Randy.

Her car wears a thick winter patina, mud and slush splattered front to back. As the Cougar approaches Danetta's on the rutted dirt road, it bumps and bounces, Sharon twisting in her seat, grimacing. The pain in her lower back that has bothered her all season is still there. A sweat will feel good. As usual, the men will go first, including Rudolph Shane, a deacon in the Baptist Church and a respected clan uncle from the Greasy Mouth clan. He's been invited to offer a special playoff blessing.

The gathering of thirty people includes two elderly women from the Bad War Deeds clan who've temporarily suspended their rivalry with the Greasy Mouths to honor Sharon. Inside the house it is crowded and smoky, everyone convivial. A new touch has been added to the decor, a safety pin to hold the frayed gold drapes together. On the TV, John Elway and the Denver Broncos are driving for a score. In the kitchen, Danetta proclaims her granddaughter is the team, conference, and state MVP.

Sharon's chances of making All-Conference seem a lock. On the season she is averaging 8.2 rebounds and 16.3 points a game, both stats second best in the league. Not bad considering she is at least two inches shorter and twenty pounds lighter than every opposing center. That Hardin won the conference and is ranked third in the state should help her chances. So should her clutch play in the team's four overtime victories.

"But she's an Indian," says clan uncle Gilbert Birdinground, "and strange things happen to Indians around here."

Danetta still believes Sharon will get a scholarship to Montana State or the University of Montana. Never mind that the coaches from those schools haven't contacted her. Or the coaches from any other school.

"How can they not give her one?" she says. "She's the best player in Montana."

After the men finish their sweat and return to the house, Danetta serves the familiar feast of beefsteak, macaroni, fry bread, and gravy. Sharon barely touches her food, leaving the table to sit on the couch and snack on Fritos.

The women clear the dishes, then Sharon is summoned back to the table. She positions herself next to Rudolph, a wiry BIA range specialist. He is forty years old, pithy, and knows little about basketball. He's never seen Sharon play. But Danetta has invited him for his wisdom and role as a Crow spiritual leader.

A soft-spoken man, he delivers his message in Crow, giving Sharon the same advice she received at the feast to start the season: she should relax and forget about the things she can't control; she should play with patience and trust her teammates; she should accept that Coach Mac is running the team and there is nothing she can do about it; she should ignore any pressure she feels from her family or tribe. As he speaks, Sharon stands straight, listening attentively, respectfully.

His sermon rendered, Rudolph heads for the door, intercepted by Danetta, who presents him a Pendleton blanket and a fistful of double sawbucks. Then he is gone, the sound of his pickup fading into the night. A few minutes later, Sharon is gone, too, off in search of Randy.

* * *

The next morning, Sharon hurriedly packs for Sidney, then rushes upstairs. A block away, her teammates are already loading suitcases into *Bulldog I*.

In the kitchen, Marlene waits, worried that Sharon is heading off to Sidney feeling too much family pressure. At the feast, it was Sharon this, Sharon that, Sharon should get a scholarship, Sharon should get more passes from Tiffany. On and on.

"Let me brush you with these," says Marlene, holding up four eagle feathers.

"Do it fast," replies Sharon. "I can't miss the bus."

Marlene also worries that Karna will come to Sidney and cause another scene. She saw her yesterday and Karna made her intentions clear. "I'm coming and there's nothing you can do about it," she vowed.

After brushing Sharon with the eagle feathers, Marlene lights four—the mystic number—bowls of cedar on the kitchen table, the incense wafting in Sharon's direction, then she prays to the Creator, asking that Sharon be protected on her journey and not give in to the pressure. Then she blows her Sun Dance whistle, a hand-carved instrument used to ward off evil spirits.

Normally, Sharon likes these spiritual offerings that connect her to tribe and family. It's an elixir. But on this morning, she doesn't have time. "I gotta go," she says, rushing to the door.

"Take this," urges Marlene, handing her a small bag of sage to sprinkle inside her shoes for protection in battle. "And give some to your teammates."

Sharon hurries down the steps, suitcase and Baggie of sage in hand. Marlene smiles, foreseeing a good journey. She believes strongly in dreams and visions, and although this isn't a vision she is having, it is special, strong and unexplainable. She has had these feelings before, sometimes good, sometimes bad, such as the one earlier in the year when she attended a workshop in Helena on shamanism and made contact with her grandfather's spirit. The experience scared her. So she quit . . . no more shamanism. But the strong feeling on this morning isn't scary: *the team will win Divisionals and Sharon will be the star.*

Sharon is the last to board the bus. Already on board are eleven players, two coaches, five cheerleaders, one cheerleader adviser, two team managers, and Louie, the driver. She moves toward the back, ignoring the cheerleaders, taking a seat in the last row with three Indian teammates.

As the bus pulls away from the school, the players are downright giddy. It isn't just the anticipation of playing in the biggest games of their careers, and possibly the last. It is the expectation of three days and nights on the road. Staying in a motel. Eating in restaurants. Missing school. Sharing a room. Talking in bed. Playing video games. Listening to boom boxes. This is a memory maker, a high school experience that will stay with them long after they've forgotten everything they read in Kafka's "Metamorphosis" back in Mr. Nelson's fourth period English class. This is cool.

Sharon feels relaxed, like she's in a cocoon, sheltered from all the pressure, glad to be getting away. It has been a hectic week. Feasts. Sweats. Pep assemblies. Family prayers. Tribal rituals. Everyone giving her advice, everyone telling her she is the best. Everyone, that is, but Randy. He'd been his same old slippery self, not returning her phone call, not showing up to meet her as promised. When she finally managed to track him down, he apologized, telling her he was busy concentrating on his trip the following week to the National Indian Rodeo in Albuquerque, his big event of the year. She asked if she could call him from Sidney. "Why are you going to Sidney?" he asked.

It is a six-hour bus ride to Sidney, with a forecast calling for snow and hazardous driving conditions later in the day. A few years earlier a bus carrying the Whitefish High wrestling team skidded off an icy road, killing the coach and five team members, but that doesn't scare Louie. He's been driving in eastern Montana his whole life, and a little swirling snow on the highway is nothing. Tiffany turns up the volume on Garth Brooks.

It takes an hour for the girls to settle down, then out come the pillows and blankets, the bus falling quiet as the storm clouds get darker. By the time *Bulldog I* nears Sidney on Highway 16, the snow is flying in every direction, visibility reduced to fifty feet. Grain elevators and water towers next to the road disappear. Louie squints through the flapping windshield wipers. The girls are now wide awake.

"Maybe I should go up there and help Louie," suggests Stacie, who had the stitches removed from her forehead and is now cleared by the doctor to play.

She clutches an imaginary steering wheel and guides her imaginary bus through the snow. "You don't seem to understand," she says. "I was an honor student in driver's training."

Sidney, population 5,973, is just ahead. Located on the west bank of the Yellowstone River near its confluence with the Missouri, and five miles from the North Dakota border, it is part of what the locals call the MonDak area, a sweeping land of rolling prairies, wide river valleys, and rippling wheat fields. It's just down the road from Fort Buford, a military post famous for the Indian prisoners it housed, including Chief Joseph and Sitting Bull. Hosting the divisional playoffs will be the biggest thing to hit the town since Vince Gill played the county fair in August.

It takes a while, but Stacie and Louie finally steer the bus into the parking lot of the Lone Tree Motel, the team's home for the next three nights. As the players file off the bus, Coach Mac hands them a photocopied message titled "It Takes a Little More to Be a Champion":

Our motel is our own little world. It is a time and place where we can be together without outside interruptions. We are a team and it is for this reason that no one other than fellow team members, cheerleaders, managers, and coaches can be in our room or visit you at the motel. It is our place to relax, be ourselves, and prepare to reach our ultimate goal as a team.

IT'S TIME
IT ALL STARTED WITH A DREAM

It is thirty-two hours until game time, thirty-two hours to kill time and build a case of the jitters. To help eliminate distractions, Coach Mac removes the phones from the girls' rooms. If Sharon wants to check up on Randy, she'll have to use a pay phone.

The team is traveling on a shoestring: $4 per meal; four girls to a room; two girls to a bed. Coach Mac puts Sharon in a room with reserves Kassi, DyAnna, and Maria. I walk by and the door is open.

"How can you make such a mess in thirty minutes?" I ask.

Stacie pops her head out of her room. "Does this joint have room service?" she asks. "I need to order up some beers."

After a shootaround at the gym, the team stops at Pizza Hut for dinner. "It's important that you get some good carbohydrates tonight," announces Coach Mac. "So I've ordered extra helpings of garlic bread sticks."

"Pinch me," says Stacie.

Sharon gobbles down two slices of pizza, then hustles off to the video game room, soon engaged in Mortal Kombat with Tiffany. With each kill, the screeching increases. But before a winner is declared, Coach Mac herds everyone back onto *Bulldog I* to return to the gym to watch the first-round game between Sidney and Miles City. Hardin will play the winner tomorrow. Everyone agrees they want it to be Sidney, the team they scored 26 straight points against the first game of the season.

Practically fused at the hip, Sharon and Tiffany enter the gym. The whole team is dressed identically, all in black, with T-shirts that proclaim: *"Lady Bulldogs—A Class Act."* The co-captains climb up the bleachers and take a seat high in the back. Sharon settles directly behind Stacie, and saying nothing, begins to rub her back, then her temples. The massage lasts through the first quarter . . . then the second . . . then halftime . . . then all the way into the third quarter. Other players take the cue, turning the last two rows into a massage parlor, everyone rubbing everyone's shoulders.

"You can bet the boys' team won't do that," observes Coach Oswald. "If I didn't know these kids, I'd think this is a little weird."

In the fourth quarter, they shut down the massage parlor to cheer for Sidney. Shoulder to shoulder, Sharon and Tiffany gyrate to the Miles City pep band's version of "We Will Rock You." Is there any high school band in America that doesn't play this song?

Tiffany grins. This is the Sharon she remembers from seventh grade, whooping and hollering, funny and silly. Such a contrast to six nights ago when it was all bad vibes. Now it's all giggles and smiles, a new harmony. She isn't sure whether to trust it, but she's happy to go with the flow.

Sidney loses. So tomorrow the Lady Bulldogs will play Miles City, their fourth meeting of the year. In the three previous games, all won by Hardin, the total margin of victory was nine points.

"Oh no," moans Sharon. "Not Wambolt again."

CHAPTER THIRTY-FOUR

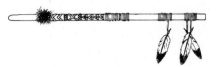

It's finally time to head for the gym. For Sharon it has felt like the longest day ever. She tried everything to speed it up . . . watching TV, listening to her Walkman, reading the tournament program . . . but none of it worked. She tried to nap, but couldn't.

She joins her teammates assembling in the motel lobby. Dressed in her tight brown polka dot dress, she approaches the front desk. "Any messages for Sharon LaForge?" she asks.

"No," replies the clerk.

She frowns. She's got more chance of Elvis calling than Randy, but still, she hopes.

With Louie warming up the bus in the parking lot, the team forms a circle near the registration desk, hands joined in the middle. "Defense!" they shout in unison, breaking the huddle.

"I'm so nervous I feel like throwing up," says Tiffany.

As the players head for the bus, Stacie is the last to exit. Wearing a slinky black miniskirt, she smiles at two young cowboys holding the door open for her, nearly melting their belt buckles.

"She's gonna be dangerous when she turns sixteen," observes Coach Mac.

*   *   *

In the dimly lit visitors' locker room, the girls hang their clothes on hooks on the wall, serenaded on the boom box by Whitney Houston's "One Moment in Time." Sitting on a bench, Sharon sprinkles a dash of sage into her shoes, then hands a pinch to everyone else.

"What's this?" asks Tiffany.

"To keep away evil spirits," answers Sharon.

Unconvinced, Tiffany sprinkles it into her shoes anyway, not wanting to offend. Anita takes the sage, too, but when Sharon turns her back, she sets it aside, thinking it is hypocritical to use it if she doesn't believe in it. She will rely on Jesus.

Coach Mac quickly reviews the game plan. It is the same as every game: zone pressure on defense, fast break on offense. Exiting the locker room, she turns to Coach Oswald. "I can't believe how calm I feel," she says. "I've got a good feeling about this."

During warmups, Sharon is distracted, her eyes searching the packed bleachers for her family.

"See them yet?" asks Amy.

"Nope."

"Maybe the snow slowed them down."

It would be easy to miss them in all the bedlam. The gym is frenetic. Students. Fans. Mascots. Cheerleaders. Pep bands. Fight songs. Half the rez. War whoops. Tip-off is still ten minutes away.

Sharon glances toward the other end where the Cowgirls are warming up. Joleyn Wambolt looks fiercer, more intense than ever, if that's possible.

The buzzer sounds, signaling the players to gather on the sidelines. As Sharon makes her way off the court, she spots

331

her grandmother standing behind the bench. The whole family is there—Blaine, Marlene, her cousins JoJo and Christie, her half-brothers, George and Clarence. But thankfully, no Karna. She's back in Crow Agency nursing a hangover.

Sharon waves a quick greeting, then turns to her teammates. "We can't let these guys beat us," she instructs.

Anita tips the opening toss to Sharon, who whirls and bounces a perfect pass to Rhea cutting to the basket for an easy score . . . exactly as Coach Mac drew it up. Then Anita steals the inbounds pass and scores again. Four points in eight seconds.

With the Hardin side of the bleachers working at full volume, the Lady Bulldog defense swarms all over the court, befuddling the Miles City guards. Another steal and another easy score. It's in-your-pocket defense, so tight that it takes two minutes and 10 seconds before the Cowgirls get off their first shot. Gary Vels, Mr. Coach-by-Intimidation, screams for a timeout. Hardin leads 10–2.

"We can't let up!" encourages Sharon.

Hardin continues the defensive pressure, keeping Miles City out of sync, bothered. At the end of the quarter, Hardin leads 16–6 and Danetta is war-whooping herself hoarse.

Coach Mac substitutes Christina for Owena, and the defensive intensity cranks up even higher. Three quick Miles City turnovers are converted into easy buckets. At halftime, Hardin leads comfortably 31–17, with Sharon topping a balanced scoring attack with eight.

Despite Hardin's great first half, reserves Amy, DyAnna, and Geri are upset. Returning to the court for the second half, they grumble to each other. "I don't get it," says Amy. "She doesn't play Christina on the varsity all year, and now she's her new pet player."

"It she wants us to go in for garbage time, I'm refusing," says Geri.

Coach Mac isn't thinking about an insurrection. She's worried the team will lose its intensity. Too many times she's watched them fail to put a team away when they had them by the throat; too many times she's watched the wheels come loose.

"Give me sixteen more minutes!" she orders.

The intensity continues in the third quarter, the lead holding at 15. Only the hustle of Wambolt keeps the Cowgirls from being blown right out into the snow.

Aside from a momentary lapse at the start of the fourth quarter, it's all Hardin, a performance worthy of a conference champ. With a little under two minutes to go and the Lady Bulldogs up by 17, Coach Mac allows herself a rare sideline smile. She can't remember any team she's ever coached playing four quarters of such consistent basketball. It has been a team effort. For the first time all season, all five starters are in double figures, Sharon high scorer with 14. Christina, the only substitute, has added instant energy during her minutes, chipping in with three assists and five steals.

Coach Mac turns to the bench and motions the second string to check in for the final 60 seconds. Maria Oswald and Stacie hop up and hustle to the scorer's table. But Geri, Amy, and DyAnna don't move.

"Hurry and check in," says Coach Mac.

"No!" answers Geri.

"What'd you say?" replies Coach Mac, disbelieving.

"No!" repeats Geri.

Coach Mac glares, first at Geri, then at Amy and DyAnna.

Amy hesitates, poised on the edge of the bench, uncertain what to do. All season long she showed up on time to practices and worked hard with no praise, no pat on the back. Most games she never got out of her sweats, and on the rare occasions when she did get in, it was for garbage time. The one game that she did get in with the score close, she played well, but then it was back to the bench. She still hasn't scored a basket. For 18 games she has watched Coach Mac treat Anita, Tiffany, and Sharon as if they could do no wrong. But something inside her won't let her disobey a coach's order. She pulls off her sweats and hustles to check in.

Coach Mac turns her back on Geri and DyAnna. She isn't going to beg them, she isn't going to let this little mutiny ruin the dance. Her team is now one win away from going to State, one win away from her greatest coaching triumph. If these sulkers want to brood and pout, that's their problem. She will enjoy the moment.

Before the subs can enter the game, there's a loose ball near midcourt and Sharon and Wambolt crash into each other in hard pursuit. The ref signals a foul on Wambolt, her fifth. Fighting back tears, she heads to the bench, a senior at the end of a noble varsity career. Sharon follows close behind, hoping to shake her hand.

Ever since the ninth grade, they have played hard against each other, fiercely competitive. But they have never talked, never shaken hands. Their only communication has been the pushing, shoving, and bumping. As Wambolt nears the scorer's table, Sharon intercepts her.

"Good game," she says, extending a handshake.

Surprised, Wambolt shakes hands, then stands frozen near her bench, the ignominy of the defeat sinking deep. Unable to hold back the tears, she begins to cry. Not little tears, but big huge pellets. She makes no effort to hide her

334

anguish, sobbing full force in front of everyone in the gym. Her body trembles.

From the crowd of white supporters behind the Hardin bench, a mother of a Hardin junior varsity player rises to her feet and points a hostile finger at Wambolt. "Sit down, you loser, you big crybaby!" she screeches.

CHAPTER THIRTY-FIVE

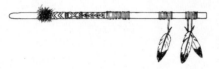

On the bus back to the Lone Tree, Coach Mac summons Sharon up to her seat in front. "I don't want those girls ruining what we've worked so hard to achieve," she says.

Sharon nods.

"I need you to do me a favor," continues Coach Mac. "You're the captain. I want you to talk to them."

"What am I supposed to say?" asks Sharon.

"Just make sure they're not going to do something disruptive."

Coach's Mac's use of Sharon is puzzling. Why doesn't she talk to Geri and DyAnna herself? Or why doesn't she just put them on the next Greyhound home? Sharon shouldn't have to do her dirty work. Then again, maybe it's a good move. Maybe Sharon's the only one who can keep a lid on something that could turn ugly at a very bad time.

Sharon promises to try.

Life is weird, or more specifically, life is making me weird. Eight months ago I had not heard of Hardin, Montana; I didn't know a Crow from a Cree; and I could count on the fingers of one hand the girls' basketball games I'd seen. Yet here I am, camped out at midnight in my room

at the Lone Tree a thousand miles from home, alone, trying to eavesdrop on the conversation of the four Lady Bulldogs filtering through the thin wall separating our rooms.
This isn't exactly the stuff of Woodward and Bernstein—
they are gossiping about Tiffany and her boyfriend—and
I'm about an inch from Dirty Old Manhood. All in the service of journalistic truth.

"She tries to be such a goody-two-shoes," I think I hear.

Evidently, Coach Mac can hear them, too. She pounds on
their door, announcing it is past curfew and they need to
turn off the light and go to sleep. I sympathize with her
task. She is in charge of a dozen teenagers on a three-day
road trip, a responsibility requiring her to be part coach
and part warden, a person entrusted with the considerable
task of guarding against alcohol, drugs, and boys. It means
sleeping with one eye open; it means answering to parents
and administrators if anything goes wrong. Earlier, she
spotted Holly zipping through the lobby. There's a party
waiting to happen, she thought.

There's a knock on my door. Is she checking up on me,
too? I open the door but it isn't her . . . it's Coach Oswald.
He just talked to his wife back in Hardin and she told him
that the tests on Amylynn Adams had not gone well and
they are air-lifting her to Denver for special treatment.

Life is not only making me weird, it's making me sad. I
have been meeting with Amylynn almost every day for
three months to help her with her writing, and in many
ways, I've come to know more about her than any of the
girls on the team. Her candor and bravery in dealing with
her disease have awed me, and now I can't sleep, thinking
about her, thinking about Sharon, thinking about how life
can take such unexpected bounces.

I stare at the ceiling. I can taste the faint bile of adrenaline at the back of my throat. I know that at tip-off tomorrow—or is it today?—I will be as tense as I was warming

up for my own debut in the majors. After more than twenty years away from sports, the addiction has reeled me back in. It isn't that I just want the girls to win Divisionals and make it to State. I want the season to never end.

I'm still up when the sun rises.

Stacie is center stage at breakfast, cutting her stack of pancakes into an outline of the United States, slowly eating the East Coast a state at a time, then dramatically swallowing the South in one huge bite.

"Do you know where Wisconsin is?" asks Anita.

"Duh!" replies Stacie, stabbing her fork into Arizona.

"How about Alaska?"

"That's easy," Stacie says, dousing the top left hand corner with syrup. "See, there's the oil spill."

At the end of the table, Sharon and Geri quietly converse in Crow, then laugh. Maybe Sharon's doing Coach Mac's dirty work . . . I can't tell. If she is, it's going well.

I'm sitting next to Yvonne Demars, the cheerleader adviser and French teacher. She seems perturbed that the girls are talking in Crow.

"Why don't they teach Crow at Hardin High?" I ask. "Wouldn't it be more practical than French?"

"French will be useful for students going into business," she explains.

"Why? Are they going to start printing John Deere manuals in French?"

She isn't amused. "There's a lot of kids at Hardin High of German ancestry, but we don't teach German," she says. "And over in Butte there's a lot of kids of Polish ancestry, but there's no classes there in Polish history or culture. So why should the Crows get special treatment?"

Stacie slowly chews California. "Could somebody get me

a toothpick?" she asks. "I think I've got a surfer caught in my teeth."

Back at the Lone Tree, a knock on my door interrupts my nap. It's Anita. She's come to invite me to join the team in Sharon's room where they have gathered to listen on the radio to a consolation bracket game between Glendive and Sidney. Should Hardin lose to Colstrip tonight, they will have to stay over another day to play in the consolation bracket for the league's second qualifying slot for State. I wonder if this invitation officially makes me an honorary seventeen-year-old girl.

The room is packed—seven Crows, five whites, and a ton of clothes strewn in every direction, including garments I don't want to see. The coaches are at a meeting to vote on the All-Conference team. I clear off a space in a corner and sit down on the floor. Sharon is sprawled out on one of the beds, wrapped in an Indian blanket. Sidney scores and everyone cheers. They don't want to play Glendive, the team that blew them out of the gym, twice. As the game progresses, I am ignored, just part of the woodwork.

A last-second shot by Glendive fails to connect and Sidney wins, sending the room into a temporary frenzy. Even Geri and DyAnna yell their approval. Sharon has already talked to them, I later learn, and all is calm on the mutiny front. It wasn't really much of a talk, according to Sharon; she just told them Coach Mac asked her to talk with them, and then they all laughed.

I pick myself off the floor and head for the door. "You go, girl," says Stacie.

As the Lady Bulldogs huddle prior to tip-off, Coach Mac extends a high-five to her co-captains, Sharon and Tiffany.

The consolation games are finished, and no matter the outcome of tonight's game against Colstrip, Hardin is going to State.

"Congratulations!" she exudes. "You guys have worked hard. You deserve this."

She lets the words sink in, then adds, "We've still got a game to play. We can't let down now. I don't want us to back into State. We have to win Divisionals!"

The team responds, playing with intensity, poise, and confidence. At halftime they lead 32–26. Other than Christina, no subs have played, Coach Mac holding to the theory that solidifying first-team chemistry and building momentum for the state tournament in Whitefish is more important than a little playing time for the scrub patrol.

A temporary loss of focus in the third quarter is cause for concern, but then Sharon kicks it back into a higher gear. On a Colstrip three-on-one fast break, she strips the guard of the ball, then takes it the length of the court hounded by two defenders, giving them the shake with a hesitation, cross-over dribble before scoring on a reverse, spin-it-off-the-glass layup. Even Coach Mac applauds.

In the fourth quarter, Hardin pours it on, building the lead to 20. With two minutes left, Coach Mac finally signals for the second unit to enter the game. One by one they file to the scorer's table, including DyAnna. Only Geri remains on the bench, Coach Mac standing next to her.

"Are you going in or not?" she demands.

Geri has been playing basketball since the seventh grade, and although she has no grand illusions about her talent, her involvement with the team is vital to her self-esteem, a chance to connect with friends, have fun, belong. But in her senior year, Coach Mac has killed all that . . . at least in her mind.

Slowly, she rises from her seat and heads toward the scorer's table, saying nothing. Caught off guard, Coach Mac reaches out and grabs her by the back of the jersey and pulls her back toward her. For an awkward instant, they stare at each other, unsure what to say or do. Without speaking, they embrace. It's not a perfunctory little hug, but a full-frontal squeeze, tight, filled with a season's worth of emotion, neither letting go. Both tear up, then finally release, still no words spoken. Then Geri checks into the game.

Watching this embrace, I am puzzled. I don't understand why some coaches, be they high school, college, or pro, refuse to sit down with their players and explain their roles. Seems like basic Communication 101. If Coach Mac had gone to the malcontents early and often, and told them they shouldn't expect to play much but that they were still important to the team's success, then the players could have accepted that or quit.

My time with Coach Mac so far leaves me with little doubt that she cares about her players, all of them. But why give Geri a hug now? It almost feels like a cheap shot . . . an olive branch after the battle has been lost. Somehow, I don't think her coaching hero, Bobby Knight, would've hugged a player who'd just told him to buzz off.

Hardin wins 58–44. Anita leads the scoring with 17, Sharon adding 16, with nine rebounds. Once again, Christina's play off the bench—six points, three steals, and a ton of defensive havoc—raises the question of why she wasn't on the varsity sooner.

After the final horn, Hardin fans pour out of the stands onto the floor to mob the team. Danetta almost smothers Sharon. "You're the one they all come to see," she gushes.

Behind them, Sharon's father, who took three days off from his job at Crow Hospital to make the trip, stays back, watching, smiling, making no effort to intrude.

The players depart for the locker room. Standing in the middle of the court with Anita's and Tiffany's parents, I can hear the squeals of the team in the dressing room. "The team is peaking at just the right time," observes Tom Hopfauf. "Their last three games are the best they've played all year."

It's true.

Bobbie Romine, the team manager, approaches. "The players want you in the locker room," she says.

Entering the dimly lit locker room, I don't see anyone, just clothes and underwear hanging from hooks. I feel weird, apprehensive. This is my first trip into a girls' locker room. Suddenly, from around a corner, the whole team appears, still in their uniforms, stampeding toward me. I have nowhere to run.

Sharon grabs one arm, Tiffany the other, and with everyone else helping, they carry me into the shower room where the cold water is running. I spot Coach Mac and Coach Oswald off to the side. They are already drenched.

"No!" I plead. "I'm wearing my new longjohns."

It isn't so bad—in fact I'm honored—until later when I walk outside in my wet clothes to the bus and the below-freezing windchill slices right through me.

After dinner at the South 40, Sidney's premier beefateria, the players reboard the bus for the long ride home. "Is everybody here?" asks Coach Mac, still bubbling.

"Where's Sharon?" inquires Anita, whose 17 points included nine of 11 from the free throw line.

"She's riding back with her grandmother," says Coach Mac.

I look out the window and see Sharon drive off into the night with Holly. I can see smoke coming out of the passenger window. Maybe it's just someone's icy breath.

The swirling snow that greeted the team on its arrival in Sidney is gone, the road ahead clear and dry. As the bus pulls onto the highway, it is followed by a long caravan of cars and pickups, most of them filled with Indians. Near the front of the line is Marlene's van, a hastily scrawled "Indian Power" sign taped to its side.

With its cargo of happy warriors, *Bulldog I* rolls homeward over the eastern Montana landscape. Three hours later, and only halfway there, I awake from a little snooze and look out the window. For as far back as the eye can see, it's a line of headlights patiently snaking through the moonless night, 150 cars, maybe more, nobody passing, not even when the bus strains over a hill at forty-five miles an hour.

It's 4:00 A.M. when we reach Hardin, the caravan still intact. In the back of the bus, Stacie stirs, staring out the window at the deserted streets. "Where's the mayor? Where's the parade?" she asks. "What kind of reception is this?"

PART VI

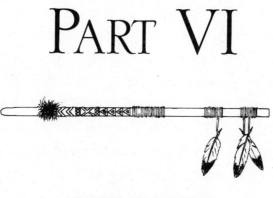

STATE

CHAPTER THIRTY-SIX

It's the send-off banquet in the jam-packed cafeteria for the Lady Bulldogs two nights before leaving for Whitefish. Black and orange streamers and balloons decorate the room. At the podium, Madam Chairman, Clara Nomee, turns to the players seated at the head table. She is already well into a speech of more than sufficient length.

"You girls are very important to me," she states. "I wasn't fortunate enough to have any children of my own, so I feel as if you're my children. In my clan I helped raise thirteen nieces and nephews, and have twenty-three grand-kids, but I always feel that all young Crows belong to me."

"Not my granddaughter," Danetta mutters at her table.

"You girls are idols to these young kids here tonight," continues Nomee. "But always remember that God gave you the talent, and without Him you wouldn't be where you are. I pray you will leave drugs and alcohol out of your lives. Please stay clean-cut. Live one day at a time. And lean on God! At one time I was an alcoholic, one of the baddest drunks on the streets in Hardin. It took God to change that. If it wasn't for God, I wouldn't be the tribal chairman today."

"I'm confused," whispers Tom Hopfauf. "I thought this was a banquet to honor the conference champions, not a church AA meeting."

Sponsored by several tribal families, the event is the first time a Hardin High girls' team has been distinguished with a public honoring ceremony. It's standing room only. With no shortage of fry bread. Or bad perfume at the dais.

"And remember, girls," continues Nomee, "you can grow up to be whatever you want. Someday, one of you could become tribal chairman."

Stacie grins.

"You're kidding, right?" I ask, incredulous.

"Nope," replies Coach Mac.

She has just informed me of the results of the All-Conference voting. Sharon and Tiffany have both been selected to the first team, Anita to the second. That makes sense. What doesn't figure, however, is the way the voting came down.

Selected by the coaches, with each coach rating every nominated player on a 0–10 scale, Tiffany and Glendive's Michelle Frenzel, the leading scorer in the league, tied as the leading vote-getters. Sharon, the second top scorer in the conference, received a zero from one coach. *Zero.*

How could it be? Sharon never played dirty, talked trash, baited the refs, failed to hustle. No player in the league scored as many clutch baskets or made the difference so often between victory and defeat.

It makes no sense. *Zero.* It's like leaving M.J. off the All-Star team.

But of course it does make sense. Some people in these parts don't like Indians.

Next stop on the Lady Bulldog Send-Off Tour is the pep assembly. But the mood is tempered. Sitting in her wheelchair next to the bleachers, Amylynn Adams has come to school with good intentions of paying tribute to her former teammates, but her presence has saddened the gathering.

The team files by her wheelchair to greet her and offer words of encouragement. She was not transferred to the hospital in Denver as earlier planned, but her condition has worsened, the injections of cortisone swelling her body to an almost unrecognizable state. She struggles just to sit. The only thing keeping her normally ebullient spirits from crashing through the floor is the nightly phone call from her newly located father in Cincinnati. I stop by to say hello and it's all I can do to choke back the tears.

Coach Mac calls the players to gather in front of the student body, then presents them the Divisional Championship trophy. Holding it aloft together, they take a brief victory lap, the pep band playing the school fight song. The cheering from the students is restrained.

Conspicuously absent from the victory lap is Sharon, choosing instead to play her clarinet with the pep band. "It's hard to explain," she later says, "but with Amylynn sitting there in her wheelchair, I just didn't feel like running around and acting all happy."

"Karna called Sharon and told her she was coming to Whitefish," says Marlene.

"How did Sharon respond?" I ask.

"She hung up on her."

It's predictable that Karna would be trying to screw up the most important week of her daughter's basketball life. All Sharon can do is hope she doesn't show up. It'll be a huge relief for her to finally climb on the bus Thursday morning and get away from all the advice, all the distractions.

She and her teammates won't be making the trip alone, of course. Her clan will be making the long trek to Whitefish. They will cram into their pickups and one-eyed Fords, leaving their little box houses; they will drive all day and night, the family squeezed in tight, clan uncles coughing, babies crying, grandmothers solemnly staring out the window, aunts pinching off sprigs of cedar for protection; they will be pinning their hopes upon her spin moves and skinny shoulders. She is the reason they will be leaving their safe place and venturing as far from home as some have ever been. *Sharon LaForge. The One They All Come to See.*

Everything she and the team have accomplished—seventeen wins, league title, Divisional Championship—none of it will matter if they bomb at State. If she is to leave a mark on the world, they have to win.

"So what will you do if Karna comes walking into the gym up there in Whitefish?" I ask.

Marlene ponders the question, then replies: "I'll escort her back out."

"And if she doesn't go?"

"Then I'll drag her out by the hair."

As the players board the bus, it's 5:30 A.M., minus two degrees, and still dark on the prairie. As usual, Sharon is the last to arrive, dressed only in shorts and a T-shirt, her Indian blanket draped over her shoulders. Packed in her suitcase are two new dresses Danetta bought for her to wear in Whitefish.

According to the map, it is 481 miles from Hardin to Whitefish, and by Louie's calculation, it's going to take fifteen hours, including stops, more if it's snowing over the Continental Divide as the forecast predicts.

"I'm bored," says Stacie as we pull out of the parking lot.

"The good news is that we're going to State," observes

Coach Oswald. "The bad news is that it's fifteen hours on a bus with Stacie."

Personally, I'm looking forward to it. We're not even out of town yet and she's reinvented herself from Betty Boop to Tammy Wynette . . . without even trying.

The Interstate is deserted as we head toward Billings. Listening to the girls chatter in the back of the bus, I am reminded of the many long bus rides I took in the minor leagues, going from places like Macon to Montgomery . . . Eugene to Wenatchee. Thirty years later I can't remember much about the games I played in those towns, but the bus rides in between are still vivid—the card games, the belching, the hot foots—those shared times that brought us together, made us a team.

An hour later, as the sun rises over the rimrocks above Billings, Stacie and her teammates have settled in for the long trek, many of them sleeping as we follow the meandering Yellowstone River and leave the prairie behind. We start the long climb over the Rockies, the scenery getting more rugged and mountainous. Near Livingston, we pass the site of a buffalo jump, where the noble Indians drove herds of buffalo off of cliffs so that they might eat two or three.

At Bozeman, known as the gateway to Yellowstone Park, we stop for breakfast. I suggest we try the Leaf and Bean, a popular espresso and scone place half owned by Glenn Close, but I am unanimously overruled. We eat at a Denny's wannabe, my grand slam special coming up a couple base runners short.

On the way out of town Stacie announces that she has to go to the bathroom.

"Why didn't you go back at the restaurant?" asks Coach Mac.

"There were no Protecto-Seats," she explains.

* * *

Onward and westward we trek, crossing the Madison and the Big Little Missouri rivers, then up and over the steep grade of the Continental Divide and down into the copper mining town of Butte, once known as the ugliest town in the west. It has sprouted a few trees since then, but surely it's still battling for the top spot, the huge open-pit mine behind the town greeting visitors like a giant scab. Still, it's a sacred place in Irish-American history because the Irish not only worked the mines around Butte, they owned them. It is also the state's major source of Democrats.

We stop in Butte for a practice Coach Mac has arranged at Montana Tech. She has studied a tape of Hardin's first-round opponent, Stevensville, and wants to practice against the man-to-man defense they employ. From what she's seen on the tape, she doesn't think Stevensville has anybody athletic enough to stop Sharon inside. So that's what the practice focuses on—getting the ball to Sharon in the post.

Leaving town, Louie informs the girls that Butte is the home of Evil Knievel and the "toughest town in America."

"How do they know it's the toughest?" asks Stacie. "Was there a big fight?"

The bus continues west on I-90 on its long day's journey through the Rockies, rolling by Galen, the site of the Montana State Psychiatric Hospital where Karna first underwent treatment for her drinking, then past Deer Lodge, the site of the Montana State Penitentiary. According to legend, some of the roughest prison hoop is played at Deer Lodge, games pitting Indians against whites where the rule of the court is: *no autopsy, no foul.*

"I'm still bored," proclaims Stacie.

"Do some homework," suggests Coach Mac.

"I'm not *that* bored."

With the predicted snowstorm stalled to the west, *Bulldog I* passes Missoula, home of the University of Montana, a school called Granola U by kids in Hardin based on the high ratio of backpacks and Birkenstocks on campus. Eight miles west of Missoula, it's a late lunch at a truck stop, then north on two-lane Highway 93, a scenic drive through the Mission Range of the snowcapped Rockies.

Night descends for the final leg through the pastoral valley of the Flathead Indian Reservation. We pass the turnoff to Glacier National Park, closed for the winter, and moonlight shimmers off of Flathead Lake.

It is nine o'clock when Ginger, Louie's wife and co-driver, wheels the bus into the Best Western Outlaw Inn in Kalispell, the team's tournament headquarters fifteen minutes south of Whitefish and fifteen long hours from Hardin. This is no minor league Best Western—it's a vast establishment set up for conventions, a four-star place with sauna, Jacuzzi, gift shop, video poker machines, cocktail lounge, and *two* indoor pools.

As the players gather in the lobby to await their room assignments, Coach Mac hands them each a printed sheet of paper:

DIVISIONAL CHAMPS
IT TAKES A LITTLE MORE TO BE A STATE CHAMPION

This is what the long hours of practice are all about. These are the last games of the year. Remember, if anyone asks you the best game you ever played, let it be the last one. Again, use the time in the motel to be with your teammates, rest, and do HOMEWORK. I am so proud of you. You are the best team, but just as impor-

tant, you are the best group of people that anyone could ever work with.

YOU REALLY ARE CHAMPIONS IN EVERY WAY!
IT ALL STARTED WITH A DREAM, AND IT'S TIME TO
MAKE THAT DREAM COME TRUE. GO LADY BULLDOGS!

After checking into their rooms (with the phones removed again), Sharon and Amy set out to explore the motel, made wide-eyed by its creature comforts. "I've never stayed in a place with one pool, let alone two," says Amy.

Sharon detours by a pay phone and pulls out Marlene's long-distance calling card. "What'ya doing?" asks Amy.

"I'm calling Randy in Albuquerque," Sharon answers. "I want to find out how he did today."

"Is he going to call you after your games?" asks Amy.

CHAPTER THIRTY-SEVEN

Wow! Looks like someone's having a bad-hair day," says Tiffany, pointing at my wet, stringy mess. Standing next to her, Sharon surveys my do and laughs.

"I just got out of the pool," I explain.

We're standing next to the highway in front of the Outlaw Inn, waiting for a break in the traffic so we can hustle across the street to Fred's Family Restaurant and join the team for breakfast. The predicted snowstorm has arrived, turning western Montana's highways into treacherous ice rinks.

"You've already been for a swim?" asks Sharon, disbelieving.

"Hundred laps," I brag, neglecting to mention that each lap in the motel's indoor pool is three strokes.

I follow Sharon and Tiffany across the recently sanded road. They are arm in arm, and if I didn't know better, I'd swear they are best friends, two teenagers without a trace of mistrust, resentment, or rivalry between them.

In the restaurant the other players are already seated. Stacie eyes my thinning, disheveled hair. "I've got three words for you," she says.

"What's that?"

"Hair Club for Men."

"That's four words," Anita points out.

"Close enough," answers Stacie.

The bus trip from Kalispell to Whitefish is ten miles, and for each of those miles, the Lady Bulldogs are game-face silent. Not even Stacie utters a peep. The snowfall has eased off, but there is still concern whether Hardin fans have been able to navigate the bad conditions over the Continental Divide. According to reports, poor visibility and swirling snow have reduced I-90 to one lane, with cars sliding off the road into snowbanks.

Whitefish is small and friendly, with cute clapboard houses, a gentrified, frontier-like downtown, and a major ski resort, Big Mountain, hovering in the background. Glacier National Park and some of America's most spectacular scenery is just up the road.

Dressed in a new short brown skirt and matching coat, Sharon is the last player off the bus. She surveys the scene outside the gym: school buses, athletes in letterman's jackets, ticket lines, pep bands, tournament banners.

"I can't believe we're really here," she says. "It's like I'm in a dream."

Eight teams have qualified for State, including number-two-ranked Ronan and top-ranked Dillon, the defending champ. Also making it is Colstrip, winner of a consolation game against Miles City to earn the Eastern Conference's second berth.

"Don't be in awe of these other teams," warns Coach Mac.

But it's hard not to be in awe, especially when you're a seventeen-year-old and Billings has been the western edge of your universe. Somehow, teams from far away loom bigger, stronger, faster, scarier. Surely the opposition must chew nails.

But Coach Mac isn't afraid of Hardin's opponent, the Lady Yellowjackets of Stevensville, a small town south of Missoula in the picturesque Bitterroot Valley. Although winners of seven of their last eight, including an upset of league champ Ronan in the Western Conference Divisionals, they are a mediocre 12-10 on the year, and judging from the tapes, they are a slow perimeter team vulnerable to Hardin's full-court pressure.

"The only way we can lose," says Coach Mac, "is if the girls cave in to the pressure and lose their poise."

After entering the gym, the team climbs to the top of the bleachers to watch Ronan play Browning. If Hardin beats Stevensville, they will play the winner of this game. Sharon isn't impressed. "We're way faster than either of these teams," she reports.

Stacie opens the tournament program and turns to the picture of the Browning Indians, a team from the Blackfoot Reservation. She reads aloud the names of the players, enunciating each name slowly and precisely: *Monica Butterfly . . . Barbara Madman . . . Carrie Iron Shirt . . . Elaine Little Plume . . . Jill Comes At Night.*

"Wow!" she proclaims. "Jill Comes At Night. Bet she's popular with the boys."

Despite the distance and the bad driving conditions, a full contingent of Hardin fans has arrived safely for the tournament. In motels around the area, many Crow families have crammed three generations into a single room. Much to Sharon's relief, an emergency trip to the dentist for a bad toothache derailed Karna's plan to come to Whitefish. Karna did tell Marlene, however, that if Hardin wins their first game, she'll find a way to get there for the semifinals, even if she has to hitchhike.

Sharon's family enters the gym, and Marlene stops just inside the door, her eyes searching the surroundings. Earlier, she had taken a side trip up to Big Mountain, stopping along the side of the road on the way back to pick up some cedar bark, a Crow symbol for good fortune. The cedar and several sprigs of sage are in her purse.

She finishes her visual examination of the gym. "Our medicine is strong here," she concludes.

The warmups are over, the starting lineups introduced. Coach Mac, the only female coach in the tournament, gathers the team around her, high-fiving her co-captains. Despite the fact that her team is about to take the court in the school's first-ever appearance at State, she appears calm. Inside, however, it's gastric fireworks.

"Just play relaxed!" she shouts, trying to be heard above the pep band. "Don't force things."

With everybody in the packed-to-capacity gym on their feet, the opening tap goes to Owena, who panics, shoveling it toward Sharon like a handful of hot rivets. Stevensville intercepts and scores.

"Calm down!" yells Coach Mac.

Tiffany bobbles a pass out of bounds; Sharon shoots an air ball; Tiffany travels; Owena misses everything. Five possessions, five screwups. A nightmare of a start.

"Relax!" Coach Mac repeats.

The horrible start ends with a basket by Sharon inside, then a fast-break layup by Tiffany. The jitters begin to subside.

Sharon hits back-to-back shots from the key. Christina comes off the bench at full throttle and the Stevensville guards can't get the ball upcourt. Anita and Tiffany hit easy buckets. In less than three minutes, Hardin reels off 13 straight points.

"Don't back off," orders Coach Mac.

They don't. At the end of the second quarter, they lead 37–19, their biggest halftime margin of the season. With the exception of her opening air ball, Sharon has played flawlessly, scoring 15.

"The game's not over," warns Coach Mac at halftime.

Yes it is. Hardin continues its domination in the second half. It is so easy, in fact, that for only the second time all season, Coach Mac plays all twelve players, keeping the starting team on the bench the last five minutes. The final score is 58–43.

"There's four teams in our conference better than that team," concludes Coach Mac.

For the night, Anita and Tiffany both score 12, with Christina contributing six points, five rebounds, six assists, and three steals. But clearly, this is Sharon's game, playing with as much poise and confidence as she has all year. She finishes with 24 points, the leading scorer of all the first-round games, her shots coming in all flavors—lefthanded hook, turnaround jumper, and a baseline drive that brought down the house.

In his postgame interview, Stevensville coach Terry Rosen offers his perspective: "Sharon LaForge is the best player we've seen all season."

CHAPTER THIRTY-EIGHT

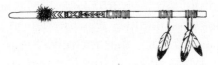

Y ou're her mother, you should be there," says Stanley Pretty Horse, holding up the sports page of the *Billings Gazette*. He points to the headline: "LaForge Leads Hardin to Win." "I'm telling you, we can make it over there in time for the game."

"Yeah, right," says Karna. "How much we got between us, twelve cents?"

They are sitting at the dining room table at Danetta's house, where Karna has crashed for the night while her parents are in Whitefish. Pretty Horse, an unemployed carpenter, gets up from the table and heads outside.

"Where you going?" asks Karna.

"I need to check something in my car," he says. "I'll be right back."

Karna rubs her jaw, then washes down three Tylenol with the dregs of her morning cup of instant coffee—she got the Tylenol from the dentist at the clinic where she'd gone for her toothache. What she really wants for the pain is a shot of bourbon, but this is Day 6 of her newest sobriety, and she's trying to stay the course.

Pretty Horse returns, holding up a map of Montana, pointing to Whitefish. "I ain't shittin'," he says, "we can make it."

"What do we have to do, drive ninety miles an hour?" says Karna.

According to Pretty Horse's calculations, all he has to do is average sixty miles an hour to get there for the 6:30 tip-off.

"How'll we pay for this, rob gas stations along the way?" she asks.

"I got that all figured out," he says. "We'll stop at a pawn shop in Billings and I'll hock my new Skilsaw. That'll give us enough."

Eight hours later, they stop in Missoula for gas and a snack, the Skilsaw hocked back in Billings. Pretty Horse checks the time. Four-thirty P.M. Still 120 miles to go. "We can make it," he says.

So far, the weather has cooperated, the pass over the Continental Divide wide open when they passed. But as they turn north off of I-90 and head up Highway 93, the snow starts to fall. Heavy snow.

"Sharon will sure be surprised to see you," says Pretty Horse.

"Yep."

Waiting in the lobby of the Outlaw Inn to leave for the game, I see Sharon standing in the corner and looking like Grumpy the Shark. Her eyes point me in the direction of Anita's and Tiffany's parents standing across the lobby.

"That pisses me off," she says. "Coach Mac made a rule that the motel was just for the team and coaches, no family. So how come the whites get to have their parents stay here and we don't?"

The answer, I later learn, is because the Dewalds and Hopfaufs made advance reservations at the Outlaw Inn and Coach Mac didn't want to tell them they had to change motels after they'd already unpacked.

But it isn't just the motel situation that has Sharon irked. Earlier, she overslept, missing the team breakfast. Then Coach Mac decided against a pregame supper, afraid the girls would be too bloated for the game. So the only thing Sharon has eaten all day is a slice of leftover pepperoni pizza she scrounged from last night's takeout order.

"I don't know why she won't let us eat," she says.

"Couldn't you have gotten something on your own?" I ask.

She shoots me the evil eye. Maybe all the pressure has finally gotten to her. Maybe this would be a good time for Coach Mac to tell her that an assistant coach from the University of Idaho approached her after the Stevensville game last night and said she liked Sharon's game and wanted to know about her grades. Not wanting to add to the pressure already on Sharon, Coach Mac decided not to tell her about the conversation until after the tournament.

I slide away from her, moving next to Amy. "Sharon's sure in a grumpy mood," I observe.

"She's pissed because she's been trying to call Randy at his rodeo thing ever since last night," she says. "He's never in his room . . . or maybe he's there and just doesn't want to answer."

The wipers on Pretty Horse's pickup squeak against the windshield, the snow continuing to fall. Traffic has slowed in the Bitterroot Valley, and the forecast on the radio warns of hazardous driving conditions.

"We may miss the start of the game," he says, "but we'll still see most of it."

Karna leans forward in her seat, co-navigating. At first, when Pretty Horse posed the idea of driving all the way across the state, it didn't sink in with her—they had no money, it was too many miles, the weather was bad—but now that she's getting close, she's starting to believe it.

Just south of Flathead Lake, they slosh through the town of Ronan, tonight's opponent. "Maybe I should put some bad medicine on this place," suggests Pretty Horse.

Karna ignores him. "I don't even care if Sharon knows I'm there," she says. "I just want to be there for her, cheer her on."

"Right on," says Pretty Horse, focused on the road.

"This is her senior year and I've missed everything, you know, homecoming, trips to the doctor, whatever . . . hear what I'm saying?"

"But you're still a good mom," he says. "You really love that girl. Anyone can see that."

"Let's get a hot dog," suggests Amy as they enter the gym.

"Screw it!" snaps Sharon. "I ain't eatin'."

"Sorry I asked," replies Amy.

While the girls head to the locker room to get ready, Coach Mac walks back outside to have a nervous smoke and review her notes on tonight's opponent.

"No way we should lose to these guys," she says. "They can't run with us. Hell, they lost to Stevensville in Divisionals, and Stevensville couldn't beat us in a hundred games."

She stamps out her cigarette and turns back toward the door, then pauses. "Remember what I told you at the start of the year about us being a team of destiny? Well, I still feel that way."

As she readies to leave the motel room, Marlene blows out the embers of the burning cedar collected yesterday from the side of the road, then puts four small bundles of sage in her purse. But when she and Blaine and Danetta arrive at the gym, she stops just inside the door.

"Something's not right here," she says, looking toward the Ronan side.

Like Hardin, the Ronan Maidens are a team of Indians and whites, with two Flathead Indians in their starting lineup. Unlike the Crows, the Flatheads (a nation of two confederated tribes, the Salish and the Kootenai), are one of the most financially self-reliant reservations in America, with an unemployment rate 60 percent lower than that of the Crows, their revenue coming largely from $10 million annual lease payments from Montana Power for Kerr Dam built on the Flathead River in 1930.

"What's the problem?" asks Danetta.

"The Ronan people have already put their medicine on this place," replies Marlene. "I can feel it."

"What's it feel like?"

"It's strong," answers Marlene. "Very strong medicine. It worries me."

Karna turns on the radio, scanning the dial, hoping to find a station carrying the game. All she gets is static. The snow falls even harder.

"How much farther is it?" she asks.

"Half hour," answers Pretty Horse.

Everyone rises for the national anthem, sung a cappella by a vocally gifted sophomore from Whitefish High. Sharon, normally fidgety just prior to the opening tap, stands in rapt attention, transfixed on the singer. "Holy cow!" she says when the song ends. "That sent a shiver down my back."

Stacie nods her approval. "That guy should be on *Star Search*."

The first half is a disaster. Hardin is outrebounded, out-hustled, and outplayed, the low point a 10-point Ronan run in the second quarter. Aside from Sharon and Tiffany, the team is playing scared, almost as if they've already given up. Earlier in the second quarter, Owena tosses up an air ball and Sharon glares at Coach Mac.

"Get her out of here!" she yells.

In the Hardin stands, Marlene turns to Danetta. "I told you so," she says. "I don't like their medicine."

With a minute left before halftime, and Hardin trailing by 12, a timeout is called. "Sharon, you have to stay in your zone on the press," instructs Coach Oswald.

"I would but I have to cover for everybody else," she steams. "Tell them to move!"

"Just worry about yourself!"

Ten miles away in Kalispell, Karna continues to fiddle with the radio dial, finally finding the game. "Shit!" she exclaims on another air ball by Owena. "What's wrong with that girl?"

Pretty Horse stops for a traffic signal.

"Run it!" orders Karna.

Pretty Horse looks both ways, then runs it.

"Hold on, my little babycakes!" Karna shouts. "Mama's coming."

If Hardin is to get back in the game, it won't be by the three-point shot. In their previous 16 games, they attempted a grand total of *zero* three-pointers compared to

LARRY COLTON

158 by opponents. As Glendive and Billings Senior did to the Lady Bulldogs in their only losses, Ronan is collapsing in the middle, conceding the outside shot.

Ronan starts the third quarter by upping their lead to 14. Coach Mac calls another timeout.

"We're running out of time, girls," she says. "You've got two choices. You can get it together and still win this thing, or you can pack it in and blow everything you've worked for all year."

On Hardin's next possession, Sharon scores with a drop-step move to her left and is fouled. She converts the free throw, and for the first time since the opening minutes, the Hardin crowd responds. The noise unnerves the Ronan guard and Christina steals a pass and scores. Then Anita hits a jumper, Tiffany scores on a fast break, Sharon flips in a little baby hook, and Anita scores again on a power drive. It's 13 straight points, and just like that, Hardin trails by only one. The noise is overwhelming. Karna and Pretty Horse are just south of town, the traffic at a crawl.

At the start of the fourth quarter, everybody in the gym is on their feet . . . and will stay that way the rest of the game. Sharon hits her first two shots, and for the first time in the game, the Lady Bulldogs take the lead. Then, for the next six minutes, the lead changes hands seven times.

With two minutes to go and Ronan up by two, Karna and Pretty Horse are a mile from the gym. "Be strong, honey!" pleads Karna. "I'm almost there." Sharon has not been out of the game. Neither has Tiffany or Anita.

With 58 seconds left, Ronan scores to go up by four. Sharon inbounds the ball to Tiffany, then heads upcourt,

366

frantically waving to get it back. Tiffany is cut off just across midcourt, but manages to overhand a pass ahead to Sharon near the free throw line. Off balance, she shoots and misses, but she is fouled.

With the Ronan fans raising the volume even higher, she steps to the line and swishes the first shot, then the second. The margin is now two with 37 seconds left.

Karna and Pretty Horse reach the parking lot.

As a Ronan guard desperately tries to bring the ball up-court against ferocious pressure, Sharon traps her near the sideline and the girl dribbles it off her foot and out of bounds. It's Hardin's ball with 32 seconds left.

"Time out!" yells Coach Mac. It's their last one.

"Shit! There's no place to park!" shouts Pretty Horse, turning down another row.

"Over there!" says Karna, pointing to a no-parking zone right in front of the gym.

Coach Mac quickly consults with Coach Oswald to plot strategy. In the second half, Sharon and Tiffany have played like All-Staters, both with 21 points. Anita has also stepped it up, hitting five of her last six shots.

"Okay, here's the play," says Coach Mac, kneeling to draw it on her courtside chalkboard. The plan is for Christina to inbound it to Anita, who will pass it into the post to Sharon for a drive to the basket.

"Come on, let's get in there!" urges Pretty Horse, stopping the car in front of the gym.

Karna doesn't budge, her ear tuned to the radio.

*　　*　　*

Christina inbounds it to Anita, who turns to look for Sharon, who is double-teamed. In a panic, Anita lobs a crosscourt, ugly-duckling of a pass toward Tiffany, who is also covered. As the ball descends, three Ronan players are waiting for it, arms outstretched. But somehow, Tiffany worms her way between them and pulls it in 10 feet from the basket.

Taking the ball strong to the hoop has never been Tiffany's strength, but on this occasion, she blows by two defenders. From a foot away, she throws up an awkward shot, half hook, half slingshot. It goes in. With 24 seconds left, the score is tied at 61.

Quickly, Ronan inbounds the ball, and their guard, Steph Irvine, angles it toward midcourt. Christina cuts her off and they collide, both players tumbling to the floor. The foul is on Christina, her fifth, sending Irvine to the line for a one-and-one.

"Come on!" pleads Pretty Horse. "We gotta get in there and put some bad medicine on that girl."

Karna still doesn't budge.

"What's wrong?" asks Pretty Horse.

"Something is telling me to stay out here," says Karna. "I'm not sure what it is. But it's strong."

Irvine shoots a clothesline, the ball banging off the back rim high into the air, then straight down through the net. Ronan back on top by one.

"My God! Have you ever seen such a lucky shot?" Danetta yells.

The second free throw is also a rocket, but this time it bounces away. There's a wild scramble and a whistle.

Sharon is fouled and will be shooting a one-and-one with 15 seconds left.

Pretty Horse pulls on Karna's arm. "You gotta go in there and let her know you're here for her," he says.

Karna shakes her head. "I'm right where I need to be," she says.

Sharon can't count the times she's stepped to the free throw line in practice or in her grandmother's yard, pretending the championship is on the line. But those were different. Those were rehearsals. There weren't *really* three thousand fans screaming themselves nuts. The championship wasn't *really* on the line.

In the stands, her family holds hands. "You can do it!" yells Danetta. Several rows behind them, Sharon's father clasps his hands in silent prayer. Nine times during the season his daughter and her teammates have either been tied or trailed by one in the last minute . . . and nine times they have pulled it out. Nine for nine, just like a cat.

The ref hands her the ball. She wastes no time—bounce, aim, fire. The ball arches high, straight on line. But it hits the front rim and bounces straight back.

Like ten vultures after a single scrap, it's another wild scramble, only this time it's a held ball. The possession arrow points in Ronan's direction. Thirteen seconds left.

"Foul 'em! Foul 'em!" screams Coach Mac.

Ronan throws a long pass to forward Jami Jackson at midcourt. At full gallop, Rhea slams into her, knocking her two rows deep into the crowd, sending her to the line for a one-and-one. If she makes them both, Hardin will need its first three-pointer in 16 games to tie.

369

She misses.

Anita grabs the rebound. There are no timeouts and 10 seconds left.

"Get it to Sharon!" screams Karna.

In the NBA, a final 10 seconds is time enough for six beer ads, two promos for *Dateline,* and 15 minutes of over-coaching. In Whitefish, it will be enough time for Hardin to get it to the other end and get off a shot . . . maybe.

On the sidelines, Coach Mac is nearly jumping out of her white slacks, waving her players upcourt.

Anita dribbles up the right side, crossing midcourt with a defender two steps in front of her and another closing fast.

Eight . . . seven . . . six.

Running slightly ahead down the middle, Tiffany heads for the basket, Rhea and Owena right behind her. They are well covered. But Sharon is all alone down the center of the court. "Anita! Anita!" she screams, waving her arms.

But Anita doesn't hear or see her. Her only hope, she thinks, is to lob it toward Tiffany in the middle of that big knot of players under the basket and hope for a miracle.

She lets it fly and as it arcs down into the key, arms and legs flail in every direction. With her last ounce of energy, Tiffany again jumps the highest and pulls it down, five feet from the basket.

Three seconds left.

As Tiffany turns to her left, a Ronan defender reaches in and slaps at the ball, nailing her hand and the ball at the same time, knocking her off balance.

Stumbling, she shoves the ball toward the basket, and miraculously it threads its way through a cover of out-stretched hands and limbs. Up and up it climbs, banging first off the backboard, then the side of the rim. But it doesn't go in.

With one second left, it caroms right back to Tiffany, and in a last wild swirl, she tries to relaunch it. But there are too many hands in the way. The buzzer sounds.

There will be no 10th time, no State Championship.

CHAPTER THIRTY-NINE

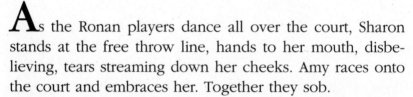

As the Ronan players dance all over the court, Sharon stands at the free throw line, hands to her mouth, disbelieving, tears streaming down her cheeks. Amy races onto the court and embraces her. Together they sob.

Still crying, they line up to shake hands with the victors, Sharon moving rapidly through the line, head down. Then she sprints off the court to the locker room to continue her despair. She can't stop crying. This is even worse than after last year's Divisionals; this time there is no next year. On the other side of the wall, the joyful celebration of the Ronan players is another knife in the heart.

She closes her eyes and thinks of the *what ifs*. *What if* Anita passed her the ball? *What if* the team didn't roll over and play dead in the second quarter? *What if* she'd eaten breakfast? And especially *what if* she hadn't missed that free throw in the last minute? She is sure that for the rest of her life she'll replay that miss in her mind, and it will never go in, never stop haunting her.

Coach Mac, also crying, approaches. She puts a hand on Sharon's shoulder and speaks, consoling words praising her for a great game and a great career and about how the sun will come up and life will go on. Sharon's tears keep falling. And when Danetta and Marlene enter to add their words of consolation, she cries even harder.

"I want to go home," she sobs on her grandmother's shoulder.

Reminded that there are still consolation games to play, Sharon shakes her head. "I'm not playing," she vows.

Wearing a new pink-and-white-striped dress suit that Danetta bought her for the trip, she exits the locker room, her eyes red and puffy. She checks a rear exit, hoping to sneak out the back and avoid the crowd, but it is locked.

On the court, conference runner-up Colstrip, a team they beat three times, is on their way to beating top-ranked Dillon for the right to play Ronan in tomorrow night's championship final. "I can't stand it," she utters.

Heading through the lobby to the bus, she hears a voice call her name, a familiar voice. For an instant, she freezes, eyes on the exit, her instinct just to keep moving and pretend she doesn't hear it. Then she turns around, spotting Karna coming toward her through the crowd, arms outstretched.

Surrounded by fans carrying cardboard crates of nachos, mother and daughter momentarily eye each other, Karna moving closer, Sharon stiffening. Then, without speaking, they embrace, and together they cry.

Sharon is the last player off the bus as it stops at Pizza Hut. Inside, the players pick at their food, barely talking. Coach Mac takes two bites of a salad, then pushes it aside.

"If we played Ronan ten more times, I'd bet everything I owe we'd beat them all ten times," she says.

She grasps for a positive spin: her players worked hard all year, the Hardin fans are the best, the loss will build character. The words are sincere, but choking back tears, she scoots back her chair and heads for the exit.

"I need some air," she explains.

With the team still inside, she sloshes through the snow to the rear of the Pizza Hut and bawls her eyes out.

On the bus back to the Outlaw Inn, she struggles to hold it together. "I've never wanted anything so much in my life as I wanted us to take it all," she says. "Not for me but for the girls."

She stares out the window at the snowy landscape, then turns to Coach Oswald. "I've never felt this low," she says. "Those kids are my family. You've got a wife and kids to go home to, a life away from the gym. I don't have anything else. This is my life. I feel so hollow."

It is 6:00 A.M. before Sharon finally falls asleep, only to be awakened a half hour later by Coach Mac pounding on her door. Cruelly, their consolation game against Columbia Falls is at nine o'clock.

"I'm not going," Sharon repeats.

But with Coach Mac's insistence, she does go, taking an ice-cold shower before the game to get herself awake. In the second quarter, Karna arrives and takes a seat high up in the bleachers, alone, quietly watching her daughter play. Across the half-empty gym, her ex-husband, Sharon's dad, also watches, alone. They do not talk or acknowledge each other's presence. If Sharon is bothered by their attendance, she doesn't show it, playing all but two minutes in a 77–67 victory. She scores 25 points, with 10 rebounds and eight assists.

After a nap at the motel, the team returns to the gym for their second game of the day, their third in twenty-four hours. Sharon plays the entire 32 minutes in a 43–42 win over Dillon. She finishes the tournament with a 20.5 per-game average, edging out Dillon's Shanna Smith, headed to Montana State on a scholarship, as the leading scorer in the tournament.

Karna is not at this game. She's back in Kalispell, pounding down shots of bourbon, her brief brush with sobriety gone.

The team remains at the gym for the championship game between Colstrip and Ronan, but Sharon can't watch, staying in the lobby the whole game, missing Ronan's victory. After the game, she and her teammates are summoned to midcourt for the presentation of the trophies.

"I'm not going," she asserts.

But again, Coach Mac persuades her to go. When her name is called for the All-Tournament team, she doesn't smile or wave to the crowd. Tiffany, who averaged 16.5 for the four games, is also named to the All-Tournament team, and when her name is announced, she smiles and waves.

The Lady Bulldogs are called forward to pose with their third-place trophy. Smiling, Tiffany kneels in the front row, her hand placed atop the trophy. Sharon stands in the back row, unsmiling. Just as the photographer presses the shutter, she ducks behind Stacie. Her image will be forever missing, third place never good enough.

Part VII

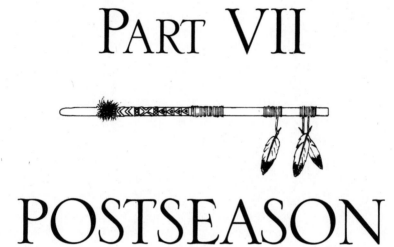

POSTSEASON

CHAPTER FORTY

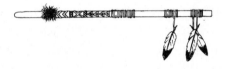

Sharon sprawls out on the couch at her grandma's, watching *Jerry Springer*. It's been six weeks since the end of the season, and a week since she's attended school. The failure notices in Senior Comp and American Government have done nothing to light a fire.

She hears a car approach. She doesn't get up, partly because she figures nobody is coming to see her, and partly because her knee is still stiff from the arthroscopic surgery she had two weeks after the season. The knee has healed enough that the doctor cleared her to play volleyball, but she still hasn't turned out for practice or come to the team's first two games, an absence noticed by her teammates. Tiffany went to Coach Sundheim and told her the team doesn't want Sharon allowed back.

She and Tiffany haven't talked since the awards banquet the week after the season. That was the night they both received certificates for being selected to the All-State team, as well as another one for making the All-Tournament squad. Statistically, they finished the season as close as two front teeth, Sharon's 17 points per game edging out Tiffany's 16.1. In the vote by the players for the Lady Bulldogs' MVP, Sharon won. Tiffany was selected to play in a statewide all-star tournament, Sharon wasn't.

The door opens and Sharon looks up, surprised to see her mother enter the room. They haven't seen each other since Whitefish. From across the room, Sharon can smell the booze.

"How come you're not at school?" asks Karna.

"How come you're not at a bar?" responds Sharon.

Sharon studies her mother's foggy glaze. "Why do you do this to yourself?" she asks.

Karna doesn't answer, retreating to a back bedroom. Sharon gets off the couch and follows. "I'll ask again. Why do you do this to yourself?"

"'Cause I'm an alcoholic, stupid!" Karna retorts.

Another car approaches. Karna moves to exit the bedroom, but Sharon blocks the doorway.

"Get out of the way!" orders Karna.

"Not until you explain why you keep doing this to yourself," says Sharon, holding her ground.

Karna lunges, catching Sharon off guard. She pulls her toward her and they tumble backward onto the bed. With a quick twist, Karna throws her into a headlock, then rolls over on top.

"Get off me!" screams Sharon, flailing to get loose.

Karna squeezes tighter on the headlock.

"You're hurting me!" yells Sharon.

The front door opens and Blaine enters the house. Hearing the commotion, he rushes to the bedroom. "What are you doing!" he yells, pulling Karna off Sharon.

Sharon springs off the bed and runs from the room. "I can't handle this anymore!" she screams.

Karna chases after her, catching up to her outside next to the rusted and bent basketball hoop. "I'm sorry, I'm sorry," she pleads.

"Can't you see what you're doing to the family?" cries Sharon. "Why do you do this?"

"Because I learned it from your grandparents," Karna answers.

"Stop blaming them!" Sharon says.

"Don't go," begs Karna. "We can go back inside and talk."

"Why? Nothing ever changes."

Karna reaches out to hug her, but Sharon pulls away. "Stay out of my life!"

Then she drives off down the dirt road, past the simple white tombstones of Custer's fallen soldiers, tears fogging her view.

Three months later . . .

Lighting another Benson & Hedges menthol, Danetta sits at her cluttered dining room table scribbling down numbers on a yellow legal pad, trying to do the math on a stack of loan applications—it's part of her new position on the Tribal Credit Committee. Outside, winter has finally turned to early spring and the coat of snow that has covered Big Horn County since November has begun to melt.

The door opens and she glances up, seeing Sharon hurry past the kitchen toward the back of the house. "Did school get out early?" she asks.

No answer.

She continues to study the applications, penciling in $1,000 for Karna, who is now one month sober and living in a subsidized apartment in Hardin, getting by one day at a time with the help of a little Prozac.

"I've got an application here from Cody, Amy's boyfriend," she hollers. "He needs $750 for bills, but I turned him down."

No response.

Danetta considers going back to check on her granddaughter but doesn't. She's noticed the change in Sharon—

moodiness, loss of interest in school, terse responses—but figures she's still grieving the loss to Ronan, or the fact that she still has not, despite all her awards, heard from a single college coach, not even a junior college. It doesn't help that Tiffany recently signed a letter of intent to accept a four-year ride to Carroll College in Helena.

"Hey, you'll be happy to know I approved the $2,000 loan for Randy so he can make the down payment on that new pickup he wants," she hollers.

No response.

"Did you hear what I said about Randy's loan?"

Still no response.

Danetta puts out her cigarette and heads down the hall. The door is open and Sharon is sitting on the edge of the bed, head down. Danetta studies her for a moment. "Is that a new hairstyle?" she asks.

Sharon looks away.

Danetta moves closer. "Your hair looks cute like that," she offers. "Stand up and let me look at it."

Reluctantly, Sharon stands, her hair combed forward, swooping across her forehead at an angle, covering her right eye. As she turns her head to the light, Danetta spots it, the familiar signature of the reservation, a black eye.

"Did Randy give you that?" demands Danetta.

"I don't want to talk about it," Sharon replies. "It's none of your damn business!"

Danetta steps back. Never has Sharon raised her voice toward her. "Tell me what happened," she presses.

Sharon doesn't answer, pulling a small suitcase from her closet and hastily throwing clothes into it.

"What are you doing?" asks Danetta.

"I already told you that it's none of your business."

She's going to Bozeman to spend a few days with Holly and to try to figure out what to do about Randy. The latest episode started when he said he'd spotted her talking to

if there's a way she can still pass. "She's only turned in two assignments all semester," he says. "I don't see how I can pass her."

I talk to Coach Mac to see if there's a small college out there that still might want to take a chance. "If there is, I haven't heard from them," she says.

I talk to Laura Sundheim, her school counselor, and ask if it's too late for her to apply to college. "Kids are already getting their letters of acceptance," she says. "It's too late, except maybe at a community college."

I even drive to Bozeman and talk with Montana State head coach Judy Spolstra. "All our scholarships have been committed months ago," she explains.

I talk to Windy Boy in Crow Agency and she restates her case that Little Big Horn College is Sharon's best option, but when I mention it to Sharon, she shows no interest. "There's no basketball," she says.

Finally, I call Mark Englert, the women's coach at Sheridan Community College in Wyoming eighty miles south of Crow Agency. His program is regarded as one of the best in the region, although I find it odd that he's never even heard of Sharon.

"Bring her down for a visit," he says. "I'd be happy to talk to her and show her the campus."

I'm leaving my duplex when the phone rings. It's Danetta. "I hate to ask another favor of you," she says, "but would it be possible for you to loan us $200 for Sharon's trip to Denver?"

We had never talked about repaying the first loan, and I was pretty sure I was kissing this money goodbye, but a few minutes later, I meet her in the parking lot behind the bank and hand her ten crisp new Andrew Jacksons. As I count it out, I remember again Ron Johnson's warning about loaning her money and how she'll just keep using me as a soft touch. I'm tempted to ask her why it is that an officer of the Tribal Credit Committee needs a loan, but I don't.

"You keep an eye on our girl down there," she instructs.

Sharon is going to Denver to play in the Eighth Annual All-West Native American Basketball Classic, and the money is for her participant fees and hotel costs. I'm going, too, and in fact, Sharon is riding down with me, a ten-hour drive. I've arranged for us to stop in Sheridan on the way and meet Coach Englert and tour the campus.

I pick up Sharon and we're on our way. It's a warm spring day and she is dressed casually in striped Bermuda shorts, penny loafers with white socks, and a Portland Trail Blazers T-shirt that I gave her for her eighteenth birthday. "Is that what you're going to wear to meet the coach?" I ask, worrying about first impressions.

"Is this a beauty pageant we're going to?" she answers.

An hour later we reach Sheridan, a ranching town of five thousand. Sharon spots the Thunderchild Treatment Center. "That's where I went to visit my mother," she says. "Jeez, that seems like a hundred years ago. I remember being there and thinking, 'This is it. Mom's finally gonna get well.' Pretty stupid, huh?"

We arrive at the campus. The way I figure it, this is Sharon's last chance to keep her playing days alive, and maybe her last chance for a college education and a shot at a better life. She seems less than enthused.

We meet Coach Englert in his cramped office, his desk cluttered with stacks of videotapes. He is a large man with a friendly, cherubic face, and he takes us on a brief tour of the campus. "Do you know what you want to major in?" he asks.

"Maybe business accounting," answers Sharon. "I've always done pretty good in math."

Bookkeeping isn't something normally associated with the rez. It's hard to envision Sharon sitting at a desk crunching numbers all day. But maybe that's what the tribe needs . . . someone to help them get into the financial swing of things. Maybe her first project can be her grandmother.

As we walk across campus, a modern facility with an enrollment of 750, we see nothing but white faces. "How many Indians go here?" I ask.

"I'm not sure," he answers. "Maybe twenty."

I can see Sharon's mind churning. Of the many roadblocks to Indians succeeding in college, one of the biggest has always been the small ratio of Indians on campus. For most young Indians, moving off the rez into an academic environment with no support system is a task too daunting.

"You'd only be an hour's drive from home," I offer.

The last stop on the tour is the gym, a golden-domed field house, the dominant landmark in town. Walking onto the darkened court, Sharon looks up into the spacious bleachers and then across the shiny floor, illuminated only by the light streaking through the open door. She smiles.

"This would be a cool place to play," she whispers.

"We really pack in the crowds," says Coach Englert.

Suddenly, Sharon looks as if she's just awakened from a long and troubled sleep. For the first time in four months I see a light in her eyes. For her, college basketball has always seemed vague and distant, unreal. Now, walking across the deserted field house with its hardwood floor beneath her feet, it's tangible. She can see the bleachers and nets and free throw lines. A coach is standing next to her telling her his teams play man-to-man and fast tempo, and if she comes to school here and makes the team she'll have to practice harder than any game she's ever played.

Her face is alive. He shows her the weight room and talks about his rigid conditioning program, and she looks like she wants to start pumping iron right there in her penny loafers. He talks about eligibility and she looks like she wants to sit down and finish all her missing assignments in Senior Comp and American Government. He asks if she has a game tape she can send him and she sounds as if she's ready to call FedEx.

He says that if he likes what he sees on the tape, he'll invite her down for an informal scrimmage. And if he still likes what he sees, well, he can't guarantee anything yet, but maybe there will be some money for room and board.

"The important thing is to fill out all the financial aid papers and take the entrance exam," he concludes.

"I will, I will," she vows.

We say goodbye to Coach Englert and head back to the car. In the nine months I've known her, this is the most excited I've seen her. "I definitely want to come here," she enthuses. "I wish the season started tomorrow."

Standing by the car, she looks back toward the field house and its golden dome glistening in the spring sun. She can't take her eyes off it; she can't stop gushing. She will give up cigarettes and pot; she will start getting in shape as soon as she gets back home from Denver; she will run, lift weights, and work on her outside shooting and ball-handling. That's what she says.

As we drive away from the campus and the golden dome disappears in the distance, I feel hope. Her life is renewed, alive again with design and direction.

"Have you seen Sharon?" I ask.

"Not in a couple days," answers Marlene. "Why?"

"I just got a call from the coach down at Sheridan College and he's got a scrimmage set up for her tonight at seven," I explain. "He liked what he saw on that game tape I sent him."

It's two weeks after the trip to Denver—where Sharon was named to the All-Tournament team—and I'm having no luck tracking her down. She hasn't been to school in two days, and Danetta hasn't seen her either. Since the campus visit, all of Sharon's big talk has evaporated and reality has set back in. She hasn't lifted any weights, worked on her ball-handling, or made up any missing assignments. According to Amy, she's still smoking a lot of "Bob Marleys." The one time I've seen her since the trip was at the Town Pump—she was buying a prepackaged burrito and looked as if she hadn't slept in days. When she looked up and saw me, she greeted me with all the warmth of a BIA agent. It was a far cry from our candid conversations driving to and from Denver.

"She's probably with Randy at his mother's house," says Marlene.

"Where's that?" I ask.

"In the Wolf Mountains," she says.

The Wolf Mountains are forty miles south. "Where in the Wolf Mountains?" I inquire.

"I have no idea," she says, "except that Sharon told me that it was way back in the woods down a long dirt road."

"Is there a phone?"

"Nope."

With no assurance that I can find the place, I give up. When Sharon finally learns two days later of Coach Englert's efforts to contact her, she doesn't call him back.

I tell Ron Johnson of my failed effort and he shakes his head. "I don't want to say I told you so," he says, "but I told you so."

Three months later . . .

"Where the hell is she?" fumes Amy, pacing, her long white wedding gown dragging the floor of the bridal party dressing room at St. Xavier Catholic Church twenty miles south of Hardin. The ceremony is set to begin in fifteen minutes, and Sharon, one of her bridesmaids, is missing.

"Maybe Mr. Not Afraid is afraid she'll talk to one of the bridegrooms so he won't let her come," jokes Geri, also a bridesmaid.

"Don't laugh," says Amy. "It's probably true. That guy won't let Sharon talk to her own shadow."

Amy walks outside to see if she can spot Sharon's car coming. She's on familiar turf, having spent most of her childhood living on the church grounds while her stepfather, Slick, worked there as the maintenance man. It is a place with lots of dark memories.

The last time I'd seen Sharon was a month earlier at graduation day. That was a big day for both of us. Thanks to the charity of two of her teachers, she graduated . . . and thanks to a vote by the senior class, I got to be the co-commencement speaker. I gathered pictures of all the kids in the class, put together a slide show to music, and delivered my top ten highlights of my year with Hardin High. Number one was having Amylynn Adams's MS go into remission and having her be my co-commencement speaker. As they say, there wasn't a dry eye in the house, including mine.

After the diplomas were handed out, I went to a huge feast in Sharon's honor hosted by Danetta, complete with canvas awnings, a side of buffalo, and a picnic table filled with gifts. Earlier, Sharon showed me the term paper she turned in that kept her from flunking American Government; it was a report on child abuse, and I was impressed at how well she had learned to write exactly, word for word, like a reporter for *U.S. News & World Report*.

Geri wonders if maybe Randy made her drive him to one of his rodeos. The week before she drove him to Pine Ridge in South Dakota, paying for his entry fee out of her first paycheck from her summer job cashiering at the Custer Trading Post.

I walk down the gravel driveway. It's hard watching Amy's anxiety attack. Given all the hard times this kid's been through in her nineteen years, she deserves a smooth wedding. The scorching heat isn't helping.

"I feel like I'm gonna sweat right through this dress," she says. She'd paid for it herself, the $200 coming from the last of the monthly Social Security checks she'd been receiving since her father's murder.

The guests file into the church, the whites to the left side, Indians to the right.

"Let's start without her," Amy finally says, signaling Cody's cousin to start the Garth Brooks tape. It jams in the boom box.

"Here she comes!" says Geri, pointing to Sharon getting out of her car and gathering up her purple taffeta bridesmaid dress to walk across the courtyard. She apologizes for being late, offering no excuse.

One glance and Amy knows. Sharon is stoned, totally ripped. Her eyes are bloodshot, she reeks of pot, and she has that vacant stare.

Inside the church, the priest, wearing a brown frock and sandals, and looking like he's auditioning for the role of Friar Tuck in a Fellini movie, decides to entertain the guests with a singing sermon about love in the 1990s. It's a cappella and unlistenable.

Finally, the ceremony begins, the bridesmaids walking down the aisle as Amy waits in the doorway, veil down, arm in arm with Slick. They are waiting for the start of "Here Comes the Bride."

"The tape's stuck again!" yells the wedding disc jockey.

It takes ten excruciating minutes to fix it, then Amy and Slick make the walk, Amy taking her place next to Cody, who is dressed in a white tuxedo jacket, black jeans, and cowboy boots.

"Good afternoon, Amy and Cory," greets the priest.

"His name's Cody," whispers Amy.

The priest begins the service, delivering a lecture on the pitfalls of modern marriage, citing statistics on the high percentage of marriages that fail. "So, when there's trouble in this marriage, as we all know there will be, there may be a tendency among those of you here today who love Amy to say, 'Cory is such a lazy beast.'"

"His name's Cody," snaps Amy.

I'm having trouble believing what I'm seeing and hearing. If this is a Hollywood script, the producers will reject it for being too weird. Sharon looks like she's going to pass out.

The priest continues. "Amy, you must hang in there when it seems hopeless. And to those of you who love Cory, he may come to you and say, 'Amy is so stupid, so emotional. I can't stand her anymore.' But Cory, you must not give up even though you don't want to be with her."

"How many times do we have to tell you, my name is Cody," he says.

Standing just to the left of Amy, Sharon suddenly collapses, eyes rolling to the back of her head, her body crumpling to the floor in a giant taffeta heap. She's out cold, fainted. The ceremony stops, everyone standing to check out the wreckage.

"It's no wonder she's fainted," says Danetta. "The poor girl has been working so hard."

From her pew in front of us, Marlene rushes to Sharon's side, cradling her head in her arms. Amy looks ready to implode. The priest begins to whistle show tunes.

Slowly, Sharon opens her eyes and Marlene carries her to a side pew as the service resumes. After more statistics from the priest on the rate of failures of modern marriages, he pronounces them "man and wife."

After the ceremonial kiss, a perfunctory little peck, Cody and Amy walk back down the aisle, escorted out of the church into the boiling sunshine by Tanya Tucker's "Two Sparrows in a Hurricane."

"What a lovely ceremony," decrees Danetta.

"She's one of the best employees I've ever had," says Putt Thompson, the owner of the Custer Trading Post. "I wish they were all like her."

It's late July and I've come to visit Sharon on the job. She's busy waiting on tourists, but as soon as she gets a break, we'll talk. Mainly, I want to know if she's had any luck persuading Randy to sit down with me for an interview. So far, he's avoided me.

"Thanks, and have a nice day," says Sharon, handing a customer his receipt for his postcards.

Am I hearing correctly? Is this really Sharon LaForge, the girl who hated to shake hands with the opposition before a game? Is this really her selling Custer postcards and bidding white tourists to *have a nice day*?

I mill around the store, checking out the racks of Little Big Horn Battlefield T-shirts and turquoise trinkets. She finally gets a break and we move to the cafe side of the trading post and have a Coke. I ask if she's sent in her application to Sheridan College, something she told me she was going to do the last time we talked. She says she has, although I'm skeptical.

"How's Randy feel about you applying to college?" I ask.

"He doesn't want me to."

"Have you had a chance to ask him about meeting me?" I inquire.

"Yeah . . ." she slowly replies.

"And . . . ?"

She pauses, hesitant to answer. "He said for me to tell you to go fuck yourself," she finally says. "He said he wanted me to make sure you understood that he's the one telling you to go fuck yourself."

I remember on the drive to Denver her telling me all about how jealous, possessive, and controlling he is, and how she's made up her mind not to put up with it anymore.

Her eyes suddenly widen. "Oh, my God," she says. "Randy just pulled up in his truck."

For an instant, I think she's kidding . . . I hope she's kidding. She's not. I turn around and see him getting out of his pickup, the new red one he bought with the money Danetta helped him get. I'm assuming that if he walks in here and sees me sitting all chummy and sipping Cokes with his woman, my ass is alfalfa, or even worse, Sharon's ass is alfalfa.

He's headed for the entrance.

I jump up from the table and retreat down the clothing aisle, hiding behind a rack of Little Big Horn T-shirts. I watch him enter the store. He looks pissed. Maybe he spotted my car in the parking lot.

He steps inside, and with his hands hooked inside his big silver belt buckle, looks around for Sharon. I suddenly realize that in my haste to hide, I left Sharon sitting at the table, my Coke still sitting there. I'm not sure how Randy did in math at Lodge Grass High, but I suspect he knows that two glasses and one person doesn't add up.

I consider my options. I can wait until his back is turned, then hightail it out the door. Or I can step out from behind the rack of T-shirts and meet him face-to-face. The problem with that option is that he might want to fight, and fistfighting has never really been my sport. I've only been in one fight in my whole life, and that's the one where I got the snot beat out of me, separating my shoulder and costing me my big-league career. Since then, I've crossed the street whenever I saw a fight coming.

Watching Randy stand there in the doorway of the Custer Trading Post, I'm keenly aware that this rodeo-riding numbskull is half my age and has the rage, muscles, and testosterone to prove it. Not to mention that he probably thinks I've got some Lolita thing going with his girlfriend.

I decide on option number one, the sneak-around plan. But there's a hitch. Randy is, for lack of a better analogy, standing in the doorway like some sort of cigar store Indian.

Finally, he walks away toward the cafe where Sharon and I were sitting. Seizing the moment, I spring from behind the shirt rack and hustle toward the exit. I glance back toward the table where Sharon and I sat. It's been neatly cleaned, and Sharon is coming out from behind the counter as pure as dishwater.

"All you have to do is remember to take little baby buffalo steps," instructs Danetta.

"Little baby buffalo steps?" I reply.

"You know, step, touch . . . step, touch."

"Whatever."

It's a warm August evening at Crow Fair, a year since my arrival in Big Horn County, and I'm about to receive one of the highest honors on the rez. I'm being adopted into the tribe.

The adoption ceremony takes place in the filled-to-capacity arbor at Crow Fair. It is Danetta who recommended me, and it is into her family and clan, the Big Lodges, that I am adopted, which I suppose has a nicer ring to it than being a member of the Filth Eaters or Greasy Mouth clans. In the tradition of the tribe, I am escorted around the arbor by two warriors in full headdress and costume. With tribal drums echoing through the night, I screw up the baby buffalo steps.

After circling the arbor two times, I'm presented with the traditional giving of gifts: a blanket; a shawl; a pair of hand-beaded moccasins; a package of Bull Durham cigarettes for the traditional sharing of tobacco. Then I'm given my new Indian name, chosen for me by a clan uncle, a name chosen from a vision or spiritual visitation. Giving me my name will be Oliver Half, the guy with the sea lion ass that I wanted to climb over in my first sweat lodge. He addresses the crowd.

"I present our newest Crow," he bellows. "Well Known War Dancer."

Sounds good to me. Oliver doesn't explain how he came up with it.

After the ceremony is finished, I spot Sharon sitting with Geri in the shadow of the arbor. "You realize, of course, that I'm now your uncle," I say.

"Whatever," she replies, stifling a smile. She lowers her head and looks away, but even in the dim light, I can see the new black eye.

It's October and in a few days I will be leaving Hardin and returning to Oregon after fifteen months in Big Horn County. But on this night, I've come to the gym to watch Anita, Stacie, and Christina try to keep the Lady Bulldogs undefeated and number one in the state. They are cashing the check Sharon helped write last season.

I haven't seen Sharon in several weeks. The start of the semester has come and gone without her at Sheridan College . . . or any other college. When last we talked, she told me she was burnt out on school and needed a semester off, maybe a year. She insisted she would eventually go back to school, but I don't think so. My time on the rez has made me a skeptic.

The reality is that Sharon now lives with Randy at his mom's house twenty miles from the nearest phone. With the tourist season over, her hours at the Custer Trading Post have been cut, and in another month there will be no work at all. She worries about how she and Randy will get by. He is out of work, seasonally laid off by Crow Tribal Housing, his payment on the pickup overdue. His rodeo winnings don't even pay travel expenses. She pays for those.

When last we met, she also talked about feeling cut off. She and Holly hadn't talked since graduation day, their relationship severed with Holly's admonition that Sharon is an "idiot" for staying with Randy. Her senior teammates, the girls she'd played side by side with since the seventh grade, have all gone their separate ways: Amy is pregnant, DyAnna is taking classes at Little Big Horn College, Geri has a boyfriend, and Tiffany is a freshman at Carroll College, already first string on the volleyball team.

Sitting in the bleachers, I watch Stacie control the opening tap against Miles City, Anita taking the ball and burying a jumper. On the season, they are both playing like All-Staters, Anita averaging 25 points a game, Stacie leading the state in rebounding.

Christina steals a pass and takes it the other way for an easy two. As I watch the ball fall through the net, I spot a familiar face enter the gym. It's Sharon and it's her first time back to see her old teammates.

She quickly walks up the bleacher stairs and takes a seat in the far upper corner, alone. I give her a few minutes, then I move in next to her. She greets me with a self-conscious smile. She doesn't look healthy. It seems like just yesterday that she was down there on that court, wrestling the ball away from her old rival Wambolt.

She focuses hard on the game, as if her concentration

will keep me from asking her anything about her life. I suspect that she's embarrassed to tell me what I already know from Marlene—that she is pregnant. I don't ask about the baby, figuring she'll tell me about it at her own speed. We watch Stacie grab an offensive board and put it back in.

"I can't believe Stacie didn't play varsity last year," I say.

"We would've won State with her," she says.

We watch in silence for several minutes, then Sharon speaks. "Have you noticed that every time Stacie gets the ball up high, the back door is wide open for Rhea," she says.

I hadn't noticed. Her observation reminds me of one of the things that made her such a good player—an intuitive understanding of the game. Her talent was more than just her physical skills and intensity. She had a grasp of the Xs and Os. She knew where players were supposed to be.

"You'd make a good coach," I say.

She shrugs.

"Do you wish you were still out there?" I ask.

She nods. "I can't believe I'm not playing basketball anymore. It was my whole life."

The horn sounds ending the half, Hardin leading by 17. "Come on, I'll buy you a Coke and some Nibs," I offer.

We walk down the bleachers and through the lobby, nobody noticing her, nobody patting her on the back like in the glory days. At the refreshment line she turns toward me. I expect her to tell me her big news.

"I need to get going," she says.

I don't argue. I walk her to the door and say goodbye, then watch her taillights disappear into the night. I fear it is the last time I will see her.

Mostly, I feel sad . . . about the night, about my year with Sharon, about the lost promise of her life. I try to make sense of it.

EPILOGUE

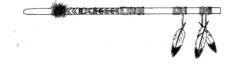

Back home in Portland, I continue to try to make sense of it, to find hope. As much as I want it otherwise, the conclusion I keep reaching is that Sharon has failed. By Crow standards, by white standards, by any reasonable standards. The facts confirm it. Last I checked she was smoking cigarettes and pot, having a baby at eighteen, blowing off college, quitting basketball, wearing shiners, and buying Cheez-Doodles with Food Stamps.

I struggle to complete the book. Sharon and I stay in touch, but just barely—a couple letters, a few phone calls, a baby gift for her new son, Roddy. She is living with Randy and I am reluctant to call, afraid he'll get jealous and take it out on her. Yet I still feel connected. Maybe it has something to do with my adoption into the tribe, but more likely it's because she's been at the center of my thoughts for two years.

In a phone conversation, I ask of her long-range plans. She tells me she wants to have another baby and maybe get her job back at Custer Trading Post. I feel disheartened, but am I guilty once again of imposing my values? Maybe raising babies and waiting on white tourists is what she wants.

"What about school?" I ask.

She tells me she plans to enroll at Little Big Horn College. Her voice has conviction, but I remember the day we visited the field house in Sheridan and her good intentions at the time . . . and then she didn't do diddly about it.

"What's Randy say about your going back to school?" I inquire.

"I haven't told him yet."

I finish a draft of the book, but a funny thing happens on the way to publication. Actually, it isn't funny at all. I write an account that has no passion, no point of view, no chance for publication. My failure is due in part to the sadness I feel about the path Sharon's life has taken. It's hard to write a story with such a bleak ending and sense of hopelessness. The project gets moved, not to a back burner, but to the freezer. I quit working on it altogether and start another project—providing support for teachers and writing in the Portland school district. But not a day goes by that I don't think about Sharon. And worry.

A year passes, and then another with no work on the book. I keep hoping for some sort of happy Hollywood ending, but the farther I get from the story and Sharon, the more hopeless her situation seems . . . which makes it even harder to start working on it again. I continue to get news updates, mainly in phone calls from Coach Oswald or from my out-of-state subscription to the *Big Horn County News*. I learn that in Stacie and Christina's senior year, the Lady Bulldogs win the State Championship and both girls make All-State. But then the following year, the team does not win a single game—0 and 18. The next year they win only three games. Coach Mac resigns.

I lose contact with Sharon, partially because I'm embarrassed about intruding on her life for all those months with no book to show for it, and partially because I'm afraid to hear what's become of her. I fear the worst. Why would I believe otherwise? Coach Oswald calls and tells me he saw her on the street in Hardin and she looked terrible, haggard and drawn.

Then out of the blue, a card arrives:

Hi there! How are you doing? I'm hanging in there. I'm going to school at Little Big Horn College. My grades for the quarter are A = Finite Math, A = History, A = Business Law, A- = Survey Anatomy and Physiology, B = Accounting. I wasn't satisfied with the B in Accounting. I really enjoy going to school. It was tough but I survived. I'm on break now so I'm enjoying every minute. Here's a picture of Roddy.

Best wishes,
Sharon

I am wondrously shocked and amazed. I write back congratulating her on her success, and for the first time since that string of miraculous overtime victories, I feel that maybe some good will come of this after all.

I let another eighteen months pass without contact. I do it because I don't want to jinx anything. It's like not talking to a pitcher in the middle of a no-hitter. Just keep quiet and hope the magic continues. I fear that if I call she will tell me that Randy has beaten her up again and she has dropped out of school.

In May 1997 another letter arrives. Judging from the envelope, it's some kind of announcement. My first thought is that Sharon has had another baby. I'm wrong. It's an invitation to the commencement exercise for the 1997 graduating class of Little Big Horn College. Sharon is graduating with an associate arts degree in Business Administration. The name on the announcement reads: Sharon Not Afraid.

Because my own daughter is graduating from the University of Oregon the same weekend, I cannot attend. But I call and congratulate her. "This is an accomplishment way better than any game you ever won," I say. "You should feel incredibly proud." Her response is subdued.

For her to have gone back to school and earn an associate's degree from an accredited community college is a feat of phenomenal proportions considering the obstacles. She has done it while raising a child and receiving little or no emotional or financial support—none from the tribe, none from her family, little from Randy, whom she married earlier in the year. She is now pregnant with their second child.

She says her plan is to continue her education, and she's already registered for classes in the fall at Rocky Mountain College, a small, academically respected private college in Billings. She will major in business finance. And what's even more impressive is that she is getting a scholarship.

"Basketball?" I ask.

No, it's for academics. According to Little Big Horn College president Janine Windy Boy, Sharon worked as hard as any student in the school's history, getting voted Student of the Year by the faculty. "Her scholarship to Rocky Mountain College is based on merit, not need," says Windy Boy. Sharon will commute to Billings from the house she and Randy live in deep in the Wolf Mountains—150 miles round-trip.

"No, I'm not going to try out for the team," she says. "Those days are over."

"Is Randy okay with all this?" I ask.

"Not really."

Sharon not only enrolls at Rocky Mountain College, she makes the Dean's List her first year, majoring in business finance. It's almost too good to be true. This is the same girl who needed a joint just to say hello. If for no other reason, it's an amazing feat because of where she lives—ten miles from a paved road, a place where elk and bear wander the front yard and in winter the snow piles as high as the corral posts. Child care is a daily scramble. Some days Danetta watches the kids, but sometimes there's no one and Sharon has to miss school.

For the next year and a half, she works toward a career in accounting, making the long drive to Billings, raising her kids, squeezing in time to study, fighting with Randy. She is scheduled to graduate in May 1999. I will be there, and when she walks across the stage to receive her diploma, I will whistle my lungs out.

Then in April 1999 she calls. She gets only a couple words out, then starts sobbing. With only a month to graduation, she has had to drop out of school.

"Why?" I ask.

"Everything is going wrong."

It's true: her car broke down and Randy won't let her use his truck to get to school; her youngest son, Michael, has been in and out of Crow Hospital for two months with a severe ear infection; her scholarship money is gone, loaned out to family; her head throbs around the clock. Danetta is concerned that it might be from a blow she received from Randy.

"All I want to do is curl up in a ball and die," she cries. "I'm so tired of hurting."

She asks if she can come to Portland with her two kids and stay with me and my wife—I finally married my long-time girlfriend, Marcie—while she sorts things out. I desperately want to help and say yes, but I know it's not the solution. I tell her no. She cries even harder.

From her description, her life with Randy is a nightmare, but somehow she can't find the strength to leave. It's a familiar story. She has moved out several times, but then he turns contrite and promises to stop the drinking and abuse. She buys the story, returns home, then it happens all over again. He promises to get her car fixed, but then spends what little money they have on booze or rodeo fees. At one point, the abuse was so bad that she moved into a women's shelter in Billings with her kids. But he tracked her down and talked her into coming home. In their latest episode, he demanded that she take off his shoes and she refused. "We got into a big fight," she says. "He kept telling me I'm the one with the problem, that I have an attitude and a big mouth. Then he took off and didn't come home for two nights."

"Did he hit you?"

"Yes."

I think back to how tough and stoic she was throughout all the chaos of her senior season, rarely letting on that anything was wrong. It feels odd that she is now pouring out her guts to me five years later, especially after we've had so little contact. She says there's nobody on the rez she feels comfortable talking to. Sad.

I call Janine Windy Boy to inform her of the situation. "It's not surprising that Randy is making her life miserable," she offers. "He's threatened by her success. I just hope Sharon can get away from him. It'll be hard."

Windy Boy knows a little something about jealous Crow males. By her account, her partner, John Pretty On Top, has accused her of sleeping with no fewer than fifty men during their eight years together. Recently she was offered the position of president of the Consortium of Indian Colleges and he said she had to choose between the job and him. She chose the job. They separated for a few months, but now they're back together.

* * *

In the summer of 1999 I return to Big Horn County to visit old friends. My first stop is Coach Mac. Sitting in her living room, I feel a bit like a traitor: this is the woman who afforded me almost total access to her team and trusted me with their story, then I wrote a book that is often critical of her. But she is a dedicated, caring professional, a coach of high school girls out in the middle of nowhere who, under normal circumstances, wouldn't have had her every move scrutinized.

As we chat, I am struck with how much more relaxed she seems. "I'm enjoying just being a teacher," she says. "My stomach hasn't bothered me since I quit coaching. Other than my relationship with the kids on the team, I don't miss it at all."

She fills me in on what has happened to most of them. It is no surprise that Tiffany Hopfauf and Anita Dewald are both doing well. Tiffany graduated with a degree in elementary education from Carroll College in Helena, where she was a four-year varsity letterman and an All-Conference selection in volleyball. After graduation, she stayed in Helena, married a greenskeeper at a local golf course, and works as an assistant volleyball coach at Carroll.

Anita, the girl everyone predicted big things for, hasn't disappointed. She graduated with a degree in marketing from Montana State, where she played three years of varsity volleyball, earned a 3.98 GPA, and was voted outstanding senior woman. After graduation, she and her husband, who was her co-valedictorian at Hardin High, moved to Alaska, where he is stationed for three years after his graduation at the top of his class at the Air Force Academy. Anita plans a career in business and is already involved in a start-up computer consulting company.

Nor am I surprised to learn that the physically gifted Stacie Greenwalt was able to continue her athletic career in college. She was offered a full ride for basketball to several colleges, but instead chose a volleyball scholarship to the University of Utah, where she was a starter her first two years before transferring to Montana State because she had conflicts with her coach. That doesn't surprise me, either.

I guess what does surprise me is that other girls on the team have done better than their high school vitas would predict. Amy Hanson, the girl who tried to commit suicide and rarely got to play, is a mother of two, still married to Cody, and working as a licensed masseuse in Hardin. Christina Chavez, a girl who battled a drinking problem and a home life from hell, moved to Arizona, completed community college, is gainfully employed, and doing well. The same for Geri Stewart, the disgruntled second-stringer and president of the Indian Club. She moved to North Dakota to attend United Tribes Technical College, where she was voted student body president. Rhea Beatty, the girl who never seemed able to please Coach Mac or her dad, is also doing well. She graduated from Little Big Horn College, married Paul Little Light, the Hardin High heartthrob, divorced him, and now lives and works in Billings.

Certainly these girls did better as a group than I expected. Did the fight they waged with Coach Mac that season stiffen their spines? I like to think so.

As delighted as I am to hear of the success of these girls, I am even happier to learn that Amylynn Adams, the girl with multiple sclerosis, is doing great. After high school, she moved to the warmer climate of Florida, graduated with a degree in English from Florida Central, got married, had two babies, and moved back to Montana, where she and her husband both work for FedEx in Great Falls. Her disease has remained in remission. She was disappointed, however, to learn from DNA testing that the man in Cincinnati was not her father. But eventually she tracked down her real father in Spokane. I accepted her offer to accompany her when she traveled to meet him and got to witness their tearful and joyous reunion.

After leaving Coach Mac's house, I drive to the reservation. Sharon knows I'm coming, but is vague about when we can meet. I suspect she's worried Randy will find out and put the kibosh on it. I head for Danetta and Blaine's house. Sharon has said she might be there, then again, she might not. It appears that some things on the rez, like Crow Time, will never change.

Sharon isn't at Danetta's. Randy took her and their two sons on a cattle drive on tribal land up Black Canyon above Yellowtail Dam. He now owns a hundred head of cattle and is moving them to a high range for grazing. Ironically, it was Tiffany's father, Tom Hopfauf, who approved a bank loan to match the tribal grant Randy received to chase his dream of becoming a big cattle rancher. The loan came just days before the notice in the *Big Horn County News* about his arrest on a public intoxication charge. Sharon has left word with Danetta that she'll meet with me tomorrow afternoon at Custer Trading Post.

It isn't long before Danetta flings a little mud on her old nemesis Clara Nomee. Despite a seemingly endless string of controversies, Nomee is still the tribal chair, now serving her fifth term, but to Danetta's joy, she has been indicted for alleged misuse of tribal funds from the Little Big Horn Casino. Nomee is now under house arrest, wearing a leg monitor, and battling the charges. Danetta and Blaine have also brought suit against Madam Chairman and the tribe, accusing them of delinquent payments for land and a water tank.

Danetta tells me she's been battling a series of health problems, as well as struggling with the drama that is her family. Karna is now living in a halfway house in Billings, ordered there by the court after being arrested for the seventh time on a drunk driving charge. Big shock there. Marlene is still working for Head Start and has just moved back in with her husband after she'd left him for, what was it?, the seventh time.

It's funny. From the day I first arrived on the reservation seven years earlier, the white folks in Hardin told me that nothing ever changes around these parts, and I'd be living in a fantasy world if I expected otherwise. By the time I had finished my research, I saw the logic of their argument. I guess that's why I've come back here . . . to see if I can see that fantasy, talk to it.

One good sign I learn from Danetta is that Sharon and her father have slowly built a relationship. It may not be the stuff of *Father Knows Best*, but Michael LaForge is now in semiregular contact with his daughter. He was there at the hospital for the birth of her second son, and he has offered encouragement, if not financial support, for her pursuit of a college degree.

"He wants to be a good grandpa," says Danetta.

But the best evidence that gives cause for hope is that the tribe, with Clara Nomee's support, has just given $3 million to Little Big Horn College for construction of a new campus. The money comes from the tribe's settlement with the U.S. government over the disputed land with their old enemy the Northern Cheyenne. It's an exclamation mark to Janine Windy Boy's efforts . . . a gift that was pure fantasy seven years earlier.

After lunch Blaine offers to take me for a sweat, but I beg off, telling him I'm fighting a cold. In truth, I have no desire to climb into that little hot box and fry my carcass. Haven't I already proved myself on that one?

As I prepare to say goodbye to Danetta and Blaine, I feel a tinge of guilt in the same way I did back at Coach Mac's. These are people who went out of their way to be hospitable to me, even adopting me into their family and tribe. Back then I wondered if I was being co-opted. Well, I'm no fool and I don't think I was, but even if it was true, I was proud to be co-opted. Still, it's hard not to worry that they will think I have betrayed them.

I sit at a table in the restaurant of the Custer Trading Post, waiting for Sharon. She is ten minutes late. I half expect her not to show, especially if Randy knows she's supposed to be meeting me.

To be honest, I'm nervous. I've heard rumors that she's been drinking lately and put on lots of weight. Another rumor has it that Randy knocked out her front teeth. I'm prepared for the worst. But what I'm most nervous about is that she'll tell me she's given up on getting her degree. If that's true, it'll kill the hope I have left.

I continue to wait. Just as I am about to give up and leave, she enters, trailed by her two sons, Roddy, four, and Michael, two. She's wearing jeans and a print shirt, and she looks terrific, pretty as ever. The rumors are false. We awkwardly hug, then order hamburgers.

"I don't have a lot of time," she explains. "I have to run a bunch of errands for Randy."

It wasn't that long ago that she was sobbing her eyes out, telling me on the phone that he was "a lying, cheating drunk." Now she's running errands for him. I ask if Randy understands how important it is for Sharon to get her degree.

"He thinks I'm going to graduate and leave him," she says.

Sounds like a plan to me. But why wait?

Our meals are delivered and she patiently cuts up her boys' burgers and feeds them, sneaking in a bite of her own in between. Michael starts to fuss, but she quickly calms him. I tell her she's a good mother.

She looks surprised. "Nobody has ever told me that before," she says.

As we eat and make small talk, I see maturity in her that wasn't there before. Part of it is age, of course, and part of it is being a mother, but some of it surely comes with her success in the classroom. She seems to have a new sense of self, a belief that she can compete in a world apart from basketball and the reservation. She is off pot and cigarettes. I ask her the big question. "Are you going to go back and get your degree?"

"Yep."

"No matter what?"

Stereotypically, Crows are not noted for making direct eye contact. She looks me square in the eyes. "This is just a detour," she says. "I will graduate."

"When?"

"When it works out."

I return to Danetta's the next day to meet Sharon again. She shows up an hour late, looking completely frazzled. She told Randy we had met and he pitched a fit, telling her it wasn't right for her to meet another man for lunch. The self-confidence I'd seen in her yesterday is gone.

"I've got to get the radiator for his pickup fixed today," she says. "A mechanic is coming by here in a little while to look at it."

I look over her shoulder at six junkheap vehicles cluttering the property, including her Cougar, a car dead before its time. It bit the dust five months earlier while she was on her way to school. On that day she hitchhiked back home in the freezing cold and had it towed back to Danetta's, where it has been gathering rust and dirt ever since, leaving her with no way to get to school. Every time she asks about getting it fixed, Randy tells her there is no money. Nobody has even bothered to see what the problem is.

"How come Randy's pickup blows a radiator one day and somehow there's money to fix it the next?" I ask.

She shrugs.

While we wait for the mechanic, we ease toward the basketball hoop to shoot a few easy baskets. She says she hasn't touched a ball in a couple of years, but drains her first five shots, all from fifteen feet. "I still can see that last free throw against Ronan hitting the rim and bouncing away," she says. "It still bothers me."

She moves with the same casual ease and athletic grace that first caught my eye. It is a natural elegance impossible to teach, and judging from her movement, hard to lose. It's beautiful to see, in part because she is so completely unaware of it.

Soon, four-year-old Roddy joins us. An eight-foot hoop stands next to the old basket, and he takes aim. I'm sure he can't get the ball that high, but he sinks his first three shots. Just like Mom. Then he turns and spots an old propane tank sitting behind the abandoned Lincoln Continental with the "Jr. Boss" license plates. "I want to rope," he states.

Sharon retrieves a lariat—or maybe they call it a lasso—from the back of the pickup and Roddy is now dialed in to roping. Just like Daddy. He misses his first toss at the propane tank from about ten feet, then hits five straight as easy as Roy Rogers. His mom takes the rope, gives it a couple of twirls, steps back to fifteen feet, and nails it. Five times in a row without a miss.

She hands me the rope. "Try it," she says.

My first toss catches on my pants leg and flops to the ground. My second goes about halfway.

I give the rope back to Roddy.

Behind us, two-year-old Michael appears on the porch, crying. He wants to join his big brother in play. Sharon moves quickly toward him, scooping him up in her long

411

arms. She cradles him to her chest, then sits down on the porch steps with him in her lap. Gently, she rocks him, dabbing at his tears, softly explaining that she doesn't want him playing outside because of his ear infection. He listens, tears from his big brown eyes slowing to a trickle.

It's hard not to be impressed. The young woman I am watching comfort her son has made it all the way to this moment in spite of overwhelming odds. She has survived an absent father, diseased mother, jealous husband, tribal corruption, her own weaknesses, and a too often brutal culture. Not to mention 150 years of repression and government ineptitude. She is not the Jackie Robinson of the reservation, or even a Janine Windy Boy. But her wins have their own dignity. These kids, I think, are lucky in their mom, the soon-to-be college graduate. She is a mom to be proud of, a warrior, one who has counted many coups.

I say goodbye to Sharon and pass through Crow Agency one last time. Driving by the basketball court in the center of town, the place where I first spotted her, I slow down, my eyes catch sight of a group of teenage boys shooting hoops at one end, then drift to the other end. There, all alone, is a slender Indian girl. I guess her to be thirteen, maybe fourteen. She has that same easy grace as Sharon. I stop the car.

In the same way that I was hooked by my first sight of Sharon, I am locked in on this girl. But there is a difference. Instead of languidly flipping up shots the way Sharon did that hot August day, this girl is working with a purpose. Starting at the top of the key, she pivots, turning her back to the basket, and dribbles slowly to the right, holding off an imaginary opponent with her left arm. Slowly, she backs her way to the basket, bending at the knees, keeping the ball low. Her technique is textbook.

When she gets to within five feet of the basket, she fakes a shot, then makes an imaginary pass to a teammate. Then she walks quickly back to the top of the key and does it again. And again. And again.

Her concentration is convincing. A missed dunk at the other end ricochets all the way to her end of the court, but she doesn't see it, too absorbed.

I sit and watch for ten minutes, amazed at her intensity. Finally, she finishes her drill and walks off the court, stooping to pick up something lying nearby. At first, I can't make out what it is, but as she moves closer, I can see it is one of those handgrips used to strengthen the wrist. She is squeezing it hard with her left hand.

My first thought is, what if Sharon had worked this hard and been this disciplined? Maybe then she might have gotten that full ride for basketball and taken her dream to another level. But that is getting trapped in the what-ifs and dark clouds, and too much of my time on the rez was spent dwelling on the bad choices and negative forces. I choose now to focus on the victories . . . and Sharon's success at a four-year college is certainly one of them. I can think of nothing in my travels that match the magnitude of her effort.

When I first met Sharon I saw a mixture of sorrow and hope. Now, in a new millennium, I still see the sorrow—one cannot visit an Indian reservation and deny it—but I still see the hope, too. It is Sharon's college degree, it is her skills as a parent, it is that next generation walking off the court in Crow Agency, squeezing a handgrip.

As I said, out here on the Little Big Horn, there has been no surrender.

INDEX

INDEX

INDEX

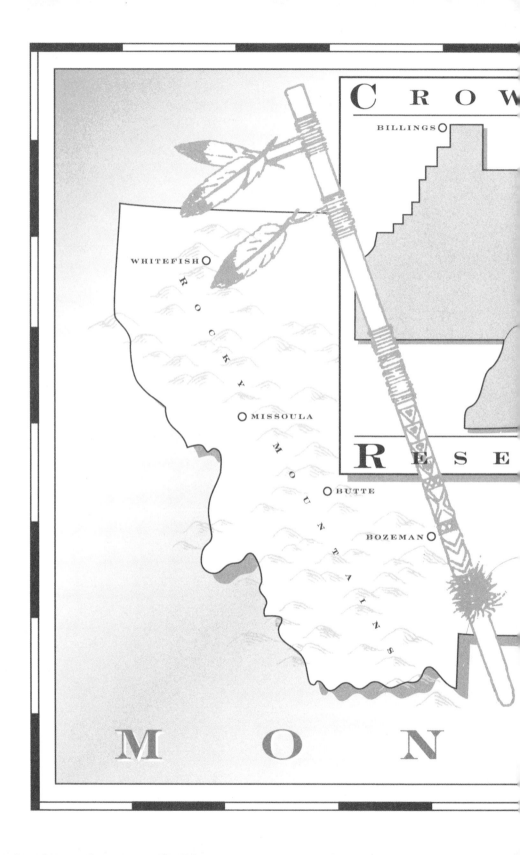